Moral Language

Moral Language

MARY GORE FORRESTER

The University of Wisconsin Press

Published 1982

The University of Wisconsin Press
114 North Murray Street
Madison, Wisconsin 53715

The University of Wisconsin Press, Ltd.
1 Gower Street
London WC1E 6HA, England

First Printing

Printed in the United States of America

For LC CIP information see the colophon

ISBN 0–299–08630–5

Publication of this book was made possible in part
by a grant from the Andrew W. Mellon foundation.

To my mother, Jim and the children

Contents

Introduction

Among the most important judgments we are called upon to make are evaluations: assessments of the worth of things, actions, and persons. Hardly a day goes by that we do not need to decide what is the right thing to do in a given situation and what is the best procedure for doing it. To this end we need to appraise objects and actions as good, bad, or indifferent. We must compare them with each other to determine which is better in some respect or other. We must choose, from what is sometimes a vast number of alternative courses of action, how to spend every moment of our lives. At least to the extent that these choices are consciously made, we make them on the basis of which alternative seems better in some way than the others.

For the most part, the guidelines we use to help us in these choices are rather firmly established in our own minds. Most of us perform the duties of our jobs before engaging in purely recreational activities. In purchasing objects we have fairly clear ideas of which best suit our tastes and purposes and of how much they are worth to us in comparison with what must be sacrificed if we are to possess them. We are generally confident about how we ought to treat other people and how they should act toward us.

That we have knowledge of what is right and wrong, good and bad, is usually taken for granted. We do not hesitate to teach our children how they ought to behave and what is good for them. We hold them responsible for their acts when we consider them to know what they should do. We even make decisions about whether an offender should go to jail or to a mental institution on the basis of whether at the time he committed the crime he *knew* the difference between right and wrong. Whenever a person reaches a certain level of knowledge and competence in a given area, we expect him to know what he ought to do. If he has, despite this, done the wrong thing, we say that he "knew better."

Yet the knowledge of what is good and what we ought to do often seems hard to come by. We ought not to lie and we ought not to cause others grief and fear, but what should a doctor say to his terminally ill patient who asks if he is going to die? A mother wishes to serve food that is both nutritious and tasty, but how is she to balance the two virtues? And to what extent should she sacrifice them both in order to save time or money? In such cases the agent is faced with conflicting principles and standards, and he must decide which is to take precedence over the others. On what grounds is he to make his decision?

Generally, the agent wants to do what is best—best for himself or best for everyone concerned—but in order to determine what is best, he must have some principle of ordering his values. If the doctor considers honesty to be more important than sparing others distress, he will decide that it is better to tell his patient the truth about his condition. The mother's primary aim is to do what is most likely to promote her family's overall health and happiness, and it is in the light of this principle that she will decide when the taste of the food she serves should be sacrificed to increase its nutritive value.

Even when a person has accepted principles by which he may resolve conflicts between less inclusive norms and values, he is apt to be challenged by those who hold different beliefs. A father who has worked hard all his life, scrimping and saving to provide for his children, may be told by his son that his efforts have been wasted: that he has neglected things of far greater value than wealth. A native of a tropical island, to whom time is of no importance, will, on coming to live in the United States, be utterly bewildered by the necessity for meeting deadlines and conforming to schedules. Looking at situations like these, it is difficult to decide whether money is more or less valuable than spiritual or artistic development, or whether one ought to try to achieve as much as possible in the time available or to enjoy life and take it as it comes. If indeed we can have knowledge about values, then surely there must be criteria by which such questions may be resolved.

It is not easy to formulate such criteria, however. Over the centuries various candidates have been proposed: that what is good is what is pleasant or conducive to pleasure; that a thing is good to the extent that it is desired; that good is what God wills; that good is self-realization; and others besides. Difficulties with each of these ultimate criteria have been pointed out by critics. The usual method of attack is to provide counterexamples. An argument against the theory that good is whatever is conducive to pleasure, for example, is that knowledge is good, whether or not it brings pleasure, and even when it brings pain, and therefore, pleasure is not the ultimate standard of goodness. As a counterexample to the position that what satisfies desires is good, it might be said that money enables us to satisfy countless desires, yet it is the root of all evil. If so, then the capacity to satisfy a desire cannot be the fundamental criterion of what is good.

If the moral philosopher whose proposal is criticized by counterexample objects on the grounds that what people *think* is good is not necessarily *really* good, his critic can reply that the philosopher must give reasons for perferring *his* suggested criterion to the beliefs of ordinary people and other philosophers. Rather than attempting to show that the judgment of his fellows on moral issues is radically at fault, most moral philosophers try either to argue that the apparent counterexamples are not counterexamples at all, or to revise their criterion in order to make it generally acceptable. Thus far, however, no one has succeeded in satisfying all critics.

Faced with these difficulties, many moral philosophers, and laymen as well, have drawn the conclusion that conflicts between evaluative beliefs cannot all be resolved by appeal to a single criterion or set of criteria. The basic criteria we use for making evaluations, they suggest, are ultimately matters of individual taste. To the extent that two people agree on a question of values, their tastes and preferences are alike. There are no absolute standards by which the validity of our moral or aesthetic claims may be judged. Still other thinkers have held that further clarification and investigation can yield ultimate standards acceptable to all rational, well-informed human beings—acceptable not merely because they are liked by all, but because they are true standards of value.

In this book I shall attempt to show that such an investigation is feasible and to point out the direction it should take. If successful, this will be a first step toward showing that moral knowledge is possible. In order to do this it will be necessary to answer those who say that there can be no appeal to universally shared criteria which are ultimate standards of rightness or goodness.

According to a number of ethical theories, the nature of moral language is such that objective standards cannot apply. In chapter 1, I will briefly sketch these views, indicating why some earlier theories have been generally discarded and what modifications have been made to those which have been retained. Chapters 2–6 consist of a sustained argument to the effect that these theories are false, even in their newest dress, and that moral language is fundamentally no different from factual language. Many of the criticisms which I shall discuss are not original with me; however, I think they need to be carried further than they have been. Also, there have been some recent efforts at defense by the proponents of the theories attacked here, which have not yet been successfully answered.

Even if moral language is like factual language, however, this is not sufficient to show that there are objective criteria for the truth or falsity of moral judgments. A sentence like "God is a spiritual being" resembles factual statements in form and syntax. It is, however, at least questionable whether we have any way of determining its truth or falsity or even of knowing what it would be like for it to be true or false. We would need to know, for example, what is meant by "God" and by "spiritual," how God would be different if he were *not* spiritual, what distinguishes God from other beings, and so forth. It is certainly not at all clear that there is agreement about the criteria for the truth of such a statement, and many would argue, and have argued, that agreement would be impossible. For this reason, such statements have even been declared meaningless.

The second task, which I undertake in chapters 7 and 8 is to show how we go about discovering the criteria for the truth of factual statements generally and to show how this method can apply to moral judgments. I will not try in this book to determine what the criteria for truth in moral judgments actually are; this requires an extensive investigation which at this time I have not completed. I will, however, point out the direction which I believe such an investigation should take.

Moral Language

1

The Problem

The question of whether there are true evaluative standards has been the central concern of moral philosophy from the time of the pre-Socratics to the present day. Throughout the history of the discipline many have answered this question in the negative. The theories offered in support of the view that there are no absolute standards are varied, but for the most part they can be classified either as forms of relativism or as forms of nondescriptivism. Relativists do not necessarily deny that any moral knowledge is possible; however, they say that what we do know is not what is good, right, etc., universally, but only what is good for some individual or group. Nondescriptivists deny that our knowledge extends even this far; moral knowledge is, strictly speaking, impossible, because matters of ethics are not factual at all. The sentences expressing evaluations are not sentences which are either true or false, but rather some other linguistic entity.

In this chapter, I will briefly discuss these two types of theory, as well as examples of each. While I will mention in passing some of the arguments which have been raised against these positions, my main purpose in doing so is not to refute them, but to show how these views have developed, especially in recent years. By the end of this chapter I hope to have presented a clear picture of the current theories which I will examine critically in the chapters immediately following.

RELATIVISM

Some who have denied the existence of absolute standards of value have been ethical relativists. *Individual* relativists, or subjectivists, hold that what is good for an individual is what he likes, or wants, or what he believes to be good. If another person wants different or incompatible things, then these will be good for *him*, though bad for the other.[1] Individual relativism has not been maintained by professional philosophers in this bald form for many centuries. It is, however, commonly held today by laymen—some of whom even consider it unquestionably true.

Cultural relativism, moreover, has the backing of a substantial number of anthropologists, although its popularity seems to have diminished in recent years. Cultural relativists maintain that the way in which a given society requires its members to act is the way they ought to act, and what the society as a whole considers valuable *is* valuable for its members. The same acts and objects, however, might be wrong or bad by the standards of some other society, in which case, they are bad for the people who live in that other society.[2] In both forms of relativism, it is held that the rules and standards applying to one person or group of persons do not apply to others, and that there is no justification for saying that one person's principles or one culture's moral code is superior to that of any other.

While relativism is popular, it has also been widely criticized. Two major objections—with which I concur—are (1) that judgments of value are of an entirely different kind from individual or societal expressions of liking or preference,[3] and (2) that relativists provide no justification for maintaining that either the individual or the society is and ought to be the arbiter of values. Those who offer the first objection point out that statements about what is good or bad, right or wrong, are not used to express a purely personal viewpoint, but are rather put forth as universally applicable. If I say, "I *like* chicken livers," I am not committed to any view about the value of chicken livers for anyone else. But if I say, "They are *good* for one," then I am so committed. I am claiming that they have certain characteristics which make them conducive to health, and, furthermore, implying that health is valuable for all. In stating what I want to do or how I want others to act, I refer only to my own attitude; however, if I say that a person *ought* to do something, then I imply that anyone in the same circumstances should do likewise.

There is a further, but related, difference between expressions of wants and likings, on the one hand, and evaluations, on the other. One's desires and preferences do not stand in need of justification, but evaluations do. While we may ask another why he wants to go on a cruise, for example, we are content to accept "I just do" as an answer. Our respondent may reply that the cruise would be a means to some end—such as getting away from office routine—and that this is his reason for wanting the trip. But such a response is not necessary; we may continue to think him a good and reasonable person without it. On the other hand, if he says that he *ought* to take a cruise, he may be called upon to defend his pronouncement. Someone who disagrees might reply, "But you'd have to go into debt to pay for it" or, "You have far too much work to attend to" or, "How can you dream of leaving the country while your mother is critically ill?" Faced with this kind of opposition, the person who had declared that he ought to go on the cruise is expected to bring forth reasons to justify his view or else to admit that it is not the case that he ought to go. If he does neither, we consider him to be to some extent deficient in rationality.

While our wants and feelings are largely independent of our control and we do not typically come to have them as a result of rational thinking, this is not the case with evaluative beliefs. We do not as a rule lose our desires simply because we cannot justify having them, nor are we expected to do so. If an evaluative belief is such that we cannot rationally justify it, however, then we *are* expected to give it up.

The situation in which A likes or wants X and B does not differs from that in which A thinks X is good and B does not. In a disagreement about likes, the parties are usually willing to accept the difference in their views, because it is one which cannot ordinarily be resolved. On the other hand, a disagreement about what is good is generally thought capable of being affected by argument. When their likes differ, B may try to get A to stop liking X, but he must do so by playing upon A's other desires in such a way as to make A begin to feel an aversion for X. Or A may persuade B to give X another try in hopes that the new experience will cause B to like X. However, one does not come to want or stop wanting a thing merely because of the reasons for doing so. Apprehension of these reasons must also produce in some way feelings for or against the item in question.

On the other hand, a person may stop thinking that an item is good solely as a result of seeing that there is insufficient reason for believing that it is good. He may continue to like or want X after B has completed his arguments, but he is expected as a rational being to give up his belief that X is good. Value judgments are considered to stand in need of rational justification, while likes and preferences are not. A person who cannot produce a reason for holding something to be good or bad, right or wrong, is held to have failed to be reasonable, whereas one who cannot adduce reasons for his desires is not.

Persuading someone to change his evaluations differs from and stops short of persuading someone to change his tastes. Suppose you have a friend who has a trait which is either self-destructive or hurtful to others—say, making witty, but cutting, remarks. To argue with him that he ought to stop, you would point out that he hurts the feelings of those to whom he addresses his barbs and that he ruins opportunities for their friendship. Consequently, there are moral and prudential reasons for him to change his ways, and you offer those reasons as grounds supporting the conclusion that he ought not to speak so unkindly. The same reasons, it is true, may be adduced to get him to want *not* to make cutting remarks, in the hope that this new desire will outweigh his desire to show off his wit. But pointing out these considerations can be effective in changing his desires only if your friend cares about the feelings and friendship of the people he hurts. Unless he does, he will not have any desire to stop hurting them; he may, however, be persuaded to the view that he *ought* not to hurt them. Pointing out that something is the case may provide a *justification* for an evaluation, but can only serve as a *cause* of a like or dislike.

It is, of course, true that we tend to change our evaluations in accordance with our tastes, and conversely. For the most part, we all want to be good people, to do what is best for ourselves, and to love virtue and beauty. Consequently, if we like a thing, we do not wish to consider it bad or ugly, and we can often persuade ourselves that it is not. If we think that we ought to do something, we sometimes persuade ourselves that we want to do it; still more frequently we can persuade ourselves that what we want not to do is not something we ought to do. We do not enjoy dissonance between our likes and our values, and often employ techniques to lessen that dissonance.

These techniques of self-persuasion typically involve a certain amount of self-deception, and in some cases can result in serious personal problems. Depending upon whether we bring our tastes in line with our values or our values into line with our tastes, a different kind of procedure is involved. Suppose you are at an art show and your eye has been caught by a particular piece of sculpture. You like it, but as you stand before it, a friend whose artistic judgment you respect comes up and remarks, "Good God, what a monstrosity!" He then begins to point out various defects he finds in the work. By now you are undoubtedly feeling thoroughly uncomfortable, and if you are like most of us, you will find it hard to admit both to liking the sculpture *and* to its being bad art. The chances are that you will either (1) attempt to persuade yourself (and possibly your friend, too) that the sculpture is *not* bad, or (2) persuade yourself that you don't really like it. If you do (1) you will point out features which are taken as reason for considering a work of art good, for example, strength, originality. You may dispute whether your friend's assessment is just by questioning his reasons for it or the applicability of those reasons. Procedure (2) is a bit more complex. You may make it easier for yourself to dislike the sculpture by dwelling upon the features pointed out by your friend as offensive and perhaps also by searching out others which displease you. You can *tell* yourself that what you liked before about the sculpture are not features you like or that the work does not have them, after all. After these endeavors, however, you have done all you can. Whether or not you cease to like the sculpture is beyond further control on your part. Your continuing or ceasing to like it is no doubt causally related to your thought processes, but it is not a conclusion which may be considered rationally justified or unjustified on the basis of the considerations which you have entertained.

Reasons for considering a work of art good, on the other hand, while they may not logically imply the truth of an evaluative judgment, do determine its reasonableness or unreasonableness. A person who accepts both the judgments that the sculpture had certain features and that these were good-making features (and that it had no bad-making features which outweighed the good), yet who evaluated the work as bad, would be lacking in rationality. The recognition that an object has features which we like or do not like, does not, however, commit us to liking or not liking the object. We are not thought stupid or irrational if our feelings about a thing, situation, or an action differ from our feelings about some specific features we take that item to have. We may, of course, withhold an evaluation—for example, we may recognize good-making characteristics in an item and no bad-making features, yet still feel uneasy about conferring whole-hearted approval. Such a stance is justified, however, by pointing out that we don't know all there is to know, and that new information might be relevant to a final evaluation. We cannot, however, as a rule, withhold our feelings of liking or disliking at will. They came unbidden, and, if not present, cannot be summoned at will. Thinking may encourage or discourage them, but cognitive processes do not have the final say.[4]

Apart from above considerations, to like a work one thinks is or may be bad is, logically, a perfectly possible position to maintain, and is, moreover, often the only one consistent with one's integrity. To engage in either procedure (1) or procedure (2) is usually to some extent dishonest. This clearly indicates that liking a thing and evaluating it positively are by no means one and the same state of affairs. Recognizing and accepting dissonance between our feelings and our evaluations is often an important step toward good relationships with others and sound mental health. Statements like the following express a healthy self-awareness: "I didn't like your criticizing me; it made me angry. But you were justified and right in doing so"; "My mother ought not to be blamed for her indifference to me; she was a sick woman. However, her neglect still hurts and angers me." In cases where statements of this kind are appropriate, denial of the just evaluation and acceptance of only the feeling can disrupt friendships and family ties. To accept the evaluation and deny the feeling, on the other hand, can create emotional time bombs capable of damaging a person's mental health.

On the whole, then, expressions of likes, tastes, and desires are different in meaning from evaluation, and evaluations cannot, therefore, be merely statements about individual feelings, or even the sentiments of cultural groups. Rather, evaluations apply universally: if they apply to one item, they apply to any other like it in the relevant respects. This means that if X is good, then anything which shares certain characteristics with X is to that extent also good. The goodness of X and its fellows has to do with the fact that they have these characteristics, and therefore their having them is a reason for thinking them good, or at least points to the existence of such a reason. If I say that Smith is a good man, I imply that anyone similar to him in some particular respects is also good. Whatever these respects may be—say, kindness, or honesty—a person's having these traits is a reason for thinking him good. To say that Smith is kind or honest is to rationally justify the opinion that he is good. If there is nothing about Smith which can be cited as a reason for thinking him good, then we need not consider anyone good on the basis of his resembling Smith. But evaluations do carry a commitment to such a universalized judgment, and in this they differ from statements about or expressions of the tastes and preferences of individuals or groups.

The second major criticism of the two general forms of relativism is that those who have held these theories have supplied no justification for supposing that the evaluative beliefs of individuals or social groups ought to be accepted as ultimate. A cultural relativist who says that cannibalism is morally acceptable for some natives of New Guinea because it is accepted by them, should be required to show why the practice would not be equally acceptable if indulged in and thought morally worthy by a small sect in California. Or, when an individual relativist maintains that what each individual wants or believes to be good *is* good, he must, in order to persuade those who disagree with him, explain why that individual's desires and principles should take precedence over the aims and laws of the community in which he lives. In other words, both individual and cultural relativists, if they are to uphold their status as rational men, must give reasons for adopting one brand of relativism rather than the other, and also for choosing that position rather than a nonrelativistic one.

The relativist may answer this objection in one of two basic ways: he may give reasons for preferring his views; or he may say that reasons cannot be given. Whichever way he chooses, his position is gravely undermined. Suppose that he does present a reason for favoring his brand of relativism. For example, he may say that following the mores of one's own culture creates stability and security. By doing this the relativist has taken the view that stability and security are not merely valuable, but more valuable than certain other ends, such as intellectual growth and technological development, which may conflict with them. Further, he must claim that stability and security are supremely valuable, not just for some particular group such as the Masai, the Eskimo, or the French, but for any society whatever. But if he takes this line in defense of relativism, he is no longer a relativist, for he has argued that people should follow the mores of their own culture because doing so is a way of achieving an end that is valuable for all men.

If the relativist then backtracks and says that the end of security and stability is not of overriding importance for all cultures, he can no longer consistently maintain that cultural norms are those every person ought to follow just because doing so creates stability and security. Either he must say that cultural norms are the final court of appeal for some further reason, in which case the same argument may be applied, or he must maintain that no such reason can be given. If he takes the latter course, he has failed to justify the supremacy of cultural norms.

Perhaps the relativist could get out of this bind by arguing that, because following the moral rules of one's society insures stability and security, it is better to follow them, since stability and security are instrumental in bringing about the goods that one's culture values. Without them, we would not be able to obtain the things that are held by the group to be good. This, however, is to argue in a circle, and it provides no defense for the relativist. The cultural relativist (or the individual relativist, for that matter) who takes this approach maintains that a certain kind of norm (cultural or individual), takes precedence over others because of certain consequences of following it, but that these consequences are valuable only because they enable us to attain what the norms prescribe.

It seems then that no particular relativist position can be further justified without abandoning relativism. The relativist may try to defend his position, however, by arguing that further justification is either unnecessary or impossible. He might say that such justification is not needed because it is a part of the meaning of the terms "right" and "good"—that what is right or good is what society (or the individual) holds to be right or good. Similarly, he might maintain that there is no criterion other than societal (or individual) adoption by which values are in fact ultimately judged. This view can be disputed on the grounds that whether or not there are any *other* criteria universally employed for determining what is good or right, acceptance by any sort of limited group—be it individual or societal—is not even a universally acknowledged criterion, much less does it have the status of a definition.[5] When someone disagrees with the evaluations made by a given person or society, he is seldom content to agree that those values are all right for those who accept them, even though they are not all right for him.

A relativist might argue that while acceptance by a society or individual is not the ultimate criterion actually used for determining what is right or good, no other criterion is universally employed. Here, however, his position is no longer that his brand of relativism is true by definition; rather it is a form of skepticism or noncognitivism. On views of these kinds, values are not objects of knowledge. If there are no criteria by which we can definitely determine whether an act is right or an object good, then we cannot know whether the act is right or the object good. If he takes this approach, the relativist has abandoned the attempt to justify his views, and he has no means of convincing those who disagree with him. No one, then, is rationally bound to accept his opinion. Even if it is true that cultural or individual values ought to take precedence over others, we have insufficient reason for thinking so.

It is because of the above sort of arguments that individual and cultural relativism have been largely discredited. The view that what an individual or a society deems good *is* good for that individual or society cannot be justified, either by appeal to some further criterion or by claiming that relativism is true by definition. A rather different sort of view, which Frankena calls *meta-*

ethical relativism,[6] does not suffer from these objections. According to the metaethical relativist, there is no way of determining that one set of values or moral rules is superior to any other. On a view of this kind, neither individual nor cultural relativism could be justified, because we cannot defensibly say that the norms of societies are right or good for those living in them any more than we can successfully argue that the moral code of any given individual or society is superior to that of any other.

What status, then, does the metaethical relativist accord to value judgments? What does he think people are doing when they alter them? Some metaethical relativists have said that value judgments are meaningless. It is clear, however, that a philosopher who adopts this approach must specify the kind of meaninglessness he has in mind. Certainly, evaluations are not gibberish; we understand each other when we make them. It has been argued that they are meaningless in the sense proposed by the Vienna Circle; that is, there is no way of verifying them empirically.[7] There are many difficulties with the verifiability theory of meaning, which it is not necessary to discuss here. However, it is widely presumed that for most scientific and empirical statements, if two rational persons agree upon the truth values of the same set of observation sentences which are relevant to the claim in question, they will agree as to whether the claim is true. They may think that, given only the available information, the truth or falsity of the claim is undecidable, but they agree on what the confirmatory or disconfirmatory effects of further data would be. Even where such agreement does not exist, it could in principle be reached eventually, provided that enough new information becomes available.

Those who, because of their adherence to the verifiability criterion of meaning, claim that evaluations are meaningless, argue that the case of value judgments differs from that of empirical statements in that two perfectly rational beings might agree on all the facts and still disagree about an evaluation. Further, they might disagree as to the relevance to, or the effect on the validity of, any given fact or observation upon a value judgment. Thus Tom and Dick might agree that telling the truth to Harry will cause him anxiety, but still disagree as to whether one ought, nevertheless, to tell him the truth. Tom might argue that one ought always to spare others pain, while Dick might maintain that a lie is wrong under all circumstances. According to the view presently under discussion, a point could be reached where no further facts would enable Tom and Dick to come to an agreement on whether lying was worse than causing pain, yet we could still consider both to be rational people.

The metaethical relativist maintains that there is no set of criteria such that items satisfying them must be agreed by all rational and fully informed persons to have certain evaluative character-istics. That something is good, he says, is not identical with its satisfying any particular set of criteria for goodness, nor does its being good entail the satisfaction of some particular set of criteria. But people do make value judgments, even if these are not veri-fiable, and they profess to understand what they are doing when they make them. Since evaluations are meaingful in *this* sense, the metaethical relativist has the task of showing what we *do* mean when we make them—or at least what we *think* we mean.

NONDESCRIPTIVISM

To remain viable, metaethical relativism must reconcile the supposed absence of necessary and sufficient conditions or criteria for the truth of evaluative judgments with their evident linguistic significance. The general approach which has been taken during the last several decades has been to argue that evaluations are not statements which are either true or false, but rather utterances playing some other role in speech. As a group, such theories are called *nondescriptivist*.

There are many kinds of expressions which are not state-ments—which do not state facts, which do not describe the way things are, and which are neither true nor false. Examples include imperatives—requests, commands, prescriptions, etc.—none of which assert that something is the case. The sentence "Hand over your jewels" is not one which can be either true or false. One can satisfy the demand, but doing so does not make the imperative sentence true, but only the declarative sentence, "You handed over your jewels."

Another kind of sentence which describes nothing and is neither true nor false is the promise—at least any sentence beginning with "I promise to. . . ." The utterance "I promise to mow your lawn" does not state a fact. I may keep the promise or not, and I may or may not intend to do what I promised. My keeping the promise and my intending to do so are states of affairs, but they are not described by "I promise to mow your lawn." Nor does "I promise to mow your lawn" describe the state of affairs which is my promising to do this task. Thus promises share with imperatives this feature of being nondescriptive, as do other explicit performatives such as those beginning with, "I recommend . . . ," "I hereby approve . . . ," or "I bet that. . . ." In addition, such expressions of emotion as "Ouch!" and "Hurrah!" describe nothing, state no fact, and are neither true nor false. Evaluations, therefore, need not be statements of fact or declarative sentences in order to be meaningful utterances. If they are like imperatives, performatives, or ejaculations, then the problem raised by the metaethical relativist of how we can understand them, even though we cannot verify them, might be resolved.

Theories in which evaluations do not state facts, describe states of affairs, or have a truth value, but have instead some other role in language, are called nondescriptivist. A variety of these have been proposed during the last half-century. One of the earliest and simplest forms of nondescriptivism was set forth by A. J. Ayer.[8] According to his view, evaluations—both moral and aesthetic— are not propositions at all, but rather are utterances which either express the speaker's feelings or which are employed by the speaker to have certain effects on others. For example, "Stealing is wrong" is either used to demonstrate the speaker's abhorrence of stealing, to arouse similar feelings in others, or to try to influence others not to steal. In the last of these functions, the evaluation serves much like the command "Don't steal!"

Ayer is careful to distinguish his view from traditional forms of relativism. While a relativist would say that "Stealing is wrong" is true if and only if the speaker (or his society) does in fact disapprove of stealing, Ayer maintains that "Stealing is wrong" cannot be true (or false) at all, any more than is "Stealing! Horrors!" According to the traditional relativist, evaluations are like such sentences as "I can't bear spiders," whereas according to Ayer, they are like "Ugh! Spiders!" or "Get that creature out of here!"

Ayer's analysis, however, is unsatisfactory for the same reasons that the other forms of relativism we have considered are unacceptable. Ethical and aesthetic judgments differ as much from mere expressions of attitude as they do from statements about what one's attitudes are. Evaluations are uttered as claims which apply to others besides the speaker. When I say, "Ouch!" I express only *my* pain; if I say, "Cheating is wrong," I imply that it is wrong for everyone. Of course, Ayer adds that evaluations are meant to have an effect upon the actions and attitudes of others. In saying, "Cheating is wrong," one not only expresses one's own disapproval, but attempts to influence others to avoid and despise cheating. "Cheating is wrong" has the force of the imperative "Don't cheat!" Still, evaluations differ from normal imperatives. Orders and requests are addressed to specific persons; they do not apply to any persons other than those to whom they are directed. But the person who declares that a certain kind of action is wrong is claiming that it is wrong for everyone, or at least everyone in like circumstances.

If evaluations are imperatives at all, they are of a different kind from ordinary commands and requests. The universality of value judgments suggests a presumption that cheating is wrong for a *reason*; it is this reason which makes that kind of act wrong for anyone to whom the reason is applicable and which also justifies the judgment. An order need not be backed up in this way; even if it is totally irrational, it may nonetheless be an order and have force as a guide to action for the party to whom it is addressed. An evaluation, on the other hand, generally loses its power to guide action when it cannot be supported by reasons. The authority of a command lies in the position of the commander, whereas the authority of a moral judgment lies in its reasonableness.

Considerations of this sort led C. L. Stevenson to propose an analysis of ethical expressions more complex than Ayer's. Reasoning, he acknowledges, plays an important role in moral arguments, and he subjects this role to close scrutiny.[9] He concludes that evaluations are conjunctions: a combination of a descriptive statement and an imperative. To say that X is good is both to say something true of X and to try to influence others to approve of X. Precisely what is asserted of X in the evaluation varies with the context and with the kind of thing X is. The speaker has different criteria for the goodness of different sorts of items. A good car may be one which runs smoothly and gets good mileage. A good man may be one who is fair, honest, and charitable. When he calls a car good, the speaker who accepts these criteria is saying that it runs smoothly and gets good mileage. When he says a certain man is good, he is saying that he is fair, honest, and charitable. If he argues that a given car or man is good, he supports his conclusions with premises asserting that the car or the man has the qualities mentioned.

To this extent, Stevenson allows for rationality in ethics. However, when one's criteria of goodness come into question, one can ultimately justify them only on the grounds that one approves of items which satisfy those criteria. Thus the fundamental analysis of "X is good" becomes "I approve of X, do so as well," where the second conjunct is an imperative addressed to anyone and everyone. If the speaker approves of those things which have properties A, B, and C, the analysis of "X is good" may be rendered as "X is A, B, and C; approve of X." Backing this latter type of evaluative analysis is the further evaluation, "I approve of things which are A, B, and C; do so as well."

In this manner, Stevenson hoped to account for the element of rationality in evaluations and evaluative arguments, as well as the action-guiding character of value judgments, and the prevalence of fundamental disagreement in evaluative matters. If the basic meaning of "X is good" is simply that the speaker approves of X by virtue of some of its characteristics, then those who do not approve of things having those characteristics are not going to change their opinion about X as a result of being shown that X has them. They will continue to disagree with the speaker in their attitude toward X, even though they may have the same factual beliefs about X. Ethical disagreements *can* be resolved, however, in some cases. If Jack and Jill approve of all things which have property F, but Jack thinks that X is F, while Jill thinks that X is not F, then their disagreement about whether X is good is based on a disagreement of belief; as such it may be resolved on the basis of factual data, for new information may enable Jack and Jill to agree on whether X is in fact F.

Although Stevenson's analysis of evaluations is more refined than Ayer's, it, like his, fails to account for the presumed universal applicability of value judgments, as opposed to both expressions (or descriptions) of personal tastes and commands, or requests. Although the imperative conjunct is addressed to all persons, there is no implication that it is more reasonable to comply than not to comply with that demand. Evaluations, however, do carry the implication that there are reasons for supposing them valid, and that they are not mere whims of the speaker. Even if our evaluations are ultimately based on our tastes and feelings, and even if they have an irreducible function of influencing the actions and attitudes of others, the difference between them and ordinary imperatives and expressions of emotion must be clearly delineated.

One may wonder why the two nondescriptivist views of Ayer and Stevenson, since they fail to resolve one of the important questions at issue, should be thought to have any advantage over those of the traditional relativists. The answer is provided by what has been called the Open Question Argument.

Although Richard Price introduced this argument in the eighteenth century, it was first made popular by G. E. Moore early in our own century.[10] Neither Price nor Moore aimed this argument against descriptivism; both held that moral judgments were either true or false. Rather they were attacking naturalistic theories in which the truth of evaluations depends upon whether the evaluated item has certain nonevaluative properties, for example, conduciveness to pleasure or to self-realization. While naturalism and descriptivism are not the same doctrine, for a descriptivist may hold that moral terms cannot be defined in terms of nonmoral expressions, certain features of the arguments used by Price and Moore have been considered by some to be equally effective against both types of theory.

In naturalism goodness and other values are defined as consisting of some set of nonevaluative qualities or relations. The failure of naturalism, according to Moore, can be seen by consideration of the various naturalistic theories. Suppose, for example, we define "good" as "pleasant." Then "good" and "pleasant" would mean the same thing. To say, "Pleasure is good" would be to utter a trivial truth, and to say, "This pleasant thing is not good" would be to contradict oneself. But, Moore argues, the former sentence is not trivial and the latter is not a contradiction. Furthermore, whatever qualities or relations we take as definitive of "good," it is always possible to raise sensibly the question of whether something possessing those characteristics is in fact good. If being good *means* having those characteristics, such a question would not be legitimate; it would not be an *open* question.

A variety of reasons have been put forth to show that Moore's argument against the so-called naturalistic fallacy is itself fallacious.[11] A number of these attempts are, I think, successful; for example, the following considerations suffice to show that Moore's argument is unsatisfactory. That the question "Are Fs good?" can be raised about any of the Fs which have been proposed as definitions of "good" can show only that the meaning of "good" has not yet been satisfactorily analyzed. By itself, Moore's argument cannot prove the impossibility of a definition of goodness in terms of nonevaluative qualities and relations. He maintains that *any* set of properties whatever must be different from that of goodness, and therefore cannot be identical with, or a definition of, goodness. He bases this claim upon the contention that goodness, like color, is a simple, unanalyzable quality. Even if the notion of a simple, unanalyzable, and indefinable quality can be made clear—a matter which I shall not pursue here—that goodness might be such a quality is but *one* possible explanation of why the definitions which have been proposed so far have seemed to fail to capture its meaning.

Aside from this failure, Moore gives us little reason to suppose that goodness is in fact unanalyzable; his argument that the definitions proposed so far *do* fail is unsatisfactory. Not all statements which are true by definition sound trivial, nor do all self-contradictory statements strike us as nonsensical. There is no absurdity in asking whether whales are mammals or whether the square root of 144 is 12. Such questions appear silly only when the answers are obvious both to those who address them and those to whom they are addressed. Therefore, the mere fact that the question "Is pleasure really good?" does not strike one as nonsensical cannot show that an affirmative answer is not true by definition.

Yet although Moore's own argument is unsatisfactory, it has been taken as pointing out a significant truth about evaluative language; namely, that there is an element of the meaning of moral and aesthetic judgments that is not exhausted by the descriptive criteria we use for applying them. A sentence saying that a thing is good or an act right is never, many believe, merely to assert something about the thing or the act, but has another function as well. If so, then no matter how one might try to define "good"— as pleasure, as satisfying desires, as the will of God—then no thing which merely possesses the supposed defining characteristics will, *ipso facto*, be good. If the judgment "This F is good," where F is any property put forth as identical with goodness, does not also have the additional function of which evaluation consists, then it is not only not true by definition, but not even true.

A variety of proposals have been made during the last three decades which attempt to reconcile Moore's suggestion that the content of value judgments is more than just a set of descriptive statements with the apparent rationality of such judgments. In general, these analyses have two tenets in common. First, evaluations may be argued for and justified on the grounds that the items evaluated have certain characteristics or satisfy certain criteria. Second, these characteristics or criteria do not constitute the meaning of, or truth conditions for, value judgments. Value judgments are neither true nor false. They do not describe anything or state facts, but they play some other role in speech. Ayer and Stevenson brought out the two main functions which have been ascribed by these later theorists to evaluations—namely, the expression of emotions or attitudes, on the one hand, and imperatives, on the other.

The major proponent of the imperativist position is R. M. Hare. Moral judgments, he maintains, are a species of imperative or prescription. Unlike commands, requests, and most other linguistic acts of this genre, evaluations are not directed to one individual on one occasion, but apply to all persons in relevantly similar circumstances, including the speaker. While "Please pass the gravy" may be asked of only one person at the table at a given meal, "You ought to pass the gravy" implies that there is something about your passing the gravy in the given circumstances which makes the speaker prescribe it for anyone—himself included—in like circumstances. This makes value judgments more rational than simple imperatives; there is a reason for each moral prescription such that if there is a reason for you to do the prescribed act here and now, then there is the same reason for me or for anyone else to do it, under the same conditions.[12]

According to Hare, a moral judgment is an expression of the speaker's commitment to the performance of the act in question by the agent(s) designated in the subject of the sentence, and not only to the agent's doing that act, but to anyone else's doing the same type of act, should relevantly similar circumstances occur. Precisely what this commitment is is not altogether clear, but it certainly entails wanting the act to be performed and is similar to the attitude one has when one assents to, or agrees to obey, a command or request, as well as to the attitude one has when one has commanded or requested something of another.

Moral judgments are thus, in Hare's view, not descriptions or statements, but they are similar to them in that they can be universalized, i.e., they apply to all individuals in relevantly similar circumstances. They may also be supported by other evaluations and by statements of fact. For example, "It is wrong to steal" may be justified by an argument with the evaluative premise "It is wrong to cause others economic loss" and the factual premise "Stealing causes economic loss." While a moral judgment can be inferred from a combination of evaluations and statements of fact, it cannot be inferred from any number of statements of fact alone. It may, however, be deduced from premises which include at least one evaluative sentence.

One may justify particular moral judgments by means of moral principles to which one is also committed, obedience to which one would prescribe for all persons, including oneself. As long as two people are committed to the same principles, if they agree also on the facts involved, their moral beliefs can also be brought into agreement. If they do not share common principles, however, then agreement may never be reached, even though there is no dispute between them over the facts of the case. There is, according to Hare, no means of deciding whose principles *really ought* to be followed. All that can be decided upon is what are the principles a given individual accepts and whether his other moral judgments are consistent with these principles. Moral reasoning can make our own evaluations mutually consistent, but it cannot tell us whether these evaluations are right or wrong, or true or false, or whether they are better or worse than the evaluations of others. One's morality is defined by the principles one has adopted: these are the principles which one follows oneself and which one desires others to follow as well, rather than those which we merely profess to hold. If we are unwilling to obey a given principle, then we have not prescribed it universally, and hence it is not truly a moral judgment.

The view that evaluations are expressions of emotions or attitudes (emotivism) has been refined and developed by Roger Scruton.[13] According to him, value judgments are fundamentally expressions of an attitude of approval or commendation. Unless this attitude is present, the person who utters an evaluative sentence has not actually made an evaluation. What the status of his utterance is in such a case is a matter of some importance and will be discussed below. It should be noted, however, that an attitude, as Scruton amply shows, is not a mere feeling, but a complex pattern of reactions. Attitudes are not, moreover, reactions to objects or persons as individuals, but as exemplifiers of certain characteristics. For example, we may contrast hating someone with despising him. Hatred is an emotion directed toward a person. While some action or characteristic of Mordred may cause me to hate him, it is not necessarily that quality which I hate, but Mordred himself. I need not hate another individual, no matter how closely he resembles Mordred, and if I learn that Mordred has changed his character entirely, my feeling for him may not alter in the least. On the other hand, I can despise Mordred only by virtue of some act he has performed or some character trait he has: for example, I may despise him for his deceitfulness. This attitude of mine is directed toward the deceit rather than toward Mordred and I would despise anyone else whom I thought to be deceitful. Should I learn that Mordred has become honest, I would cease to despise him. If a reaction to something is an attitude and not merely an emotion, then it must be possible for the person who has it to give some reason for having that attitude. For example, "Why do you admire Jones?" must be answered by something like "I admire him for his wisdom" or "Because of the kindness he shows his friends." If no answer can be given, the speaker does not really *admire* Jones; his feeling for him is more akin to love or awe, and these are emotions, not attitudes.

If, therefore, I have an attitude toward an object, person, or action, I have at least one belief about the item in question—that it has some property, F, which partly explains the attitude I have. On the view that evaluations are expressions of attitude, then in saying that X is good I imply that there is some property F which X has and by virtue of which I approve of X. That X is F is my reason for approving of X; not only do I have a reason for approving of X, but I am committed to holding that other F things are also good—approving of them as well. If I dispute about the goodness of X with someone else who also approves of Fs, then we reach agreement when we agree that X is F. For this reason, rational discussion about value judgments is possible.

On the other hand, if two disputants, A and B, do not approve of the same kinds of things, and neither can change the attitudes of the other, then, even if they agree on all the factual matters involved, they will still have irreconcilable disagreements about values. Like Hare, Scruton holds that there is no court of appeal by which such disagreements may be resolved. There is no set of superior standards which will tell us whether A or B approves of the *right* things. Indeed, value judgments are not true or false, although they may fail to be consistent with one's other values.

There is a similarity between the two types of analyses, examples of which have been expounded above. Those things of which we approve and also those things which we command or request are generally things we *want*—things we choose to have rather than not to have. This is recognized by Nowell-Smith. He points out that evaluative expressions have a wide variety of functions; for example, to express feelings, to praise, to recommend, to persuade.[14] In situations where standards of goodness for some kind of item are clearly specified and agreed upon by the group to which the speaker belongs, they may even describe. Sentences which set forth the standards, however, are not descriptions, but have one of the other nondescriptive functions mentioned. All of these functions have in common the feature of *choice*. What we evaluate positively—what is good, right, virtuous, or beautiful— is what we choose, or tend to choose, to have, to experience, or to bring about. This is what Nowell-Smith calls having a *pro* attitude toward these items. That which we evaluate negatively is what we choose against and toward which we have a *con* attitude.

Like Hare and Scruton, Nowell-Smith holds that we choose (and evaluate) as we do because of certain properties of the evaluated items. These properties do not, however, constitute the *meaning* of the evaluative terms; their meaning is the function of expressing a pro or con attitude. Rather, the properties are considered criteria of goodness, rightness, etc., because we have the requisite attitudes toward anything with those properties. That we do direct our attitudes toward properties makes evaluations universal judgments rather than mere expressions of feelings toward objects, and it makes rational discussion of evaluative matters possible up to a certain point. But while value judgments are universal in that the speaker is committed to maintaining that if X is good because it is F, then any other thing is also good to the extent that it is F, they are not universal in another respect. That F is a reason for me to think X good does not necessarily make F a reason for you to think X good. If you do not approve of or prescribe things because they are F, then being F is not, for you, a reason for a positive evluation. In this way evaluations differ from descriptive statements, in which if being F is a reason for me to call X a G, it is also a reason for you and anyone else to call X a G.

The common core of all the theories discussed above, as well as that of a number of others, is the thesis that the *illocutionary force* of evaluations is necessarily something other than asserting, describing, or stating facts.[15] The illocutionary force of a sentence is the linguistic task it performs; that of most sentences is assertion—stating something about the world. But other sentences do not do this and have a different illocutionary force, for example, imperative or action directing ("Present arms!") and promissory ("I swear that I will repay you"). When uttered, such sentences usually create specific demands on those to whom or by whom they are directed, but they do not have truth values.

Often descriptive statements (i.e., assertions) have an illocutionary force which is nonassertoric as well as one which is assertoric. For example, "I want you to bring me that money" not only describes something about my wishes, but is meant as a demand that you bring me the money. It serves both as an assertion and as an imperative. Likewise, "I will go to the meeting" describes a future state of affairs, but in certain circumstances it is also a promise. On a given occasion of utterance each of these statements may have at least two illocutionary forces at the same time: assertoric and imperative in the case of the first, and assertoric and promissory in the case of the other. On the other hand, "Bring me that money" and "I promise to go to the meeting" are not assertions at all. Their illocutionary forces are only imperative and promissory, respectively. According to the nondescriptivist theories, evaluations are akin to "Bring me that money" and "I promise to go to the meeting," rather than to "I want you to bring me that money" and "I will go to the meeting." The former pair of sentences never have the illocutionary force of assertion, whereas the latter pair normally do, regardless of whether a given utterance of them has some other force as well.

Evaluations, according to nondescriptivists, always have a nonassertoric illocutionary force; most also maintain that evaluations are never assertions, although a few do not hold this. One of the exceptions is Stevenson, who, as we have seen above, argues that evaluations are correctly analyzable as conjunctions consisting of (1) a description of, or assertion about, one's attitude, and (2) an imperative. For the majority of nondescriptivists, however, the factual content of evaluations, that is, the properties by virtue of which we prescribe or commend the evaluated item, form no part of the meaning of the value judgment. These properties could be entirely different without affecting the sense of the evaluation. "X is good" means the same, regardless of whether one considers F things or non-F things to be good.

In the next five chapters I shall attempt to show that nondescriptivism is false. Hare, Scruton, and Nowell-Smith are the most representative nondescriptivists, and their positions are the best developed. However, what I have to say applies not only to their positions but to all forms of nondescriptivism.

2

Sentences and Speech Acts

The difficulty, if not impossibility, of reaching general agreement on moral and other evaluative questions has, as we have seen, led many to the view that value judgments are not statements, but are sentences having some other linguistic function. They have been compared with imperatives (commands, requests, prescriptions, etc.), and with such attitude-expressing acts as approving and commending. Like "Turn off the motor," "I approve the minutes," "I recommend Joe for that position," and "I hereby commend your courageous action," evaluations are, these writers maintain, neither true nor false. If evaluations are sentences of a kind similar to one of the above examples and are not descriptive statements, assertions, or declarative sentences, then it is only reasonable to expect their logical and grammatical behavior to resemble that of nonassertoric sentences rather than that of assertions.

On the contrary, however, it appears that ethical and other evaluative sentences behave more like assertions than like nonassertoric sentences. Nonassertoric sentences (most of which are termed "performatives" because their central feature is that to utter them is to perform some specific action such as to promise, to give a warning, to issue an order) do not seem to be usable in some of the contexts in which we employ both assertions and evaluations. For example, "I am doing the right thing" can appear in question form ("Am I doing the right thing?"), in an expression of doubt or deliberation ("I wonder whether I am doing the right thing"), and as the subordinate clause of a conditional sentence ("If I am doing the right thing, then I don't care what others will say").

The same cannot be said, however, of commands, promises,

recommendations, or any other performatives. Compare, for example, "I wonder whether I recommend Joe," "Do I promise to feed your dog?" and "If turn off the motor, you will not damage it further" with the sentences in the above paragraph. To the extent that such strings of words make sense at all, the performative phrases have a different meaning from that which they have when they appear as the categorical sentences "I recommend Joe," "I promise to feed your dog," and "Turn off the motor." "Do I promise to feed your dog?" is asking whether I have made or will make that promise, but "I promise to feed your dog" does not say that I *have* so promised or *will* do so, but is actually (in appropriate circumstances) the vehicle of making the promise. "I wonder whether I recommend Joe" is—if anything—to say that I am undecided about whether I will recommend him or whether I ought to do so, while "I recommend Joe" does not say that I will recommend him, or ought to, but represents the utterance whereby I actually do recommend him. "If turn off the motor, you will not damage it further" makes no sense at all. One can make a meaningful sentence by changing it to "If you turn off the motor . . ." or "If I tell you to turn off the motor . . . ," but in neither case is the new clause any longer an imperative. We can, it is true, say, "Turn off the motor, and you will not damage it further," but the first clause is no longer the antecedent of a conditional, for the whole sentence is an abbreviation of "Turn off the motor, and if you do, you will not damage it further," or simply, "If you turn off the motor, you will not damage it further."[1]

The fact that nonassertoric sentences can be used in these contexts only by changing their meaning puts great difficulties in the way of their being used as the premises and conclusions of arguments. For example, arguments like "If Roger washed his car today, then it will rain tomorrow. Roger washed his car today. Therefore, it will rain tomorrow" are valid. They conform to the schema: If p, then q; p; therefore, q. No matter what sentences we substitute for p and for q, the truth of q follows from the truth of the premises. But when we substitute an imperative or some other sort of performative for p, we run into difficulties.[2]

To see this, consider the following sentences:

27

> If, John, pass this course, you (John) will turn in your paper
> by Friday.
> John, pass this course.

We do not have an argument here, for the first premise makes no
sense and no conclusion can be drawn. On the other hand, from:

> If you are going to pass this course, you will turn in your
> paper by Friday.
> John, pass this course.

or from

> If John is going to pass this course, he will turn in his paper
> by Friday.
> John, pass this course.

I cannot conclude anything either, for the second premise is not
the same sentence as the antecedent of the first. Only with premises like:

> If you are going to pass this course, you will turn in your
> paper by Friday.
> You are going to pass this course.

or

> If John is going to pass this course, he will turn in his paper
> by Friday.
> John is going to pass this course.

may I conclude, "You will turn in your paper by Friday" or "John
will turn in his paper by Friday." But if I do this, then the second
premise is no longer an imperative, but an indicative sentence,
which is either true or false.

The same sort of situation holds with respect to other performatives: Consider:

> If I thee wed, I will bring thee thy slippers and pipe every
> evening.
> I thee wed.

The antecedent of the first premise is not to be taken as a perform-

ative, but as a statement of the condition under which my promise to bring your pipe and slippers is to be fulfilled. "If I thee
wed . . ." in the antecedent means "In case I should marry
you . . ."; it is not a performative utterance in a marriage ceremony, but describes the situation of the ceremony's taking place.
The second premise, however, is a performative, and, consequently, is a sentence with a different meaning. No conclusion,
therefore, can be drawn from the two premises. One may be
drawn only by changing the second premise to something like "I
shall wed thee," where this is taken as a statement of fact.

It seems then that there are, at the very least, serious difficulties
in the way of constructing arguments of the form "If p, then q; p;
therefore, q," in which p is represented by a nonassertoric sentence. When p is an evaluation, however, such arguments appear
perfectly straightforward. For example,

> If you were wrong to say that, you had better apologize.
> You were wrong to say that.
> Therefore, you had better apologize.

and

> If brewer's yeast is good for you, you ought to eat it.
> Brewer's yeast is good for you.
> Therefore, you ought to eat it.

In both examples, the same sentence serves both as the antecedent
of the first premise and as the second premise, thereby making
the argument valid. The difference between these arguments and
those in which p represents an imperative or other performative,
and what creates difficulties for the latter, is that in the latter p is
barred grammatically from serving as the antecedent of a conditional. Yet if arguments of the form "If p, then q; p; therefore, q"
are valid, they can be so only under the supposition that p in the
first premise also appears as the same sentence in the second
premise.

The above observations suggest that the grammatical and logical behavior of evaluations resembles that of assertions, descriptions, or declarative sentences much more closely than it re-

sembles that of such types of nonassertoric sentences as imperatives and commendations. In what follows I shall argue that what appears to be so in this case is so: that any logic involving nonassertoric sentences must be radically different from the logic of arguments involving only assertions, but that the logic of evaluations is the same. In order to show this, it will be necessary to discuss in detail what would be required for a logic of nonassertoric, nondeclarative sentences.

Over the past three decades there have been a large number of articles debating whether valid inferences involving imperatives are possible. Recently the issue has become enlarged to include the question of whether performatives and nonassertoric sentences generally may be premises or conclusions of valid arguments.[3] In some cases it appears that they can. For example, the command "Thou shall not commit adultery, and thou shalt not bear false witness" surely seems to entail "Thou shalt not commit adultery." Likewise, the following argument appears intuitively to be valid:

> If you, Jacob, give me, Esau, a bowl of soup, I promise to give you my birthright.
> Jacob gives Esau a bowl of soup.
> I, Esau, promise to give you, Jacob, my birthright.

Despite such examples, the thesis that there are valid nonassertoric inferences faces at least one serious difficulty. An argument containing only declarative sentences is valid if the conclusion must be true whenever the premises are true. But nonassertoric sentences are neither true nor false, so if the notion of validity is to have any meaning in arguments containing them, it must be reinterpreted.

The usual approach to this problem is to select values for nonassertoric sentences which are analogous to "true" and "false" for assertoric sentences. If we let 1 stand for "true" and its analogues for nonassertoric sentences and 0 stand for "false" and its analogues, then we might say that *any* argument is valid in which the conclusion must always have the value 1 whenever each of its premises has the value 1. There remains the problem of how to interpret 1 and 0 for such nonassertoric sentences as commands, promises, warnings, recommendations. I shall discuss this issue in chapter 3. Prior to this, however, some other matters must be cleared up.

MEANING AND ILLOCUTIONARY FORCE

Before we can intelligently consider what values might be substituted for truth and falsity for nondeclarative sentences, we must talk about the meaning and structure of sentences in general. In particular, I must give some indication of how meaning is related to illocutionary force, for knowing this is a necessary condition of understanding what values may serve as analogues of truth in sentences which have nonassertoric illocutionary force. My account will borrow heavily from those of Austin, Searle, and Hare, as well as from the semantic theories of several contemporary philosophers and linguists, but the end result differs in some respects from all of these.

The first essential distinction to be made is that between the meaning of a sentence and its use upon particular occasions. That there is a difference between meaning and use does not preclude their being closely related. They are. Still it is clear that "I am going to George's party" has the same meaning whenever it is uttered, even though it may have a different illocutionary force in different circumstances. Normally, it has the force of an assertion, and is used to convey information. However, it may, in addition, be used to make a promise. If the circumstances in which I utter the sentence entitle you to count on my going to the party, then my utterance has the illocutionary force of a promise. As I am actually using the sentence in this book, however, it is neither an assertion nor a promise, but an example used to illustrate a point. *This* use I am making of the sentence is certainly not identical with its meaning. Likewise, an actor uttering the same sentence would be neither asserting nor promising, but only pretending to assert or promise; his use of the sentence would be still different from any of the above.

What a speaker or writer does in uttering a sentence has been called by Austin its illocutionary force.[4] The illocutionary force of a sentence does not, however, include all the possible things that can be done or acts that can be performed as a result of uttering the sentence. For example, should I say to you, "Please wash your face," I may well hurt your feelings, but hurting your feelings is not the illocutionary force of the sentence. Rather, the sentence has simply the illocutionary force of an imperative, or, more specifically, a request. The illocutionary force of an utterance depends little upon its content, but rather on its grammatical features and certain circumstances of its utterance. That an utterance has imperative force is determined by the following, at least: (a) some feature of the sentence or context of utterance which normally conveys the speaker's intention to direct his audience's action, e.g., the verb's being in the imperative mood; and (b) its being uttered by a person who has the right or the authority to command or request actions of the person to whom it is addressed. If either (a) or (b) fails to hold, the utterance is not an imperative. If (a) does not hold, the speech act has some force other than imperative, and if (b) does not hold the force is that of an attempted, or perhaps pretended, imperative only. In the latter case, the utterance is in a sense an incomplete speech act.

If my saying, "Please wash your face" hurts your feelings, this is not a consequence of (a) or (b), so much as it is your reaction to the content of the sentence and to the fact that I would see fit to utter it. Austin accordingly distinguishes between *illocutionary* and *perlocutionary* acts: between what a person does *in* uttering a sentence and what he does *by*, or as a result of, uttering it.[5] The difference is somewhat like the difference between raising a window and giving the baby a cold. Both could result from one's pushing the window upwards, but it seems right to say that what one is doing in pushing the window up *is* raising it, whereas giving the baby a cold is not what one did in raising the window, but rather a consequence of that action.

It is not easy to draw the distinction between what is an integral part of, or even the whole of one's action, and what is simply an effect of the action, and the same difficulty besets the illocutionary-perlocutionary distinction. Austin himself suggests that the features in (a) and (b) are conventions. In normal circumstances the speaker uses them to signal his intention that his utterance has a given illocutionary force, and his audience recognizes this intention. The normal effects of employing these conventional devices give the utterance its illocutionary force, whereas its perlocutionary force is dependent upon features of the situation in which the utterance is made.

Normal utterances of "Please wash your face" occur when the speaker has the right to make the request and there is a mutual understanding between the speaker and the hearer that the speaker is attempting to direct the hearer to wash his face. In these standard circumstances, the use of the imperative mood virtually guarantees that an illocutionary act of the request type has been performed. On the other hand, whether or not the request hurts your feelings depends upon other circumstances which are not a part of the standard set. Of course, there are many situations in which "Please wash your face" may be uttered in *non*standard circumstances, and then an illocutionary act of the request-type will not have been performed. For example, if you and I are actors, then the mutual understanding necessary for completion of a request is not present, and the speech act I perform is not a request. This is analogous to the situation in which I push a window upward, but, because I am feigning weakness, I do not raise it. I am only pretending to try.

It is clear that the perlocutionary force of an utterance, that is, the perlocutionary acts it may be used to perform, does not determine the meaning of the utterance. That my saying, "Please wash your face" hurts your feelings is not a part of the meaning of "Please wash your face." Suppose that Sharkley's telling me that he is going to sell all his shares of U.S. Steel will cause me to buy up all the U.S. Steel stock I can afford. Since I know that he means to deceive me, my buying the stock is a perlocutionary effect of his saying, "I shall sell all my shares in U.S. Steel." However, this effect is most certainly not a part of the *meaning* of Sharkley's utterance.

That illocutionary force is not a part of the meaning of an utterance is less obvious. My saying to you, "Please wash your face" in real life differs in illocutionary force from my uttering the same sentence in a play, yet the sentence has the same meaning on both occasions. On the other hand, there are very important differences in meaning between "Please, Alice, wash your face," "Alice will wash her face," and "I hereby promise that Alice will wash her face." These differences, however, are not differences in illocutionary force.

That each of the three conveys something different, regardless of the circumstances under which it is uttered, is obvious. The differences in what the three sentences convey is a function of the words of which they are composed and not of the circumstances in which they might be spoken. Hence they are differences of meaning and not of use. Furthermore, these differences are intimately related to the tasks we would normally expect the sentences to perform when uttered. Clues as to what these tasks are are given by certain features of the sentence, for example, phrases like "I promise" and the mood of the verb.

The same features distinguish the following trio of sentences from each other: "George, put the cat on the mat"; "George will put the cat on the mat"; and "I, George, promise to put the cat on the mat." The first of each trio is an imperative, the second an assertion, and the third a promise. At the same time, however, the members of each trio of sentences are like one another, but differ from those of the other trio, in the state of affairs which they indicate. That the first sentence refers to Alice's washing her face (at some future time) and the second to George's putting the cat on the mat (at some future time) is conveyed by other features of the sentence and is independent of particular circumstances of utterance. These features, like those mentioned above, also contribute to the sentence's meaning.

It seems then, that we may distinguish between two components of the meaning of a sentence, which I shall call the *mood* and the *propositional content*. This distinction has been recognized by many.[6] While the mood of a sentence is closely connected with, although not identical with, the particular kind of illocutionary force its utterances normally have, the propositional content designates the kind of state of affairs the sentence indicates. The propositional content is a description of a kind or type of state of affairs, rather than a particular state of affairs, for the description incorporated in that content is, in any sentence, compatible with a variety of possible states of affairs. This is true, even of eternal sentences—those which spell out the time and place of which they are asserted to be true, and which identify uniquely all individuals mentioned in them.[7] This is so because there are many different ways in which a cat can be on a mat—even one particular cat on a particular mat in a particular spatio temporal region—any one of which, if it held, would make the sentence "The cat is on the mat" true.

It would seem, then, that the propositional content of a sentence does not denote individual states of affairs but either classes of, or attributes of, states of affairs. It would be desirable to have a way of characterizing this relationship without making any decision as to whether classes and attributes exist, and something like the following might do. The description incorporated in the propositional content, when heard, thought, read, or otherwise apprehended, triggers in the person who understands it a mechanism which enables him to recognize states of affairs which satisfy it, and, for states of affairs which he observes or which are described to him, to tell whether they satisfy that description. What this mechanism is is a question for neurophysiology, psychology, and linguistics, rather than philosophy, but it must be present in a person, and capable of being activated by a given string of words, if that string is to have meaning for the person—i.e., for him to understand it.

In learning words and phrases we hear them in association with specific situations and we come to understand them when we are able to identify the features which those situations have in common and to recognize them when they occur. We have, moreover, the still mysterious and awe-inspiring ability to put words together into sentences and identify the situations in which they are true or false—not only sentences we have heard before, but indefinitely many that are entirely new. Just as words come to stand for particular features of situations—"cat" for being a cat, "on" for a spatial relation between objects, etc.—so do descriptions of states of affairs—"The cat's being on the mat" for individuals of two specific kinds being related in a particular sort of way.

The meaning of the relation "standing for" is not clearly settled. If a term F stands for some feature, two things at least must be true. (1) Some individual must associate F with that feature (take that feature as being spoken, written, or thought of, when F is heard, read, or recollected by him), and use F to re-present that feature when he speaks, writes, or thinks of it. This association of term and feature may occur with imagery, but not only is imagery inessential, but, when it does occur, it varies from one person to another, and from occasion to occasion with a given individual. The association takes place when there is a sense of appropriateness (or inappropriateness) of using the term in par-ticular situations—but even here actual feelings are usually ab-sent. In fact, when correct terms are being used, this is generally signalled by the absence of dissonance.

Linguistic competence seems to resemble the competence of an experienced seamstress, who can not only tell what sorts of dresses a particular pattern could be used to make, but who can invent her own patterns. One's vocabulary and grammar are, by this analogy, comparable to the seamstress's supply of patterns, and they are related to as much of the world that one can describe, as her patterns are related to the clothes she might make. Just as we need not suppose that all (or even any) of the clothes for which the seamstress has patterns exist, or even could exist, we need not suppose that the things and situations whose features terms stand for exist or are even possible. And while pattern pieces exist, we need not suppose that the sizes and shapes of the garment pieces they determine are existing entities. These sizes and shapes may characterize garment parts, just as various features may charac-terize states of affairs and objects, but they need not have inde-pendent ontological status. It is enough that the resemblance between the garments she might make with a given pattern be recognizable for the pattern to be usable, and it suffices, for a word to be meaningful, that a resemblance (in a particular re-spect) between objects or situations have been recognized and made note of by speakers of the language in question.

(2) Aside from some individual's having to make an association between a term F and some feature, for F to *stand for* that feature, a number of persons must agree to accept that association. This amounts, I shall argue below, to a tacit agreement to accept as true a statement to the effect that when and only when the feature occurs in a situation, sentences asserting that F applies in that

situation are true. In other words, agreement about the meaning of a term among a significantly large group of persons, which is necessary for that term to stand for anything, in turn necessitates a conventional acceptance of certain beliefs. What this involves will, I hope, become apparent below.

The propositional content of a sentence in language L is, then, a description which specifies features of states of affairs. The speakers of L normally associate the description with those features. Furthermore, there is a general tacit agreement among the speakers to make this association. This rough account does not commit us to the existence (or nonexistence) of propositions or meanings, nor even to the existence (or nonexistence) of classes, attributes, or states of affairs, and it leaves open as well the mechanisms by which words and sentences become meaningful to us. As a result, the account serves only to indicate where an investigation of this aspect of meaning should begin and is no more than a rudimentary start toward a theory of meaning.

The other aspect of sentence meaning—mood—differs considerably from propositional content. For each of the two sets of three sentences considered above, the members differ in mood from one another. In each set we have an indicative sentence ("Alice will wash her face," "George will put the cat on the mat"), an imperative ("Please, Alice, wash your face," "George, put the cat on the mat"), and a performative (the promises, "I hereby promise that Alice will wash her face" and "I, George, promise to put the cat on the mat"). The mood of a sentence is the manner of representing the kind of state of affairs specified in the propositional content. The indicative mood represents that a state of affairs of that sort holds. The imperative mood represents someone's being directed to bring about a state of affairs of the kind indicated by the propositional content—i.e., to make it hold. The interrogative mood represents someone's asking whether a state of affairs of that sort holds (yes-or-no questions), or which of a possible range of kinds of states of affairs of that sort holds (what, where, why, when, etc., questions). Various performative moods represent someone's committing himself to bringing about some such state of affairs (promising), someone's making such a state of affairs hold by fiat (approvals, pronouncements), someone's making a wager that a state of affairs of the kind in question has or will come to hold (bets), and so forth.

The mood of a sentence is indicated by certain morphemes, or meaning-bearing elements of the language. These include: specific words, such as "I promise"; the mood of a verb (e.g., indicative or imperative); word order, as in the placing of all or part of a verb phrase before the noun phrase in questions; and deletion of certain words, such as "you" in imperatives. The presence of these morphemes makes it possible to tell what the mood of a sentence is, apart from the context of utterance.

Like the descriptive terms in the propositional content, the mood morphemes have become meaningful through being associated by speakers of the language with situations in which sorts of states of affairs were represented in particular ways, and by tacit agreement among the speakers to make such associations.

The reader will have noted that my use of the term "mood" here is somewhat broader than its usual employment in grammar. This is deliberate, for although I am applying the expression to more than the simple grammatical mood of a verb, I want to point out the similarity of these other mood indicators with verb mood. Each of the indicators of mood—in my sense—is a linguistic feature of the sentence itself and has some effect upon the sentence's meaning. These indicators are to be distinguished below from those features of the context of utterance of sentences which determine their illocutionary force,-that is, the specific acts performed when they are spoken on particular occasions.[8]

The propositional content and the mood of a sentence are but two of the factors which determine what a person does on a specific occasion of uttering that sentence. They make sentences appropriate instruments for performing particular illocutionary and perlocutionary acts under particular conditions. That "Mend the fence" has its verb in the imperative mood makes uttering it a means of commanding someone to do something; its propositional content informs the hearer of *what* it is he is being commanded to do. More conditions than these, however, must be fulfilled before a command to mend the fence has been uttered, and still others must obtain before the speaker actually gets the hearer to mend the fence. If the speaker has no authority over the addressee, he has not issued a command; the most he has done has been to request or to attempt to command. If the addressee does not respect the speaker's authority, even the speaker's having given a genuine command may not suffice to get the hearer to do as he was told. If the speaker has no authority, he has not performed the illocutionary act of commanding; if he *has* authority, he *has* commanded, but if his authority is not respected, he may fail to perform the perlocutionary act of getting the addressee to mend the fence.

In order to perform a given illocutionary or perlocutionary act it is not necessary—as a rule, at least—to use sentences having some particular propositional content or mood. The sentence "The wind blew down the fence last night," for example, can serve as a command to mend the fence, and uttering it may have the effect of getting someone to mend the fence just as well as uttering, "Mend the fence." Likewise, if you say, "I promise to stop beating my wife," this tells me that you have been beating your wife just as well as would your saying, "I've been beating my wife." Each member of the two pairs of sentences differs from the other in both components of meaning—propositional content and mood—yet both members may, if conditions are right, be used to perform the same speech act.

It may be that the meaning components of a sentence, although neither necessary nor sufficient determinants of the speech acts which may be performed by uttering this sentence, are nevertheless themselves determined by the kinds of speech acts they are used to perform. That this is so has been maintained by Alston, among others.[9] That the meaning of a sentence should be a function of the sorts of illocutionary acts that one could perform by uttering the sentence under different circumstances, has much plausibility. Speaking is, after all, a kind of action, and we perform different actions by making different utterances. To spell out a meaning-function in terms of the illocutionary act potential, so that it could be shown what illocutionary acts would be performed under what circumstances by the utterance of any particular sentence, would be a task of great complexity. Complexity alone, however, is no reason for pronouncing a task misconceived, and

I have no theoretical objections against the possibility of such an account of meaning.

Whether or not such an account might be acceptable, a fair amount can safely be said about the relationship between the propositional content and mood of a sentence, on the one hand, and the speech acts the sentence may be used to perform, on the other. Earlier I mentioned sets of standard conditions which, when fulfilled, make illocutionary acts of certain types the normal result of utterances of certain types. Under the standard conditions for imperative illocutionary acts, for example, the utterance of a sentence in the imperative mood will result in the performance of an imperative illocutionary act. These conditions include the right of the speaker to direct in the manner in question (command, request, prescribe, etc.) the actions of the person to whom the imperative is addressed, and an intention on the part of the speaker that there be a mutual understanding between him and his addressee that he mean his utterance as a directive, or else that features of the context conventionally indicate such an intention.[10] Just as descriptive terms are associated with features of states of affairs, and mood morphemes with manners of representing sorts of states of affairs, these standard conditions are associated with kinds of illocutionary acts—not only for individuals, but for all the speakers of the language. The conditions mentioned are examples of what Austin called the *felicity* conditions of a successful speech act.[11] These conditions must be satisfied if the uttering of an imperative sentence is to be a command, a request, or a prescription.

Other felicity conditions are not necessary for an utterance to be an act of a given kind, but are necessary if it is to be in some sense proper. For example, whether or not a speaker means what he says, i.e., is sincere, makes no difference as to whether his utterance constitutes a given sort of illocutionary act. "I promise not to disclose your secret" is still a promise, even if I am already gloating over the sensation I will create by revealing what you have said at this afternoon's bridge club. My saying "Doris is madly in love with Ellen's husband" is still an assertion, even if I am lying, provided only that I utter it in such a way that the persons addressed take me as declaring this state of affairs to obtain and that I mean for them to do so. A college president may confer degrees upon students about whose qualifications he has grave misgivings, but the students have the degrees, nevertheless, for the illocutionary act of conferring has been performed. That there is, however, something off-color about lies, promises one has no intention of keeping, commands which one does not want obeyed, and recommendations of persons whose qualifications one does not think adequate, is a reason to call them *infelicitous*.

When the felicity conditions necessary for the performance of an illocutionary act of type I are not fulfilled, then the utterance in question constitutes some other type of illocutionary act, I'. For example, "Swear that you love only me" must, to be an entreaty, be uttered by one person to another in a situation which has features that are conventionally recognized as indicating that both persons understand that the one is expected to respond with an oath sincerely meant. When uttered on the afternoon soap opera, however, both the utterance designated and whatever utterance was made as response would be acts of pretending—pretending to make an entreaty and pretending to swear an oath in response to an entreaty. That the sentence is in the imperative mood is a partial cause of its utterance's being in the one case a speech act of entreaty and in the other an act of pretending to entreat. Also, that the propositional content of the sentence specifies a kind of state of affairs in which one person swears exclusive love for another is a partial cause of its being an entreaty or pretended entreaty that such a swearing take place.

The utterance of a given sentence may fit under several speech act descriptions. "I'll give you your money tomorrow" can, as we have seen, be both an assertion about a future event and a promise. If the circumstances are not such as to conventionally indicate that the speaker intends for the addressee to count upon his so returning the money, he has not made a promise, but only an assertion. (It does not follow, however, that the speaker is not obliged to return the money on the following day, as a result of having—even inadvertantly and without actually promising—aroused expectations.) Sometimes the speech acts (illocutionary as well as perlocutionary) constituted by a given utterance may be very different from those usually performed by uttering sentences having the same mood or content. For example, hinting is a way of saying that one wants something and also of asking for it, by making some assertion or asking a question which actually means something quite different from a request or expression of desire. "My birthday is next Friday" could be uttered in order to request some remembrance of that occasion from the addressee, and "Do you want that last piece of pie?" can be asked as a way of letting the addressee know that the speaker would like to have it himself.

That sentences can be used to perform acts of speech which are very different from those they are normally employed to perform may be explained in terms of rules like those which Grice has proposed for conversational implicature.[12] One such rule is that we normally make as strong a statement as the evidence warrants. For example, if I say, "It looks like an aardvark to me," I suggest that I am not sure that what I see is an aardvark. Were I sure, I would normally have said, "That is an aardvark." In making the weaker statement I perform a speech act of declaring doubt, even though the sentence I utter does not have as a part of its meaning *that* I doubt. It is perfectly possible for me to add something to what I have said which cancels the conversational implicature, for example, "And what's more, I feel perfectly sure that it *is* an aardvark." The two utterances are quite consistent with each other, so the negation of the second is neither entailed by, nor part of the meaning of, the first.

There are a vast number of conventional understandings similar to this conversational rule that we make the strongest statements warranted by the evidence. Another such rule is that we do not utter sentences without having some point in doing so. We do not, for example, mention an approaching birthday unless we wish to convey some information thereby, or to elicit some action on the part of another. Because of certain other understandings we can tell whether another is serious or joking in making a given utterance. For example, if what the speaker says is too outrageous to be believed, then we assume he does not mean what he says. Still other conventions tell us whether what is normally a simple assertion is to be taken also as an order or a promise or a warning. If, for example, the hearer is in a position to take an action and the speaker makes an assertion which suggests that the action would be dangerous, that assertion may also be a warning. What illocutionary act is performed is a function of the meaning of the sentence uttered (both its propositional content and its mood) and the circumstances in which it is uttered. These circumstances include various rules of conversation, the speaker's tone of voice, the social relationships between the speaker and his audience, and specific rules and customs followed by the participants in the conversation.

Whether meaning is, in turn, a function of the kinds of illocutionary force the sentence may have on different occasions of its use is not a question I think necessary to pursue here. All that I wish to make clear is that there is a distinction between meaning and illocutionary force—that the one is not identical with the other. Propositional content and mood, on the other hand, are essential components of sentence meaning. Sentences differing in propositional content, specifying different sorts of states of affairs, are also different in meaning. Likewise, if sentences have different moods, they differ in meaning, e.g., "Affirmed will win the Derby," "Will Affirmed win the Derby?" "I hereby bet $800 that Affirmed will win the Derby."

Another reason for the necessity of distinguishing between sentence meaning and illocutionary force is that a sentence considered in isolation from any context of utterance has a meaning, but it does not have any illocutionary force. Only when uttered in speech or writing by some person is it the performance of an action and only then can it have illocutionary force. At most, the unuttered sentence has illocutionary force *potential*. Yet we can understand a sentence even when we do not know what illocutionary force it has. I know what "I'll see you tomorrow" means, regardless of whether I know that its utterance is to be taken as a promise or as an assertion only. The illocutionary force of a speech act depends heavily on features of the context in which the sentence is uttered. For this reason the terms and structure of the sentence itself are insufficient to determine force. The *meaning* of the sentence, on the other hand, is generally considered to be a characteristic of the sentence whether or not it is uttered, or, if it is, in what circumstances.

Meaning, Truth Conditions, and Conventions

The distinction between meaning and illocutionary force, and the recognition of propositional content and mood as distinct components of meaning, fit well into the major theories of meaning which are currently being discussed, such as the analysis of meaning in terms of truth conditions. In the case of declaratives at least, understanding the meaning of a sentence has some close connection with knowing the conditions under which the sentence would be true. In the case of nondeclaratives, such understanding requires knowledge of the truth conditions of the corresponding declarative; that is, the sentence which would be formed by changing the mood of the sentence from the imperative, for example, to the indicative. I cannot understand the request "Please change the cat box" unless I can understand the indicative sentence "I will change the cat box," and I cannot understand the latter unless I know the circumstances which would make "I will change the cat box" true. This knowledge is quite independent of the knowledge of the conditions under which either sentence is uttered, and hence of the knowledge of its illocutionary force.

Defining meaning in terms of truth conditions has difficulties. This can be seen from a brief consideration of Davidson's attempt to do so.[13] He has suggested that for every sentence S of a language, there can be constructed a meaning postulate of the form "S is true if and only if p." The sentence represented by p states the truth conditions for S—that is, what must be true if S is true and what must not be true if S is false. Thus the sentence "Fred is a bachelor" is true if and only if Fred is a man who has never been married. Fred's not having been married is both a necessary and a sufficient condition of the truth of the sentence stating that he is a bachelor. That this is so seems to be a good reason for saying that "Fred is a bachelor" *means* that Fred has never been married, for a person who truly understands the meaning of "Fred is a bachelor" will *ipso facto* know that if that sentence is true, then Fred has never been married.

Davidson's theory has a very serious drawback, which his critics have not been slow to point out.[14] Take any pair of true statements whatever—"Snow is white" and "Grass is green" are favorite examples—and the one will be true if and only if the other is true, since neither is false. Let S be "Snow is white" and p be "Grass is green." Then the sentence " 'Snow is white' is true if and only if grass is green" is true. But according to Davidson's theory, this makes "Snow is white" *mean that* grass is green! Yet clearly the whiteness of snow has nothing to do with the greenness of grass. Should grass cease to be green, this would make no difference to our belief that snow is white. On the other hand, if Fred gets married, he ceases thereby to be a bachelor.

Davidson's analysis of meaning in terms of truth conditions, needs, therefore, to be revised in such a way that "Fred is a bachelor" can mean "Fred has never been married," while "Snow is white" does not mean "Grass is green," even though the members of each pair of sentences are true simultaneously. A possible modification of Davidson's view is that the meaning of a sentence consists not of the whole set of its truth conditions, but of the much narrower set of its conventionally recognized truth conditions. The sentence S has p as a conventionally recognized truth condition when the speakers of a language have some kind of mutual commitment to denying that S can be true when p is false, and conversely. The nature of this commitment should be clear from what follows. Since no one, if confronted with evidence that grass is not green, while still believing that snow is white, would have qualms about denying "Snow is white if and only if grass is green," the greenness of grass is not a conventionally recognized truth condition of "Snow is white." On the other hand, if our friend Fred should find himself a wife we would not allow that he was still a bachelor. If we give up the belief that he is unmarried, we also give up the belief that he is a bachelor, and we do this rather than deny "X is a bachelor if and only if X is an unmarried man."

We feel a resistance to giving up "X is a bachelor if and only if X is an unmarried man" which we do not feel to giving up "Snow is white if and only if grass is green." Why is this? In what follows I want to argue that in the case of the former sentence we have a mutual understanding or convention to accept its truth which we do not have in the case of the latter. It is understandings of this kind, I shall maintain, that establish sameness of meaning.

Sameness of meaning differs from causal and evidential relations. If we think that p's being true is a cause of, or evidence for, S's being true, we are certainly reluctant to admit the possibility that p might be true while S is false. The difference between causal and evidential relations and relations of meaning equivalence or synonymy seems to rest on the reasons for our being reluctant to give up convictions that the truth of one sentence is dependent upon that of another. My belief that a track in a cloud chamber is evidence of an alpha particle is a consequence of my belief that certain postulates of nuclear physics are true. These beliefs are based in turn upon my belief that the scientists who have developed such theories have made certain observations and calculations which have confirmed the theories. Should further evidence indicate that these theories were *not* true then my confidence that a certain kind of track in a cloud chamber was evidence for the existence of an alpha particle might be shaken. If this were to happen, it would be new evidence, empirical data, which would undermine my original belief.

Besides beliefs based on strong evidence, there are many which we are reluctant to give up because relinquishing them would require a radical readjustment in our outlook on the world, or because of a particular kind of interest we have in upholding a general agreement that they are true. Some beliefs we cling to because they are pleasant; others because we will be ostracized if we doubt them openly; still others because we would hardly know how to conduct our lives if we disbelieved them. None of these underlies a belief in meaning equivalence. There are others, however, that we cling to in order that we may understand and be understood by those with whom we speak. These include beliefs in statements we call "true by definition." People who went about speaking of married bachelors, four-sided triangles, and objects that are both red and green all over would *not* be understood. If they were to communicate anything to others, they would have to reword what they were saying in such a way as to remove the implication that there are such things as married bachelors, etc. If we are to be able to communicate with each other, we must agree on the truth of some sentences. Without some fixed points of agreement, we could not be sure that we were speaking of the same objects. Suppose, for example, that we did not agree that triangles had three sides. Then the reference of the term "triangle" would be in doubt, for we could not be sure what other kinds of figures might be designated by the term.[15] One might, of course, set forth some other property as a criterion of triangularity, but unless there was agreement as to the truth of sentences asserting that triangles had *that* property, then that property could not serve as a criterion. In other words, if we are to know what our fellow speakers are talking about, we must know to what items they refer. But we can know this only if there are more or less fixed criteria for identifying these items. This can be so only if it is agreed that sentences, which assert that items of the kind in question satisfy the criteria, are to be acknowledged as true. Furthermore, sentences of this kind must be acknowledged to be true even under adverse circumstances, if they are to continue to be criteria-stating. Suppose, for example, I see a three-sided figure, of which one side is very much shorter than the other two. It does not really look like a triangle, and I am tempted to give it another name. But since three-sided figures, however odd, are considered triangles by definition, I will, to the extent that I have grasped this, resist the temptation to deny that the figure is triangular.

Likewise, suppose that Fred lives in a city apartment, has frequent parties, and entertains a variety of women, none of whom appears to reside with him on a permanent basis. It is reasonable to suppose that Fred is a bachelor. However, if I were to be confronted with incontrovertible evidence that he is in fact a married man, I would discount all the indications of his bachelorhood and maintain, despite them, that he is *not* a bachelor. Any person who, while admitting that the evidence shows Fred to be married, continues to affirm that he is a bachelor would be considered not to know the meanings of the terms involved in the relevant sentences.

The thesis that the meaning of sentences is determined by truth conditions which are made so by some form of convention among the speakers of a language needs some qualification. One difficulty is that the said speakers are often unsure of their reasons for being reluctant to abandon their belief in a given statement in the face of what appears to be unfavorable evidence. This is true not only of naive persons who may mistake wishing to retain some comfortable opinion for the desire to be able to communicate with one another, but of the more sophisticated as well. Two examples from the history of science will illustrate the point. When it was discovered that mechanical energy could be converted to heat, the question arose as to whether this constituted a violation of the law of conservation of energy or whether heat could be considered a form of energy and the conservation law retained. The law was too useful to be abandoned lightly, yet heat certainly had differences from mechanical energy. Heat and matter in motion were, however, comparable in certain respects, and heat was in the end accepted as a form of energy; indeed it has come to be defined in terms of the mechanical energy of molecules. Yet accepting this as a truth of physics and defining energy in such a way as to include both heat and mechanical energy seems to have been done as much as a matter of theoretical convenience as to allow physicists to communicate with one another.

The discovery of pterodactyl fossils required hard thinking by taxonomists. These creatures had wings and the general shape of birds, but they differed in other respects. It seems unlikely that biologists would have ceased being able to speak to each other had pterodactyls been admitted into the company of birds, so the classification of these creatures as reptiles seems to have been at least as much motivated by the need for taxonomic simplicity as by the necessity for mutual linguistic understanding.

It is certainly true that the choice of which characteristics of particular items are taken as identifying criteria is often partly dependent upon which will result in the greatest convenience for those who speak about those items. That a choice must be made, however, in the kinds of situations depicted in the above examples, indicates that communication cannot proceed satisfactorily unless there is some agreement as to what properties shall serve as criteria for certain items, that is, that there is some agreement as to which sentences will be held to be true, even though there are temptations to reject them. While physicists may have been tempted to deny that heat, light, matter, etc., were forms of energy, their agreement to uphold the definition of energy as the capacity to do work (which entailed that heat, light, and matter, given the empirical properties they exhibit, were forms of energy) enabled theoretical physics to develop further than it would have, had such agreement not been reached. One can well imagine the confusion that would reign, if physicists could not agree on how to define energy or upon the truth of any single criterion-stating sentence. Nor could we expect many advances in taxonomy if biologists could not agree that all and only birds had feathers or upon some other criterion-stating sentences. Without agreement to accept some such sentences as true, there could be no sciences.

For many, many terms, of course, there are no criterion-stating sentences which spell out a set of necessary and sufficient conditions for their correct application. But no matter how vague or imprecise a term may be, if it is of any use whatever in a language, there are some restrictions upon its employment. The general acknowledgement of these restrictions entails a conventional acceptance of some sentences as true. There may be disagreement as to what does or does not constitute a game, but no one would consider World War II to have been a game. Wars are not games because what enables an event to count as the one are restrictions against its counting as the other. That cities are not actions and that colors are not living creatures are truths which we accept, and our acceptance of them as holding regardless of circumstances constitutes part of the meanings of the terms in question. That we accept these and other restrictions on their use makes such terms meaningful, even though there may be no sets of necessary and sufficient conditions for the use of "city" or "living creature."

Which truths we accept as holding in all circumstances varies with time, with our interests, and with the theoretical framework by which our knowledge is organized. That this is so, however, need not count against the view that the meaning of sentences consists of their conventionally recognized truth conditions. There have been few in recent times who have wanted to deny that the meanings of terms and of sentences change. All that is necessary is that at any given time there are some sentences which are accepted as true in all possible combinations of circumstances. It does not follow that these sentences cannot lose this status, but it does follow that they cannot lose it without some explicit or tacit readjustment of the system of sentences having this status. When such readjustments take place, we have changes in the meanings of at least some words and sentences.[16]

Changes of meaning occur when questions about reference or what is being talked about arise. Some beliefs are hard to give up, but the difficulty does not consist of our not knowing what we would be talking about if we did not assume their truth. The discovery of black swans, for example, necessitated the abandonment of the belief that all swans are white, but there was no question that the black birds were *swans* and that their color was *black*. On the other hand, should swan-shaped entities be discovered which were cleverly designed robots, we *would* wonder whether they were swans.[17] It would then be necessary to decide whether the extension of the term "swan" would include these new creatures. Depending upon which decision was made, the meaning of "swan" might change. It could be decided, for example, that the robots were not swans, but later, after discovery of many other objects which were also robots closely resembling different kinds of creatures, people might decide to call them all by the names of the animal they resembled. Thus robot-swans would be included in the extension of "swan" and the meaning of that word would have changed.

Consider any sentence of the form "All Fs are G." For the most part, if some item which appears to be F and not G is found, no difficulties arise; the universal statement is held to be false. But if the question arises as to whether the object which is not G is, after all, an F, then it is possible that "All Fs are G" can count as analytic or as a meaning postulate of the language. This is likely if we find it extremely hard—apart from the strangeness and unexpectedness of the event—to accept the possibility that any item could fail to be G yet still be counted as an F.

Quine has argued that there is no clear criterion for determining whether "All Fs are G" is analytic or synthetic, and hence that the distinction is spurious.[18] To an extent I agree with this conclusion; however, there are many instances in which there is no question whether the not-G item is also an F, and these can be distinguished from the cases where there is such a question. Of the cases in which there is a question, it is not always possible to say whether "All Fs are Gs" is analytic or synthetic, but what does happen is that a decision about meaning is called for. These decisions can be changed with a resulting change in meaning. Once these decisions are explicitly made, however, the analyticity of particular sentences is determined by fiat. Such decisions are not, however, irrevocable. I do not want to rule out the possibility that analyticity can be discovered, as well as assigned. It seems only reasonable to suppose that in many cases the current use of a term F makes it clear that its reference is fixed by a criterion G, and that the admission that some F might not be G would result in a change of the meaning of G. Nevertheless, as long as no problems of reference come up, it does not greatly matter whether a firmly held belief is analytic or synthetic and there is undoubtedly no feature which sharply distinguishes analytic from synthetic statements. It is only when doubt as to what things we are talking of arises that decisions on this question are made. Such decisions are to some extent arbitrary and they need not be made for all time. They are made to serve the needs of the moment and in such a way as to be most convenient to those who use the terms involved. They do, however, fix reference and determine meaning, if only temporarily, and serve to distinguish analytic statements from the synthetic.[19] Artificial though the distinction may be, it not only makes communication possible, but it enables the body of truths to be extended. If it is settled, for the time being, at least, that the sum total of matter and energy is conserved, that birds have feathers, that triangles have three sides, etc., then we are free to determine more facts about matter, energy, birds, and triangles, knowing *what* it is these facts are facts about.

Given that the meaning of a statement consists of its conventionally recognized truth conditions, we need to consider further what these conventions are. Certainly it is only rarely that any group comes together and legislates decisions about what terms mean or what is to count as the truth conditions of sentences. Linguistic conventions usually grow up informally without any explicitly formulated decisions. Dictionary entries are compiled long after the conventions they record are established. Conventions of many kinds, linguistic conventions among them, result

from people's finding it useful to do as others do in like circumstances. This point has been developed by Lewis.[20] It is particularly useful for people to use signs and symbols in the same way,
for otherwise, it would not be possible for anyone to understand
how any such sign or symbol was being used without knowing
the special language (if it could be called that) of the individual
speaker. In their use of words children imitate their parents and
teachers; teenagers imitate their peers and favorite entertainers;
adults imitate the authors of the books and plays to which they
are exposed. Since we want to be understood, we try to use words
in the ways we think others will use them, and we allow ourselves
to trust that others will use words as we do and will take us as
employing them in the way that others employ them. This element of trust, as Lewis puts it,[21] is necessary for the possibility
of communication. That we have it is made clear in those cases
in which we realize that someone else is using an expression differently from the way we use it. Our surprise shows how much
we expect and count on others' employing terms as we do.

However this expectation might arise, the fact that it is there
makes language possible. That we can expect others to use terms
as we use them entails that, by and large, these terms will have
the same reference for all the speakers of the language. This
means that the same criteria will be used for identifying the same
referents, and, further, that there will be agreement that if a term
applies correctly to an item, then that item will satisfy those criteria. Not only will there be agreement in this belief, but there
will also be a determination to retain this belief even in the face
of apparent counterexamples, unless and until a new convention
is generated. This determination is at least partly grounded in the
realization that it is needed to retain the mutual trust and expectation that others will use expressions as we do. As a rule, of
course, we are quite unaware of any determination to cling to
certain beliefs come what may, or our reasons for doing so. Only
if a belief is challenged are we likely to consider whether we
would be willing to relinquish it, and if not, what would be our
reasons for retaining it. But when we do have to consider such a
matter, we often do realize that relinquishing certain beliefs
would have serious repercussions upon our ability to understand

what others are talking about. It would be virtually impossible to discuss the relevant subject matter with someone who denied, for example, that triangles are three-sided figures, that all bachelors are unmarried, that eight and seven are fifteen, that red is a color, or that it is not the case that an object can both have and not have a given property (at the same time and in the same respect). When we find it difficult to perceive how we could communicate with someone who denied some statement, this suggests that the statement's being held true is a convention of the language in question—that it states, or is implied by a statement of, the truth conditions for some sentence which are mutually agreed upon by the speakers of the language. Belief in the truth of these sentences can, of course, be relinquished by many speakers, in which case the conventions, and, consequently, the meanings of the terms involved, will change. But given the convention, so long as it persists, so will the determination to hold the relevant statements to be true.[22]

More needs to be said about what the mutual agreement to hold certain sentences true amounts to. This agreement has an element of belief and an element of intention. In the first place, the speakers of the language already believe, by and large, in the truth of the sentences. Secondly, they intend not to accept any evidence as counting against their truth—or, at least, they intend this in situations when they are presented with facts which might be taken as such evidence. This intention is present because the retention of the belief is necessary in order to carry out their further intention of being able to communicate with one another. In particular, these intentions are (a) to specify kinds of states of affairs, and (b) to represent them as holding, or as someone's being directed to make them hold, or as someone's being committed to bringing them about, etc.

It has been argued by a number of recent writers that the intentions of speakers must be taken into account in an adequate theory of meaning.[23] To the following extent, I think they are correct. First of all, we have intentions to do the particular jobs of which communicating consists (informing, commanding, questioning, etc.). Secondly, we intend to fulfill a necessary condition of accomplishing these tasks—namely, to retain a belief in the truth of certain statements. This last amounts to a determination to use words in a certain way—to *mean* something specific by them. Furthermore, it seems clear that for someone to *mean something by* an utterance, he must intend to bring about some effect by uttering it. It does not follow, however, that *what the utterance means* must be defined by the intentions the speaker has in making it. The earlier discussion of the difference between meaning and illocutionary force makes this, I think, apparent. That the meaning of an utterance might be defined in terms of the intentions which are conventionally recognized as being expressed by that utterance, is a view which might well be successfully developed, however.[24]

To summarize thus far, I have argued that the propositional content component of the meaning of a sentence consists of those truth conditions for its indicative form which are conventionally recognized. If p represents the conventionally recognized truth conditions for sentence S, then S means that p, and there is a mutual understanding and expectation among the speakers of the language containing S that the sentence "S if and only if p" is to count as true in any combination of circumstances. When there is no set of necessary and sufficient conditions, which is conventionally recognized, for the truth of S, there may still be partial meaning rules: for example, that "S only if p" is to count as true in all circumstances, or perhaps "S if and only if p or q or r."

The sentence "S means that p" in which p is a complete specification of the meaning of S and where S is an indicative sentence, can be analyzed as follows:

> There is a convention—a mutual understanding and expectation among those who speak the language in which S appears—that the sentence "S if and only if p" is to count as true in all circumstances.

Where p is not a complete set of necessary and sufficient truth conditions, we may have meaning rules like,

> There is a convention, etc., that the sentence "S only if p or q" is to count as true in all circumstances.

When S is not an indicative, some adjustments must be made in the above account, and in order to do this, I shall introduce some symbols which should be helpful in making the required distinctions. Earlier in this chapter, I have, following others, distinguished between the meaning of a sentence and the illocutionary force of an utterance of that sentence, and also between the two components of the meaning of a sentence, namely, its propositional content and its mood. A similar set of distinctions has been made by Hare.[25] He uses the term *phrastic* for the propositional content of a sentence and the term *trophic* for its mood. The actual illocutionary force of a given utterance of the sentence he calls its *neustic* or *sign of subscription*. In what follows I will let φ stand for the propositional content or phrastic of a sentence, τ for the mood or trophic, and v for the illocutionary force, or neustic. Any sentence may be analyzed as τ(φ), where φ may be replaced by a description of a state of affairs and τ by some symbol representing mood; for example, ⊢ for the indicative or assertoric mood, ! for the imperative mood, Pr for promising, ? for questioning, R for recommending, and so forth. Thus "Jim will feed George and Martha, and Sarah will feed Jessica" can be represented as ⊢(Jim's feeding George and Martha, and Sarah's feeding Jessica), while "Jim, feed George and Martha, and Sarah, feed Jessica" can be represented as !(Jim's feeding George and Martha, and Sarah's feeding Jessica), and "I recommend that Jim feed George and Martha and Sarah feed Jessica" as R (Jim's feeding George and Martha, and Sarah's feeding Jessica).

We can relate the distinction of propositional content and mood to the analysis of meaning as conventionally recognized truth conditions in the following way. The sentence τ(φ) means that p if and only if there is a convention, etc., such that the sentence "⊢(φ) if and only if p′" (where p′ is the indicative form of p) is to count as true in all circumstances, and there is a convention, etc., according to which a speaker using the morphemes designated by τ is representing some state of affairs φ in the manner M. Just as truth conditions are dependent upon the mutual understandings and expectations of the speakers of a language, so also are the mood indicators, such as the words "I promise," the use of an imperative verb, or inverted word order.

Speech acts may be represented by speech act operators being applied to sentences. Where v is the speech act operator and S the sentence, we have v (S), or, applying a mood operator τ on propositional content, v [τ (ϕ)]. Consider, for example, the sentence "I'll meet you at six." It is an indicative, meaning that the person denoted by "I" will meet the one denoted by "you" at the time denoted by "six." We may represent it as ⊢(My meeting you at six). In most circumstances in which that sentence is uttered, however, it constitutes a promise as well as an assertion. Given that conditions are such that the speaker's uttering it under them are, by the conventions of the language, intended to arouse expectations in the addressee, and that both parties can therefore be expected in normal circumstances to be mutually aware of an intention to arouse this expectation, we may indicate the presence of this circumstance by the illocutionary force indicator Pr, which represents a promise's having been made. The speech act as a whole can be represented by Pr [⊢(My meeting you at six)]. Since the utterance is also an assertion by the speaker, as well as a promise, we can indicate the dual nature of the speech act by representing it as {Pr and ⊢ [⊢(My meeting you at six)]}.

It would not be so easy to represent indirect speech acts, such as a request for a present conveyed by saying "Tomorrow is my birthday" in a notation like the above, nor will it be necessary to do so for what follows. Perhaps the following would do. v {[τ (ϕ)]$_u$, [τ' (ϕ')]$_a$}, where the subscript u applies to the actual sentence uttered, and the subscript a to what would have been said had a direct speech act been used. The operator v represents the actual illocutionary force type the act has. In this way the birthday hint might be represented as ! {[⊢(Tomorrow's being my birthday)]$_u$, [!(Your giving me a present)]$_a$}.

The above method of representing the meaning components of sentences and the illocutionary forces of sentences will be useful in the discussion of the logic of nonindicatives which follows in the next chapters.

3

Nonassertoric Inferences

We have seen that one of the problems with developing a logic for sentences which are not declaratives is that such sentences cannot be either true or false. Yet the central notion of logic as we know it is that of the valid argument; that is, one in which the truth of the premises guarantees the truth of the conclusion. For sentences that do not have truth values, it is difficult to see how there can be valid arguments containing them, and it is also hard to make sense of a kind of logic in which validity has no role.

In this chapter, I shall undertake the following: (1) to show that the truth-value analogues hitherto suggested for nonassertoric sentences can only be expressed in assertoric sentences and in terms of truth and falsity, so that the nonassertoric logics proposed so far must be stated in the language of assertoric logic; (2) to show that in our reasoning with nonassertoric sentences we actually employ only assertoric premises and draw only assertoric conclusions, and that where these conclusions appear to be nonassertoric on the surface, they are in fact metalinguistic, i.e., statements asserting something about nonassertoric utterances; and (3) to spell out the formal structure of nonassertoric reasoning. If I am successful in this it will be clear that the role of nonassertoric sentences in our reasoning is very different from that of assertions. A comparison of evaluations with both assertoric and nonassertoric sentences will show that their role is much more like that of the former than that of the latter. Therefore, to the extent that meaning is a function of grammatical and logical behavior, evaluations will be seen to be more like assertions in meaning than like nonassertoric sentences.

PROPOSED ANALOGUES OF TRUTH FOR NONASSERTORIC SENTENCES

Those who have tried to develop satisfactory nonassertoric logics have endeavored to save the notion of validity by introducing values for nondeclarative sentences which are different from, but analogous to, the values "true" and "false." Then a valid argument can be defined as one in which, if the premises are all either true or have the value analogous to "true," the conclusion must also be either true or have the value analogous to "true." The values proposed as substitutes for "true" and "false" for imperatives and performatives have been of three basic sorts: (1) satisfaction vs. nonsatisfaction; (2) commitment, endorsement, or acceptance vs. rejection; and (3) justification, validity, or being-in-force vs. nonjustification, invalidity, or the contrary of being-in-force.[1]

In what follows I shall argue that the conditions for applying any of these values to a nonassertoric sentence can be expressed only in terms of assertoric, declarative sentences and their truth or falsity. It will be seen that a consequence of this is that the validity of an argument containing nonassertoric sentences as either premises or conclusion can be made comprehensible only through the use of a number of definitions, unstated premises, or rules of inference, none of which are necessary for understanding the validity of arguments containing only assertoric statements. The necessity for these presuppositions makes nonassertoric arguments differ from assertoric arguments in ways in which arguments containing evaluative sentences do not. If I succeed in showing this, as I hope to do by the end of chapter 4, there will be good grounds for concluding that evaluations are assertoric rather than nonassertoric sentences.

Let us now consider in turn each of the kinds of pairs of values which have been proposed as analogues for "true" and "false."

(1) Satisfaction vs. nonsatisfaction. For all sorts of illocutionary acts, there is a sense in which each kind may be said to be satisfied. An imperative is satisfied when a command is obeyed, a request granted, or advice followed; a promise is satisfied when it is kept; a bet when it is won; an assertion when it is true; a

prediction when it comes true; a warning when it is heeded; a recommendation when it is followed. Orders disobeyed, promises broken, bets lost, false assertions, and warnings, advice, or recommendations ignored are cases in which illocutionary acts are not satisfied. Sometimes the satisfaction of a performative is hardly distinguishable from the successful performance thereof. For example, "I approve the report" is satisfied when the report is officially accepted by the speaker, and the act of utterance in the normal context *is* his official acceptance. And "I confer upon you the degree of Doctor of Philosophy" is satisfied precisely when your doctorate is officially bestowed upon you by means of the speaker's uttering these words. The term "satisfied" does not sound natural in some of these contexts, but I think it will do as a generic term for the successful achievement of some state of affairs referred to in the sentence whose utterance is the illocutionary act in question, and as a general substitute for "obeyed," "followed," "acknowledged," "won," "honored," "kept," etc.

The values "true" and "false" apply, in traditional assertoric logic, to sentences rather than to speech acts of assertion, and if nonassertoric logic is to parallel assertoric logic, it seems reasonable to apply the value "satisfied" to sentences as well as to illocutionary acts. Thus, "obeyed" as a species of "satisfied" would apply to sentences in the imperative mood, "kept" to sentences beginning with the words "I promise . . . ," "heeded" to sentences beginning with "I hereby warn . . . ," and so forth.

The replacement of "true" and "false" with "satisfied" and "not satisfied," with the latter values including such pairs as obeyed-disobeyed, accepted-rejected, answered affirmatively-answered negatively, etc., seems initially plausible. The same sentence—and the same illocutionary act—cannot be satisfied and not satisfied by the same agent on the same occasion, nor is it possible for a sentence or illocutionary act and its contradictory to be satisfied simultaneously. It would seem that I cannot obey "Thou shalt not commit adultery and thou shalt not bear false witness" without obeying "Thou shalt not commit adultery," and that Esau cannot keep his promise to give Jacob his birthright in exchange for the soup if, when Jacob does give him the soup, he fails to relinquish his birthright. Using "satisfied" and "not satisfied" as values, it appears possible to understand validity in terms broader than those of truth and falsity alone.

The application of the value "satisfied," however, to a nondeclarative sentence, or to an act performed by an utterance of that sentence, can be done only under the assumption that certain declarative sentences are true. If such a sentence or speech act is satisfied, certain states of affairs must hold. If ϕ designates a state of affairs, then $!(\phi)$, $Pr(\phi)$, etc., are satisfied only if $\vdash\phi$ is true. The imperative "Polish your buttons!" is not obeyed unless the person to whom it is addressed does in fact polish his buttons. Not only must ϕ hold, but other conditions must be fulfilled as well. An order cannot be obeyed if it has not been issued; unmade promises cannot be kept, nor can unmade bets be won. My polishing my buttons would not constitute obedience to the command "Polish your buttons!" unless someone had *told* me to do so. Nor could I keep a promise to polish the buttons simply by polishing them; I would first have had to assure someone that I would perform that task. If your request that I do A has been honored or satisfied, this entails not only that I have done A, but also that you have made the request. Not only is it impossible to obey an unissued order, but it is also impossible to disobey one. Neither can unmade promises be broken nor unmade requests be ignored. The satisfaction values for nonassertoric sentences can apply only if an illocutionary act employing them has been performed.[2]

For any sentence $\tau\phi$, where τ represents the mood of the sentence, $\tau\phi$ is satisfied only if the state of affairs designated by ϕ holds, i.e., $\vdash\phi$ is true. Besides this, a speech act must have been performed of the kind represented by ν, where ν corresponds to τ in designating the kind of speech act usually performed by utterances of sentences having the mood represented by τ. There is one exception to this second rule, however. The truth of $\vdash\phi$ is independent of whether any speech act has taken place which asserts that $\vdash\phi$ has taken place; consequently, the only satisfaction condition of assertions is the truth of the sentence asserted; that p has been asserted is not one of the truth (or satisfaction) conditions of p, where p is a declarative. On the other hand, the fact that $!(\phi)$ has been ordered is one of the satisfaction conditions of

!(ϕ). The exact sentence !(ϕ) need not perhaps have been uttered for !(ϕ) to be satisfied, but *some* sentence must have been uttered which would constitute a speech act of commanding what is expressed in !(ϕ).

The satisfaction conditions of sentences of any mood are the holding of certain states of affairs. That these hold is expressed in assertions, and it is unlikely that they could be expressed by nonassertoric sentences or in terms of the satisfaction of nonassertoric sentences. To see why this is so, let us consider the possibility that for a given propositional content ϕ we might have a symmetrical relationship between the sentences ⊢(ϕ), !(ϕ), Pr(ϕ), etc., and their satisfaction values, "true," "obeyed," "kept," etc., such that ϕ's holding is ⊢(ϕ)'s being true, !(ϕ)'s being obeyed, Pr(ϕ)'s being kept, etc. If so, there would be no grounds for giving primacy to assertion and to truth.[3] But no such symmetry exists, since ϕ's designating an existing state of affairs is not a sufficient condition, although it is necessary, for !(ϕ)'s being obeyed, Pr(ϕ)'s being kept, etc., while it is both necessary and sufficient for ⊢(ϕ)'s being true.

The other satisfaction conditions for !(ϕ), Pr(ϕ), etc. can be expressed as assertions, but they cannot be expressed as commands, promises, etc., or the satisfaction thereof. Suppose that instead of having as a satisfaction condition of !(ϕ) that the command !(ϕ) is one which has been issued, we try to express this condition as "Issue the command that !(ϕ)!" This, however, would not inform us that the condition was fulfilled. Nor would "The command, 'Issue the command that !(ϕ)' is satisfied," do as an expression of the necessary condition. This is not a satisfaction condition of !(ϕ), for !(ϕ)'s being satisfied is not dependent upon whether any such command as "Issue the command!(ϕ)!" was ever made; that is, whether anyone was commanded to issue that command. The attempt to express the satisfaction conditions of the imperative in terms of the satisfaction of imperatives as opposed to the truth of assertions leads to an infinite regress, for no command can be satisfied which has not been issued, and if we must express the fact that the command has been issued in terms of the satisfaction of yet another command, there is no end to the iteration of commands. The same remarks apply to promises, bets, questions, recommendations, and so forth, but not to assertions, for whether a statement has been asserted is irrelevant to its truth.[4]

An attempt to impose symmetry between assertions and their truth and nonassertoric sentences and their forms of satisfaction might take the following lines. We could make a distinction between the truth of an assertion and its being satisfied such that while the assertion may be *true* even if it is not made by anyone, it cannot be *satisfied* unless it is both true and has been made by someone. Similarly, we might distinguish between the normal sense of obedience to a command and a sort of obedience which can occur without the command's having been issued—that *had* the command been issued it *would* have been obeyed. We could similarly distinguish between the normal sense of keeping a promise and a sort of promise-keeping which can take place even when no promise has been made. We could then indicate whether a command had been obeyed in the normal sense or in the modified sense, whether a promise was kept in the normal sense or kept in the modified sense (independently of whether a promise had been made), etc. We might then generalize so that for any sentence represented by $\tau\phi$, $\tau\phi$ has the value "satisfied" (in the modified sense) if and only if $\vdash(\phi)$, whereas $\tau\phi$ can be normally satisfied only if $\vdash(\phi)$ and also some illocutionary act (represented by $\nu\tau\phi$, where ν corresponds to τ in the sense of "correspondence" indicated above) has taken place. Very likely, other conditions would also be necessary for actual satisfaction, depending upon the type of performative in question. The state of affairs ϕ's holding is the same thing as $\vdash(\phi)$'s being true in the normal sense, or as $!(\phi)$'s being obeyed, $Pr(\phi)$'s being kept, etc., in the modified senses, but is *not* identical with $\vdash(\phi)$'s being true in the modified sense, or with $!(\phi)$'s being obeyed, or $Pr(\phi)$'s being kept in the normal senses.

Rescher has proposed a method of this sort in connection with commands.[5] A command is what he calls *terminated* when, if it *had* been issued, it *would* have been obeyed. The command $!(\phi)$ is terminated if and only if $\vdash(\phi)$ is true, and nonterminated if and only if $\vdash(\phi)$ is false. It seems plausible to extend the notion of termination to all sorts of performatives, so that any sentence $\tau\phi$

is terminated if and only if φ holds. Unlike satisfaction (in the ordinary sense), termination can apply to sentences even when there is no actual performance of an illocutionary act of the kind usually performed by utterances of the sentence having the mood in question.

An extension of this solution to nonassertoric sentences generally appears on the surface to be promising. It seems to provide a way of developing a logic which incorporates both assertoric and nonassertoric sentences, and uses the values of termination and nontermination. An argument would be valid in such a logic if and only if when its premises were all terminated, its conclusion must also be terminated. Unfortunately, as Rescher himself recognizes, and as was pointed out long before by Alf Ross, such a logic would admit too many arguments as valid.[6] For example, from "Donald will close the door" we could deduce "Donald, close the door," and conversely. Both these sentences would entail and be entailed by "I, Donald, hereby promise to close the door."

Further restrictions clearly need to be made on the kinds of arguments which will be admitted as valid in a logic which includes nondeclarative sentences. This would probably have to be done in one of the following three ways: (a) by defining termination values more fully, so as to encorporate the specific characteristics of the mood of the sentences; (b) by requiring that premises be added to the arguments which will prevent sentences having one mood from being inferred indiscriminately from sentences having another mood; or (c) by the introduction of supplementary rules of inference which will license only the kinds of inferences we wish to allow. Each procedure will require an analysis of the concepts of values for nonassertoric sentences and the validity of nonassertoric inferences expressed in terms of assertions.

(a) We might try to give some account of the meaning of termination for promises, bets, recommendations, etc. For example, we could introduce meaning-rules like: "!(φ) is terminated" means that if the command ![!(φ)] had been issued, it would have been obeyed, or "Pr(φ) is terminated" means that if a promise to the effect Pr[Pr(φ)] had been made, it would have been kept. The argument "Donald will close the door. Therefore, Donald, close the door!" is no longer valid. As Professor George I. Mavrodes pointed out in commenting on an earlier version of this manuscript, even if "Donald will close the door" is true, the corresponding command might not be terminated, since Donald may be the sort of person who would make a point of not doing what he was commanded to do, even if it was something he normally would have done on his own.

Consequently, the above meaning-rule will block the undesired inference. It also blocks, however, those inferences which we would want preserved. For example, suppose the head nurse says to a new aide, "Do everything you can to keep from spreading Smith's infection to other patients. Wear a gown, mask, and gloves whenever you go into his room; wash your hands and arms thoroughly when you leave; place his soiled linen in the isolation bag; and serve his meals in disposable dishes." Suppose that the aide obeys these orders completely. It follows that she serves the patient's meals in disposable dishes. It does *not* follow, however, that if the nurse had said simply, "Serve Smith's meals in disposable dishes," that the aide would have obeyed *this* order. The first order is given in such a way as to explain the point of each part of it. The second is not, and the aide, if she does not understand why it ought to be obeyed, might be tempted to flout it, especially if it requires extra work when time is short.

In general, whether commands are obeyed depends very much both on the manner in which they are given and the attitude and circumstances of the person to whom they are issued. That a particular command, "X, do A" would have been obeyed if issued does not suffice to show that "X, do B" would have been obeyed, even if X's doing A entails his doing B. The same considerations hold for promises, warnings, and all other performatives.

That the proposed meaning-rules given above were not adequate does not, of course, show that a satisfactory set might not be developed. There is, however, a feature of any such rule which demonstrates the primacy of assertion which cannot be avoided in a nonassertoric logic.

The rules themselves, it will be noted, are assertions, and it is difficult to see how they could be anything else. "Apply 'terminated' to !(ϕ) whenever, if the command 'Issue the command that !(ϕ)' had been issued, it would have been obeyed" does not do the same job as the translation rule. In it we are told *what to do*, but not that the meaning of the two expressions is the same. I do not think it is necessary to try the same experiment using promises, bets, or recommendations in place of commands as vehicles for expressing the translation rules or meaning postulates.

(b) Additional premises might enable us to restrict the number of allowable inferences in either of two ways. We could include in each argument premises which would give definitions of the kind of termination involved, and which would state both that the premises were terminated and that whenever there was termination of the premises, there would be termination of the conclusion. In this way the inferences to which objections were raised earlier might be rendered innocuous. For example, "Donald will close the door," and " 'Donald will close the door' is terminated," and "If 'Donald will close the door is terminated' then 'Donald, close the door!' is terminated," entail jointly that "Donald close the door!" is terminated.

Even this does not seem entirely satisfactory. It would seem that what we are trying to infer from the stated premises is "Donald, close the door!," but—according to Rescher's analysis (which, as indicated above, is unsatisfactory)—all that we can infer is that *if* Donald had been told to close the door, that imperative would have been obeyed in the ordinary sense. This peculiarity need not bother us from a technical standpoint, however. Saying that we infer from the above premises "The command, 'Donald, close the door,' is terminated" is analogous to saying that we infer from certain premises "The statement 'Donald will close the door' is true." We can, in fact, do this in assertoric logic, for, assuming the Tarskian definition of truth, the statement p is true if and only if p, so that any premises which entail p also entail that p is true. We do not, however, normally speak of inferring that p is true, rather than, simply, p. That it seems more natural, and, indeed, is only correct, to say that what we infer in the argument considered above is "The command . . . was terminated" rather than the command itself, tells us something about what we actually do when we make inferences concerning nonassertoric sentences. This is a point to which I will return later in this chapter.

(c) The similarity of the added premise "If 'Donald will close the door' is terminated, then 'Donald, close the door!' is terminated" to the rule of inference *modus ponens* in traditional logic will, very likely, have been noted by the reader. This suggests that it may be more promising to develop nonassertoric logic by providing it with additional rules of inference than by tacking on ad hoc premises to every argument. Such an approach has been taken by Welker and McArthur, who have proposed several rules of inference which govern valid nonassertoric arguments.[7] Their rules include criteria of validity which are restrictive in nature; instead of permitting the Donald inference even in an innocuous form, they would rule it out. It seems more plausible to take an approach of this kind than either of those considered so far.

Although Welker and McArthur use a value different from satisfaction in place of truth, it will be useful to consider at this point the kinds of rules they suggest. Adapting these rules to my own terminology, one of them states that if the conclusion of an argument has the mood τ, at least one of the premises must also have the mood τ. This rule would eliminate entirely the offensive Donald inference.

The rationale for such a stipulation is that the validity of any inference must take into account the mood of the premises and conclusion, since these are, after all, a part of what the sentences mean. Assertoric sentences are satisfied when they are true; when a state of affairs of the kind described in the propositional content holds when a command is satisfied, then it is terminated, and termination is defined in terms of obedience. Obedience, in turn, is the bringing about of a state of affairs which one has been directed to bring about. Thus the specific kind of termination which is applicable to imperatives is dependent upon what is common to the meaning of all imperatives; namely, their mood, or their manner of representing their propositional content—as, for example, someone's being directed to bring about the state of affairs it designates.

Something quite different is going on when sentences having other moods are terminated. A promise sentence is terminated when it is kept, or would have been kept had it been uttered in appropriate circumstances. Keeping a promise *is* bringing about a state of affairs which one has committed oneself, in a certain way, to bringing about. The meaning of keeping a promise is thus related to what promising—and promising sentences—mean. In a valid argument the value that is preserved from premises to conclusion can only be the same for both: truth in the case of purely assertoric arguments; and other values, analogous to truth, but different from it, for nonassertoric premises and conclusions. No argument, for example, in which truth is applicable to the premises, but command termination to the conclusion, is valid. Here the means of representing the propositional content of the one differs from that of the other. Where mood differs, what the sentence expresses differs, and it seems only natural to require that sentences which entail others should share mood with those others.

In the logic proposed by Welker and McArthur, the relation of entailment holds between sentences considered as potential speech acts. What kind of speech act the utterance of a given sentence would be is determined not only by its mood, but what conditions of utterance would constitute its felicity conditions, that is, the circumstances which would make the utterance be the performance of a particular type of action. Thus, for a sentence to be a conferring of a degree it must be uttered by an appropriate authority under special conditions—here, a college president at a graduation ceremony. Among the rules of inference that Welker and McArthur propose as criteria of the validity for nonassertoric arguments are (a) when all premises and conclusions are transformed into assertions, the premises must imply the conclusion by ordinary assertoric logic, and (b) the conditions which would make at least one of the premises an illocutionary act of a given kind must entail the conditions which would make the conclusion an illocutionary act of the same kind.

For example, the inference of "Stand at attention!" from "Stand at attention and present arms!" satisfies (a), since "You will stand at attention and present arms," entails "You will stand at attention." The inference can only be valid, however, if, in addition, the same speaker were authorized to order the same addressees to obey the orders represented in both the premise and the conclusion. Otherwise rule (b) would not be followed. Thus Private Bailey's obeying Sergeant Snorkel's order to stand at attention and present arms will not entail Private Diller's obeying Captain Scabbard's order to stand at attention. However, the sergeant's order to Bailey to stand at attention and present arms may, according to McArthur and Welker's system, entail an order from the sergeant to Bailey to stand at attention, since the conditions of the premise are identical with, and hence entail, those of the conclusion.

Their system is much more elaborate than I have indicated here, and I shall subsequently discuss another aspect of it. It is clear, however, from the foregoing, as Welker and McArthur themselves acknowledge, that nonassertoric inferences are heavily dependent upon assertoric logic. No such logic in which the premises are not supplemented by assertoric meaning-rules or rules of inference above and beyond those required for assertoric logic can suffice to allow inferences from nonassertoric premises or to nonassertoric conclusions.

(2) Commitment, endorsement, or acceptance vs. rejection. A more popular analogue for truth than satisfaction is that of commitment (by the speaker or perhaps others), endorsement, or acceptance. An imperative "X, do A!" is satisfied only if X does A, that is, "X does A" is true, but Y's being committed to X's doing A does not seem to be dependent upon "X does A"'s being true. Nor does it seem essential that the command "X, do A" have been actually spoken. It is not always clear, however, how speaker-commitment should be interpreted, but considering the other views of the leading proponent of commitment logic, Hare, it probably means something like this. Y is committed to "X, do A!" if Y intends or prescribes that X do A, or if Y would so intend or prescribe under certain conditions.[8] Extended to include all kinds of illocutionary acts, the notion of speaker-commitment might be interpreted as follows: the person who performs the illocutionary act $\nu\tau\phi$ is committed to $\nu\tau\phi$ if he intends, prescribes, or wants it to be the case that $\vdash(\phi)$ or would do so under specified conditions.

Even though the truth of $\vdash(\phi)$ is not a necessary condition of anyone's being committed to $\nu\tau\phi$, the truth of other assertions is. Unless X wants—or has *some* investment in—the realization of the state of affairs φ, he is not committed to ντφ. Furthermore, any meaning-postulate which expresses this relationship is an assertion. We cannot alternatively interpret the postulate as, say, a command, for linguistic and logical postulates are not imperatives, but statements of what are the criteria for the correctness of certain procedures. They are not like the directions on a package for assembling the contents. A logic of commitment, like a logic of satisfaction, must at the very least be partially formulated in terms of assertions.

A logic of speaker-commitment has a difficulty not shared with a logic of satisfaction. In the former, if a nonassertoric argument is valid, the speaker cannot be committed to the illocutionary acts represented in the premises without being committed to those represented in the conclusion. If X's doing A requires his doing B, then it is desirable in theories of nonassertoric inference for τ(X's doing A) to entail τ(X's doing B). Yet anyone may want or intend or be committed to X's doing A, and still not want or intend or be committed to X's doing B, even if he knows that X's doing B is a necessary condition of his doing A. No law of logic or psychology requires that our desires be consistent.[9]

Desires or commitments are called inconsistent, not when it is logically impossible to entertain them simultaneously, but when it is logically impossible to realize both the desired states. According to logics of commitment, if we are committed to ντφ and ⊢φ entails ⊢ψ then we must be committed to ντψ. But we need not be so committed, because we may want, intend, or prescribe φ but not ψ. Anyone committed to both φ and not-ψ is, of course, committed to realizing two mutually inconsistent states of affairs. We know that two states of affairs are logically incompatible because the statements describing them cannot both be true. The rules of a logic of commitment are dependent upon assertoric logic in that they can only be clarified in terms of the truth and falsity of assertions—in this case, descriptions of states of affairs.

Logics of commitment might license inferences from nonassertoric premises or to nonassertoric conclusions by the introduction of rules of inference or additional premises. One criterion of validity for arguments might be, for example, that for every fully rational agent, if he is committed to the argument's premises, he would be committed to the conclusion as well. Such a stipulation would, of course, be an assertion.

Alternatively, it might be possible to make a logic of commitment dependent upon a logic of satisfaction—to say that we must be committed to $\nu\tau\psi$ if we are committed to $\nu\tau\phi$ and $\vdash\phi$ entails $\vdash\psi$ because $\vdash\phi$ and $\vdash$ not-ψ cannot both be true. But as we have seen already, a logic of satisfaction must in turn be expressed in terms of assertions.

Apart from the fact that a nonassertoric logic of commitment cannot be coherently expressed except in terms of assertions, there is a further difficulty with treating commitment as a value of sentences analogous to truth. The problem is apparent when we consider mixed arguments, i.e., those with both assertoric and nonassertoric components. Let us examine the following:

> I promise to sign, only if it is legal to do so.
> I promise to sign.
> It is legal to do so.

Let us suppose that in addition we have a premise or a rule of inference which entitles us to assume that this is an inference which will be made by a completely rational being: that is, one whose desires, as well as whose thought processes, are thoroughly consistent. Given this, does the conclusion follow? Clearly, it does not. If the perfectly rational speaker is committed to the two premises all that follows is that he *believes* (on good grounds, of course) that signing the paper in question is legal. It does not follow that it *is* legal.

Here is another example:

> If the plants are dry, water them.
> The plants are dry.
> Water them.

Even given the assumption that the speaker is rational, the conclusion does not follow from the premises. That he is committed to "Water them" is not a consequence of (a) his being committed to the first premise and (b) the truth of the second, for, unless he believes that the plants are dry, he need not endorse the conclusion. Furthermore, if he believes falsely, although with good reason, that the plants are dry, it follows from his perfect rationality that he is committed to "Water them."

It seems that the value which corresponds to "commitment" here is not truth, but something like belief. A logic which adopts these values could form the basis of a logic of acceptance or endorsement of the kind suggested by Castañeda which would show what sentences should be accepted, given the acceptance of other sentences.[10] Here acceptance would be something different for each sort of illocutionary act: to accept an assertion would be to believe it true; to accept a command would be to intend to obey it; to accept a warning would be to heed it. A logic of this sort would be different from the kind suggested by Hare, and, as Castañeda himself recognizes, it would be equally dependent upon truth-functional (assertoric) logic. It is rational to accept a sentence $\tau\psi$ whenever we accept another sentence $\tau\phi$ on the grounds that $\vdash\phi$ implies $\vdash\psi$, just because the state of affairs described by ϕ cannot be realized consistently with the nonrealization of the state of affairs described by ψ. Any inferences using a logic of acceptance depend upon other inferences concerning what states of affairs are compatible according to truth-functional logic. We do not know that it is always irrational to accept $\tau\phi$ and $\tau(\text{not} -\psi)$ unless we know that $\vdash\phi$ entails $\vdash\psi$.

(3) Justification, validity, or being-in-force vs. nonjustification, invalidity, or the contrary of being-in-force. The third way of ascribing values to nonassertoric sentences has concerned notions of the validity of sentences. Castañeda has developed a logic of imperatives based on the value he terms *orthotic*.[11] The context in which an imperative is uttered, which includes certain ends or goals of the persons concerned and the conditions which obtain at the time of utterance, may be described by a set of indicative sentences, which I shall represent as C. If C entails (by standard truth-functional logic) the realization of the state of affairs represented in the imperative (i.e., ϕ, when the imperative is $!(\phi)$), then the imperative has the value *orthotic*. In other words, it is justified by the ends, given the circumstances which hold. If $\vdash$ not-ϕ is entailed by C, then $!\phi$ is *an*orthotic, but if neither $\vdash\phi$ nor $\vdash$not-ϕ is entailed, $!\phi$ is orthotic. If obeying the imperative would frustrate the ends in question, the imperative is unjustified,

while otherwise it is not. Obviously, the value that the imperative has must be inferred by means of assertoric logic from the statements describing the context, and to that extent Castañeda's system is dependent upon truth-functional logic.

The same may be said of a logic of being-in-force. That an illocutionary act is in force means, among other things, that some utterance has not only been made, but made under those conditions which make the performance of the speech act in question successful. Frequently when an illocutionary act is successfully performed, one or more persons incur obligations. If you have no right to command me, I have no duty to obey you, and no orders issued by you are binding upon me; they are not commands which are in force. If they were, any consequence of them would also be binding upon me, i.e., in force. But whether a command has been issued, whether the conditions under which it was issued are felicitous, and whether anyone is bound to obey it, are facts describable by declarative sentences which have the values "true" or "false."

Besides this, the consequences of a command which are binding upon me are determined by what it is necessary for me to do to satisfy that command, and the same may be said for other sorts of performatives like promises, advice, or warnings. If I am obliged to bring about a state of affairs, I may also be obliged to bring about any state of affairs which is a consequence, according to truth-functional logic, of the former state. If "X does A" entails "X does B," then if X is bound by a promise to do A, he is also bound to do B, since it cannot be true that he does A unless he also does B. While he has not promised to do B, his obligations are the same as they would have been if he *had* so promised. Because what X is obliged to do is determined by the truth-functional consequences of what is true if he meets the obligations to which he directly commits himself by his speech acts, a logic of being-in-force is dependent upon truth-functional logic.

Of the nonassertoric logics proposed so far, then, all appear to be parasitic upon assertoric logic in that whatever values analogous to "true" and "false" are used, it is whether certain assertions are true that determines if these values can be applied to a sentence. It does not follow from what I have said that no logic of performatives could be developed. I shall now argue, however, that such a logic would have no practical value, since it would not reflect the reasoning we actually carry out which involves nonassertoric sentences.[12]

THE USE OF NONASSERTORIC INFERENCES

There is something highly artificial about the examples of non-assertoric arguments which philosophers set forth. People simply do not argue in that way. The performative sentences contained in these arguments are presented in a vacuum. We really do not know what to make of something like:

> I promise either to go to New York or to go to Chicago.
> I promise not to go to New York.
> Therefore, I promise to go to Chicago.

unless the context is specified. I cannot know whether the conclusion is in force or whether I am bound by it except from the context. Nor can I know whether any promise has actually been made in either of the premises or in the conclusion; the bare words are not sufficient to indicate this, for the speaker might be joking or play acting and consequently doing nothing to arouse the expectations of others. *If* promises have been made by me in each of the premises, then I know that I cannot keep them unless I go to Chicago, and I know that I am as much bound to go there as I am bound to keep both of the promises expressed in the two premises. On the other hand, if I promise to go to New York or to Chicago under normal circumstances, but promise not to go to New York only under duress, I must use other considerations to decide whether the second promise is binding upon me in any way and what I shall do. I know that I cannot keep both promises without going to Chicago, but this is just because I know that "Either X goes to New York or X goes to Chicago" and "X does not go to New York" jointly entail "X goes to Chicago."

The above example suggests that we can make no inferences involving nonassertoric sentences except from the context, and that by varying the context different inferences are possible. We frequently take into account in our reasoning the commands, promises, recommendations, and predictions which are issued by those around us. But these utterances do not serve as premises in our arguments, nor as their conclusions. Rather, we infer that because we have been ordered to do A, and doing A entails doing B, we must do B in order to satisfy the command. Or, because we have promised to do A under a given set of circumstances, and those circumstances are now realized, we conclude that we are as much obligated to do A as we were to keep the conditional promise. From our knowledge that certain illocutionary acts have been performed and our knowledge of the circumstances in which they were performed, we are able to draw conclusions about what others expect of us, what we are obliged to do, or what rewards or penalties we can expect as a result of certain actions. These conclusions are not themselves nonassertoric sentences, but statements of fact (apart, possibly, from statements of obligation, though I do not think these are exceptions), and the premises from which they are inferred are also statements of fact. The arguments we actually use which involve these illocutionary acts are, consequently, assertoric arguments.

Some performative inferences do, however, have the appearance of being valid, even without additional information about the context. For example,

> If I order you to pull, haul me to the top of the cliff.
> Pull!
> Haul me to the top of the cliff!

Yet this argument is valid only under the supposition that the imperative "Pull!" does in fact constitute an order. In the example it is natural to suppose that the speaker has the authority to command the agent, but the second premise as given here does not make the fact apparent. Even given this assumption, it is not clear what we are inferring when we conclude "Haul me to the top of the cliff!" Not, certainly, that this command has been issued, but rather that the action to which it refers is necessary if I am to obey the order given in the first premise, or perhaps that I am obliged to haul up the speaker, or that I can expect blame or punishment if I do not.

Let us consider still another example:

I recommend someone for promotion to full professor only
if he is good.
I recommend Bumstead for promotion to full professor.
Therefore, Bumstead is good.

Whether this inference is legitimate depends upon whether the
context is such that the second premise can count as a recommendation of Bumstead. Normally it does, in which case the premise
actually used for inferring that Bumstead is good is "I am recommending Bumstead . . ."—a declarative statement, not a performative. The second premise may, however, not be a recommendation. If I and all those listening know full well that
Bumstead is totally incompetent, then it is clear from the context
that I am only jesting and not making a recommendation at all.

We might change the first premise to "I recommend Bumstead
for promotion only if he is good," in which case it becomes a
conditional recommendation. But even if the context is such that
this premise is to count as some kind of recommendation and is
not a joke, this need not be the case for the second premise as
well. Only if we know that *both* premises are recommendations
may we conclude that Bumstead is good. We make the inference
not from the recommendations, but from the fact that they have
been made.

Declarative sentences also are uttered in jest, of course. If such
statements are put into arguments, those who hear them, knowing
the context, do not draw the normal conclusions. But this has no
effect upon the arguments' validity. For example:

If Bumstead has proved the existence of monads, then he is
good.
Bumstead has proved the existence of monads.
Therefore, Bumstead is good.

If the utterance of the second premise is accompanied by loud
guffaws, no one is apt to draw the conclusion that Bumstead is
good. The laughter makes it clear that the second premise is false.
This does not, however, change the fact that the argument is
valid. The arguments discussed above concerning the recommendations of Bumstead are, however, not only unsound, but invalid,

for they are incomplete. In normal circumstances we are justified in drawing the conclusions, but the arguments are not formally valid.

The reason for the difference between assertoric arguments and supposed nonassertoric inferences seems to be this. When we are given an assertoric premise or conclusion we are also given a truth condition which is both necessary and sufficient for the application of the value analogous to "true" for that sentence; namely, where p is the sentence, the condition that p. In nonassertoric sentences, however, when taken out of context, the conditions for the application of the values are not all given. Not only do we not know *whether* they hold, but it is not stated *what* they are. Only if the necessary context is presented in a formal system of nonassertoric logic as additional premises, meaning-postulates, or rules of inference, will the conditions for the application of the values be given. As yet, no such system is in use, although I hardly want to deny that one may be in the future. If there is, however, it will be dependent upon truth-functional logic, for the reasons given earlier in this chapter.

As things stand now, we do make inferences from the fact that certain values apply to nonassertoric sentences and we also infer that certain values apply to nonassertoric sentences. But the premises and conclusions of such inferences are statements of fact, i.e., assertions. If the arguments are to be valid the context must be given in such a way that it is stated that values of satisfied, endorsed, etc., do apply to the nonassertoric sentences. What we have, in fact, are metalinguistic assertions *about* the imperatives, promises, etc., that appear in the arguments. It may be that these metalinguistic statements can be paraphrased out, but I am convinced that they will only reappear as the semantical rules which would interpret some nonassertoric logic. Such rules would also be assertions.

THE STRUCTURE OF INFERENCES INVOLVING NONASSERTORIC SENTENCES

Given certain nonassertoric sentences and perhaps also statements about utterance conditions, we infer what actions or further conditions are needed for the sentences constituting the premises to be satisfied in the ordinary sense as characterized above (pp. 62–63). Some examples follow. If there are one or more commands in the premises, what must I do to obey them, and are conditions such that I *can* obey them? If one or more promises, what action on my part is necessary if I am to keep them? If one or more predictions, what state(s) of affairs must obtain if my prediction is to come true? Thus, if "I promise to be home by twelve" was uttered by me and "I won't get home by twelve unless I leave now" is believed by me, I may conclude that I will have to leave now if I am to keep my promise. This in no way entails a promise on my part to leave now, although I am, under the circumstances, *obliged* to leave now.

This sort of inference may be further illustrated by the following example. Suppose I say, "I bet five dollars that if she passes his two club opening, he will hit her," and then suppose she does indeed pass. I conclude that if I am to win the bet he will have to hit her.

The validity of these inferences is dependent upon the validity of another kind of argument—namely, that resulting from the transformation of all the nonassertoric premises into assertoric statements. Thus I can conclude that I will win the bet if he hits her just because the following argument is valid:

> If she passes his two club opening, he will hit her.
> She passes his two club opening.
> He will hit her.

A sentence $\tau\phi$ can be satisfied only if $\vdash\phi$, and if $\vdash\phi$ entails $\vdash\psi$, then $\vdash\psi$ is a necessary condition of the satisfaction of $\tau\phi$. Thus if the command to bring about ϕ is obeyed, the promise to make it true that ϕ is kept, the advice or recommendation to bring it about that ϕ is followed, then if $\vdash\psi$ is a logical consequence of $\vdash\phi$, $\vdash\psi$ must also be true. For this reason, since the occurrence of a state of affairs describable by ψ is a necessary condition of the satisfaction of a sentence, and if $\vdash\psi$ is a necessary condition of $\vdash\phi$, then the satisfaction of the sentence requires that $\vdash\psi$. Thus, if $\vdash\phi$ entails $\vdash\psi$, that $\tau\phi$ is satisfied also entails $\vdash\psi$. This fact justifies the conclusion that if a given sentence is satisfied, some other statements (most often one describing an action) will be true. This kind of reasoning constitutes the basic pattern of inference involving nonassertoric sentences. An example of it is the following. The sentence τφ (e.g., "Go sit on a tack!") can be satisfied only if ⊢φ is true (here, if the addressee does in fact sit on a tack). If ⊢φ entails ⊢ψ, then ⊢ψ is a necessary condition of τφ's being satisfied. (Since "X sits on a tack" entails "X sits," that X sits is a necessary condition of satisfying "Go sit on a tack.")

Using this basic pattern of inference, whose formal structure is spelled out in the appendix to this book, we may infer that, if I have promised to take my children to the circus, provided that the weather is good and that they behave all week, and if these conditions are fulfilled, I can only keep my promise if I take them to the circus. As a second example, if a robber orders me to give him everything in my purse, and a copy of Wittgenstein's *Tractatus* is in my purse, then I may infer that if I am to obey the robber, I must give him the *Tractatus*. As another example, if I promise to give you the Philosopher's Stone, it follows that a necessary condition of my keeping my promise is that the Philosopher's Stone exists. I may also infer that since there is no such object I will not be able to keep a promise to give it to you.

Frequently we use the basic inference to draw conclusions about our obligations or interests. Knowing that I am obliged to keep the conditional promise I make in the first example, I know that I am obliged to take the children to the circus. I cannot fail to do so and still keep the original promise. In general, a conclusion drawn in this basic pattern of reasoning is a sentence having the form "If τφ is to be satisfied, then ⊢ψ." Normally, if the agent is obliged to satisfy τφ and ⊢ψ describes an action of that agent, then the agent is obliged to perform that action.

If the consequent is not an action, however, there is no transfer of obligation. Should I promise to feed your cats, I cannot fulfill that promise unless you own cats. I do not, however, have any obligation to make it true that you own cats by giving you one if you haven't any. Furthermore, if X is obliged to satisfy τφ and τφ can only be satisfied if another individual Y performs an action described by ⊢ψ, X is not obliged to bring about ⊢ψ, and neither is Y. For example, if I guarantee that I will check Jim's homework, I incur an obligation to do this. Yet I cannot fulfill the obligation unless Jim does his homework. That I am obligated to check it does not, however, entail that Jim is obliged to do his homework, nor does it oblige me to make him do it.

Likewise, if it is in my interests for a nondeclarative sentence to be satisfied, it is in my interests for the consequences of its satisfaction to be true. If the situation depicted in the second example above arises, then if I know what is good for me I will give my copy of the *Tractatus* to the robber. Prudentially, I ought to do so. But unless, as in this case, the consequent is an action on the part of the agent in whose interest it is that the sentence be satisfied, we cannot conclude from this alone that any person *ought* to make the consequent true.

In addition to the above inferences in which we draw conclusions from and about what is necessary for the satisfaction of certain sentences, we also draw conclusions from the fact that some illocutionary act has been performed. The statements that I have recommended Bumstead and have recommended him only if he is good entail that Bumstead is good. From "Anyone who bets on a three-legged horse is a fool," "Dobbin is a three-legged horse," and "I have bet ten dollars on Dobbin," it follows that I am a fool. Validity of the argument is not preserved if "I hereby bet ten dollars on Dobbin" replaces "I have bet ten dollars on Dobbin," for we have no criteria of validity for nonassertoric arguments apart from context.

In general, it appears that the inferences we actually make concerning nonassertoric sentences and illocutionary acts can be interpreted as inferences in an assertoric metalanguage, the validity of which is determined by the rules of truth-functional logic. The premises and conclusions designating a nonassertoric sentence are statements to the effect that some illocutionary act has been performed; that it has been satisfied; that *if* it is to be satisfied, some condition must hold; or that if a person is obliged to satisfy a given sentence, and doing so entails some further action's being done by him, he is obliged to perform that action.

Such statements may be construed as statements about nonassertoric sentences; for example, "The command 'Wash my jeep' was given by Captain Scabbard to Private Diller"; "My saying

'I'll be home in time for dinner' constituted a promise which I am obliged to keep"; and "If I'm to win the wager I made when I said 'I'll bet you a hundred dollars that the Yankees will win the pennant,' the Orioles must lose the next doubleheader." The utterances in single quotation marks may be eliminated entirely and the above sentences translated respectively as "Captain Scabbard ordered Diller to wash his jeep," "I'm obliged to keep my promise to be home in time for dinner," and "I can win my one hundred dollar bet that the Yankees will win the pennant only if the Orioles lose."

Whichever form the sentences take, they are still assertions and only as such do they take part in our reasoning. If I hear you say "Get out of my sight!" it is *that* you have ordered me out of your sight that is a premise in whatever I reason about what is true or what I shall do as a result of your utterance.

Of course, we make metalinguistic statements about assertions as well; for example, "Sarah said, 'My piece is bigger than yours,' and this made him furious" and "'Parallel lines never meet' is true, only if space is Euclidean." These in turn may be written so as to eliminate the utterances. These sentences, however they are written, are themselves assertions. Thus, while inferences of the sort we actually make concerning nonassertoric sentences can be fully spelled out only in assertoric language, inferences involving assertions need not be expressed in any nonassertoric manner, and probably cannot be. This is another indication of the primacy of assertion and of truth-functional logic.

My conclusion is that the nonassertoric logics which have been suggested must have some of their basic notions, especially that of validity, explained in assertions. Furthermore, any logic which defines the validity of inferences in terms of values other than "true" and "false" as applied to assertions does not reflect the way in which we actually reason with nonassertoric sentences. Nonassertoric sentences do not function alone as the premises or conclusions of real arguments; while I do not want to deny that a logic in which they did could be developed, such a system would be a significant departure from actual reasoning.[13]

4

The Illocutionary Status
of Evaluations

Having discussed the meaning and logical features of imperatives and other performatives, I will now attempt to show that the
linguistic behavior of evaluations is very different from that of
nonassertoric sentences. Evaluations appear to function in arguments in precisely the same way that assertions do, while nonassertoric sentences cannot. In chapter 3, I argued that we cannot
infer one nonassertoric sentence from others or from other nonassertoric sentences in combination with assertions, nor can we
infer assertions from nonassertoric or mixed sentences, without a
number of additional premises, meaning-postulates, or rules of
inference, above and beyond those which are required for the
validity of assertoric arguments. I argued further that in actual
practice nonassertoric sentences do not serve as the premises or
conclusions of arguments. Rather our reasoning concerning performatives employs indicative sentences about nonassertoric sentences and speech acts, and is thus conducted in standard truth-
functional or assertoric logic.

Evaluations, on the contrary, frequently appear as the premises
and conclusions of arguments. Inferences to and from evaluations
are considered valid without recourse to the supplementary rules
and premises which are the minimum requirements for an adequate nonassertoric logic. An argument like, "If he needs you,
you ought to go to him. He needs you. Therefore, you ought to
go to him," is valid as it stands. We do not need to fill out the
argument with statements about the context in which it was uttered, as we would if the sentence "You ought to go to him" were
replaced with "Go to him" or "I promise to go to him."

Evaluations Have at Least One Descriptive Component

In chapter 2, we saw that a pair of sentences like "If learn this material, you will pay attention while I explain it," and "Learn this material!" cannot by themselves be the premises of a valid argument, since the first makes no sense grammatically. This would be so in any situation in which a nondeclarative sentence was used as the antecedent of a conditional, and even a system of nonassertoric logic would not help. If the first premise were altered to "If you are going to learn this material . . . " or "If I tell you to learn this material . . . " we still cannot draw the conclusion "You will pay attention while I explain it," for the second nonassertoric premise is a different sentence from the assertoric antecedent of the conditional first premise.

Thus we cannot have an argument of the form "If p, then q. But p. Therefore, q." or an argument of the form "q, only if p. Not-p. Therefore, not-q," where p is a nonassertoric sentence. For in the first premise of such arguments, p could not be the same sentence that it is in the second premise. Consequently, if evaluations were nonassertoric, we could not have arguments of the two forms mentioned immediately above in which p represented "X ought to do A" or "X is good." But we do have arguments of this sort; for example,

> You will be punished only if you have done wrong.
> You have not done wrong.
> Therefore, you will not be punished.

and

> If that is a good film, the reviewers will praise it.
> That is a good film.
> Therefore, the reviewers will praise it.

What makes these arguments valid is that the same sentence appears in both the conditioning clause of the first premise of each and the second premise of each.

Arguments of the forms "If p, then q; p; therefore q" and "q, only if p; not-p; therefore, not-q" are valid only if p is an assertion. In a conditional sentence we state what must be the case if another sentence (the conditioned clause) is to be true or analogous to true. What must be the case is described in the conditioning clause. The sentence variable that appears in the conditioning clause represents a descriptive statement, because that statement tells us what state of affairs will be the necessary, or sufficient, condition of the truth (or analogous value) of the conditioned clause. For this reason, the conditioning clause has a sentence that represents a state of affairs as holding, and it is therefore indicative. Such a sentence could be a metalinguistic statement asserting that some nonassertoric sentence has certain value; as we saw in the last chapter, however, that kind of statement would be indicative. We may conclude from the above that where an evaluation is the antecedent of a conditional, it must represent a state of affairs as holding; that is, it must be an assertion.

Since to make these arguments valid, the second premise must represent the condition described in the conditioning clause of the first premise as being fulfilled, it, too, must be indicative; that is, be a descriptive statement which is either true or false. If the conditioning clause is an evaluation, it is a description, and when it appears as the second premise, it is a description there also.[1]

In arguments of the forms discussed here, the second premise need not, however, be identical with the sentence represented by p in the first premise.[2] The argument, "If p, then q; p and r; therefore, q," is valid, but the second premise is not identical with p. It does, however, include p, and, if p is descriptive, then we can at least say that the second premise is a conjunction that contains a descriptive statement. Consequently, evaluations, at the very least, contain an indicative conjunct, even if they also contain nondescriptive conjuncts. In the following chapters I will argue that they do not have nondescriptive conjuncts, but as yet I have not eliminated this possibility.

The argument from the fact that nonassertoric sentences do not appear as the conditioning clauses of hypotheticals may appear to rest upon an accident of grammar.[3] "If p, then q" and "p, only if q" can also be stated as "Not-p or q." While we cannot meaningfully say "If learn this material, then you will pay attention while I explain it," there is nothing peculiar about "Either don't learn this material or you will pay attention while I explain it." In combination with "Learn this material" we might, given an appropriate system of nonassertoric inference, be able to conclude that you will pay attention while I explain it. At the very least, we could construct assertoric arguments to the effect that the two imperative premises could not both be satisfied, unless the conclusion was true, or that no person could consistently endorse the two premises unless he believed in the truth of the conclusion.

Does not the validity of arguments of the forms "If p, then q; p; therefore, q" and "q only if p; not-p; therefore, not-q," where p is an evaluation, rest upon the fact that such arguments can be put in the forms "Not-p or q; p; therefore q" and "Not-q or p; not-p therefore not-q" respectively? Let us consider the following:

> If you ought to clean the house today, then don't dawdle.

This is equivalent to:

> Either not-(you ought to clean the house today) or don't dawdle.

From this statement and "You ought to clean the house today" we can infer, assuming a satisfactory system of nonassertoric logic, the imperative "Don't dawdle!" Alternatively, we may conclude that the imperative "Don't dawdle!" must be satisfied if the imperative constituting the first premise, and the second premise, both have a value analogous to truth.

The problem facing one who maintains that evaluations are not assertions is the interpretation of "Not-(you ought to clean the house today)." There are two ways in which illocutionary acts, and sentences used to perform them, may be negated: internally and externally.[4] The internal negation of $\nu\tau\phi$ is $\nu\tau(\text{not-}\phi)$, where ν represents the same illocutionary force indicator and τ represents the same mood indicator in both. Thus the internal negation of "X, do A!" is "X, do not-A!" or "X, don't do A!" The internal negation of "I promise to do A," is "I promise not to do A" and the internal negation of the assertion "Grass is green" is the assertion "Grass is not green" or "It is not the case that grass is green."

The external negation of a sentence normally used to perform an illocutionary act of kind ν is a denial that an act of that kind has been performed. The external negation of "X, do A!" is "X,

I'm not telling you to do A." The external negation of "I promise to do A" is "I don't promise to do A," and the external negation of "Grass is green" is "I'm not saying that grass is green." While the internal negation of a sentence is a sentence having the same mood as that of the sentence it negates, the external negation of a sentence need not. Generally, the external negation is an assertion, but sometimes it has a different mood—namely, that of a performative refusal to become committed to some course of action.[5] Even in the latter case, however, the refusal is couched in the form of an assertion, just as "I will be there at nine" is an assertion even in contexts where it is also a promise.

Assuming that the above remarks apply to evaluations as well as to other sentences (both assertoric and nonassertoric), we may suppose that the internal negation of an evaluation has whatever mood and illocutionary character the evaluation has, and that the external negation of an evaluation is an assertion. The external negations of "X is good" and "X ought to do A" are "I'm not calling X good" and "I don't say X ought to do A," respectively. The internal negations of these sentences would be "X is not good" and "It is not the case that X ought to do A." The latter pair of sentences are evaluations, while the former pair are not.

The internal negations of evaluations, however, do not correspond to the internal negations of imperatives and performatives, but rather to the internal negations of assertions. If "X ought to do A" were an imperative like "X, do A!" then, since the internal negation of "X, do A" is "X, don't do A!", we would expect the internal negation of "X ought to do A" to be "X ought not to do A." This, however, is not an adequate translation of "It is not the case that X ought to do A." Should our nondescriptivist attempt to cut the knot by declaring that only "X ought not to do A" is the internal negation of "X ought to do A" and that "It is not the case that X ought to do A" is simply a refusal to evaluate, he is then forced to distinguish between the latter and "I don't say X ought to do A." The sentence "It is not the case that X ought to do A" is clearly an evaluation, whereas "I don't say X ought to do A" is a refusal to evaluate, and the nondescriptivist needs to explain the difference.

To save his case the imperativist must look for an imperative which corresponds to "X, do A!" in the same way that "It is not the case that X ought to do A" corresponds to "X ought to do A." One possible candidate might be "Don't bother to do A." But while "It is not the case that X ought to do A" contradicts "X ought to do A," "Don't bother to do A" does not contradict "Do A!" It is possible to satisfy both "Do A" and "Don't bother to do A" by the simple expedient of performing A, but without taking any special pains in doing so. Consequently, "Don't bother to do A" does not do the job required of it, and there do not appear to be any other imperatives which will.

In the argument being considered above; namely,

> Either not-(you ought to clean the house) or don't dawdle.
> You ought to clean the house.
> Don't dawdle.

the sense of "Not-(you ought to clean the house)" is "It is not the case that you ought to clean the house" rather than "You ought not to clean the house." If I can show that I merely am not obliged to clean the house, the first alternative is satisfied and the alternation is true (or has a value analogous to true); I do not have to show also that I am obliged *not* to clean the house, in order to satisfy the first alternative. But there is no imperative corresponding to "It is not the case that you ought to clean the house." If this evaluation is not an imperative, then the claim that all evaluations are imperatives is false.

The same considerations operate against the other major form of nondescritivism—namely, the view that evaluations are expressions of approval or commendation if positive, and expressions of disapproval or condemnation if negative.[6] The following argument:

> Either it is not the case that the food at the Greasy Spoon is
>   bad, or you ought not to eat there.
> The food at the Greasy Spoon is bad.
> Therefore, you ought not to eat there.

is valid. But if to say that the food is bad is not to make an assertion but to perform an act of condemnation, then what performative will correspond to saying that the food is *not* bad? Certainly, it is not "I commend the food at the Greasy Spoon," for the first alternative of the first premise does not say that the food is *good*. Nor is saying the food is not bad a refusal to evaluate, as "I'm not calling the food at the Greasy Spoon bad" would be. In saying that the food is not bad, we are ruling out one possible range of values as applying to it, so we *are* evaluating. We are not, however, expressing any particular attitude toward the food, which we would have to do if all evaluations were expressions of attitudes. By saying the food isn't bad, I may deny that I have a condemnatory attitude, but I do not express any *other* attitude. I express neither favor nor indifference. Thus "The food at the Greasy Spoon is not bad" is an evaluation, but it is not an expression of an attitude (except when used colloquially as an understatement for saying the food is good), and hence it is not a performative of the kind in question. Therefore, it is not true that all evaluations are expressions of approval or commendation and disapproval or condemnation. I shall argue this point at greater length in the following chapter.

It seems clear then, that the fact that "If p, then q" is logically equivalent to "Not-p or q" does not damage the argument I have presented in this chapter. Where p stands for an evaluation such as "X ought to do A," then not-p represents "It is not the case that X ought to do A." If the evaluation were an imperative, a commendation of doings of A, or any other nonassertoric sentence, the only negation available, which would have the same mood, and whose utterances would have the same type of illocutionary force, and which could function in arguments, would be "X ought not to do A." Yet if not-p is given this latter interpretation, it means something quite different from what we mean by the negation of "X ought to do A."

Another objection to the sort of argument I give here has been made by Hare.[7] Consider the following argument:

> If I promise you a lily, you will be grateful.
> I hereby promise you a lily.
> You will be grateful.[8]

I have contended that this is invalid because the second premise is a performative, while the antecedent of the first is a description which asserts that the illocutionary act of promising has been done (or rather describes the condition of its having been done). I have argued that performatives are not equivalent to and do not entail statements to the effect that the performance in question is done. If they were, they would have a description as a fundamental part of their meaning.

Hare maintains that in any assertoric argument of the form "If p, then q. But p. Therefore, q," p has a different function in each of its two occurrences. In the second premise, p is asserted categorically, while in the first it is not asserted at all; only the conditional of which it is the antecedent is asserted. Thus the mere fact that imperatives and performatives do not have identicial functions in the antecedents of conditionals and in categorical sentences does not suffice to show that arguments of the above form in which p is an imperative or a performative are invalid. In such arguments, the phrastic, or content, and what he calls the trophic, or mood indicator, are the same, but the neustic, or sign of subscription, which indicates the kind of speech act being performed, differs in the two occurrences. In the second premise, a promise is made. The sentence has the illocutionary force of a promise there, but not as the antecedent of the first premise. Likewise, when I say, "If the cat is on the mat, the mice won't play," then I am not asserting that the cat is on the mat, as I do when I say, "The cat is on the mat."

Even given that categorical premises and conclusions of assertoric arguments are always illocutionary acts of assertion (which they are not; I am hardly asserting, or claiming truth for, each premise and conclusion of the arguments I have used as examples in this book), Hare's argument fails. If, as he contends, the performative or imperative premises retain the same phrastic and trophic in the antecedents of conditionals that they have in categorical premises, his view would be correct. But they do not. The sentence "I promise to give you a lily" has a promising mood or trophic. In the sentence "If I promise to give you a lily, you will be grateful" the mood of the antecedent is no longer one of promising, but rather indicative or assertoric. It does not have the same mood as "I promise to give you a lily" any more than "I am telling you to jump" has the same mood as "Jump!" Both members of the latter pair of sentences may, in appropriate contexts, be *used* as commands, but only the latter has an imperative mood.

To save his thesis, Hare would have to show that the lily argument can be valid even if the only thing shared by the second premise and the antecedent of the first is their phrastic or propositional content. But this cannot be. The antecedent of the first premise designates a condition whose fulfillment suffices for the consequent to hold. Unless the second premise states that that condition is fulfilled, the conclusion, which is the consequent of the first premise, cannot be validly drawn. And if the second premise is not an assertion, but a promise, then it cannot do the job required and the argument is not valid. Furthermore, the propositional content of the antecedent of the first premise and that of the second premise differ. The former is "My promising to give you a lily," while the latter is "My giving you a lily."

I think I have shown that evaluations are assertions, which describe states of affairs and which, as such, are either true or false. It is probable that most of those working in moral philosophy today agree with this position. However, there are some who will grant this, but who wish—perhaps from fear of dogmatism—to avoid the apparent consequence that it is, at least in principle, possible to discover definite answers to moral and other evaluative questions.

One way of escape is to show that, although evaluative sentences are indeed descriptive, they assert of things and actions that they fit, or fail to fit, the standards and principles which are our fundamental criteria for making evaluations. But these standards and principles, though they serve to justify particular evaluations, are not themselves true or false. They may satisfy criteria of a certain sort, but ultimately, they are simply chosen by us, as a part of our way of life, and neither can nor need be justified further. Such a view is held by Paul Taylor;[9] if it is true, it is tantamount to saying that, although ordinary evaluations are descriptions, sentences expressing our standards must be prescriptions of some kind. The latter cannot be descriptions, since they have no truth value, but only express our choices, rational or otherwise.

Let us consider the consequences of the view that, although most evaluations are descriptions, they describe conformity of particular items to the norms we have adopted, but that these norms are not themselves descriptions. Two features of norms must be recognized by those who hold this kind of theory. First of all, norms are evaluative sentences, or expressible as such; that is, they state that we ought to perform acts of certain kinds, or they affirm the goodness, beauty, etc. of certain sorts of things. Secondly, we use these norms to justify our more specific evaluations. We say that a child ought to share his cookies with his brother, because it is the fair thing to do and fairness is a standard of behavior, a norm, which we ought to live up to. Evaluative standards serve as premises in arguments; this is, as we shall see, an important feature.

The following adaptation of an argument I used earlier will, I think, show that any moral or other evaluative standard is a declarative, descriptive statement. Standards are generally expressible as conditional sentences. The antecedent consists of a factual statement, giving the conditions under which one ought to do something. What one ought to do is stated in the consequent. "One ought to treat equally those for whom one has equal responsibilities" becomes "For all X, Y, and Z, if X has equal responsibilities for Y and for Z, X ought to treat Y and Z equally." Likewise, "Any student who scores above 80 percent on this examination has done good work" becomes "For any X, if X is a student and X scores above 80 percent on this examination, X has done good work." Conditionals that give the necessary rather than the sufficient conditions for an evaluation may also serve as standards; for example, "For any X, X is a great work of art only if X provides spiritual uplift."

It is also true that we frequently employ hypothetical sentences in which the antecedent is an evaluation; for example, "If it would be wrong of me to say that, then I will not do so."

Now arguments of the form "If p, then q. If q, then r. Therefore, if p, then r." are valid. If we have moral arguments of this form in which the statement of the form "If p, then q" is a fundamental moral standard, then we may argue that such a standard is a declarative, descriptive statement. That we may conclude this can be shown as follows. We have seen that an evaluation that appears in the conditioning clause of a hypothetical statement must be a statement that is descriptive and either true or false. Let us suppose that such a statement is "If q, then r" in an argument of the form to which I just alluded. If the argument is to be valid, the sentence represented by q must be the same in both "If p, then q" and "If q, then r."

Let us see whether a moral argument that meets the indicated specifications is valid. Suppose that the standard in question is "For any X and t, if I am in a position to help X at t, then I ought to help X at t." In conjunction with "If I ought to help X at t, then X can count on my help," the inference to "For any X and t, if I am in a position to help X at t, then X can count on my help" is valid. Since this is a valid argument only if "I ought to help X at t" means the same in both premises, if "I ought to help X at t" is descriptive in the second premise, it is also descriptive in the first. Thus an evaluative statement in the conditioned clause of a hypothetical is descriptive, provided that such a hypothetical may serve as a premise in the form of argument indicated above.

Now a conditional sentence has the mood of its conditioned clause. "If it is nine o'clock, go to bed" has an imperative consequent, and is, as a whole, an imperative. "I promise to help you, only if what you are asking me to do is legal" has as its conditioned clause a promise, and is itself a promise. "If you put this sugar in water, it will dissolve" has a descriptive consequent and is itself a descriptive statement. Thus if norms or standards have descriptive consequents or conditioned clauses, they are also descriptive. Unless it can be shown that a fundamental standard is such that it cannot be rendered as a hypothetical statement with an evaluative sentence in its conditioned clause, or that, if it can be, arguments of the sort mentioned above are not valid or usable in evaluative contexts, then it appears that we must accept the conclusion that moral and other evaluative standards are descriptive, assertoric statements, rather than imperatives or performatives or some other nondescriptive linguistic item.

Now unless evaluative standards are expressible as hypotheticals with evaluative sentences in the conditioned clause, it seems difficult to see how they can be used to justify standards of a lower level or particular acts or evaluations. Consider the process by which we use standards to justify an action. We do this by asserting that the action is of a certain sort, and that actions of that sort are such that we ought to perform them. In doing so, we have constructed a valid argument of the form "If X is F, then X is G. X is F. Therefore, X is G." Such arguments cannot be constructed unless we suppose that the standards can be stated in the form of the first premise. If they do have this form, however, they are descriptive statements, according to the argument given above. Thus the function of evaluative standards as evaluations that enables us to justify less general evaluations necessitates the conclusion that standards, like other evaluations, are descriptive and are either true or false.

As in my earlier argument this conclusion is subject to the following qualification. Not only is the argument "If p, then q. If q, then r. Therefore, if p, then r" valid, but so is "If p, then q and s. If q, then r. Therefore, if p, then r." Thus even though q must be a declarative in such an argument, the consequent of the first premise, which determines the mood of the whole sentence, may have a nondeclarative conjunct s. If so, then categorical evaluations—for all that I have yet shown—may consist of a declarative conjunct and a nondeclarative conjunct.

So far, my argument has presupposed the validity of certain kinds of arguments involving evaluative sentences. It has been suggested to me[10] that this assumption is not justified. Perhaps these arguments are not valid, after all. To make this objection stick, more is needed than a mere "perhaps." These arguments seem intuitively to be valid, just as do arguments involving only nonevaluative, declarative sentences. To maintain successfully that arguments containing evaluations are not valid, while those containing nonevaluative declaratives are, some relevant difference between the two must be cited—apart from the fact that the one kind of argument contains evaluations and the other does not. Thus far, to my knowledge, no one has cited such a difference, and, consequently, I think I am justified in supposing (at least tentatively) that none exists. While we should hardly be justified in supposing that our intuitions about logic are infallible, they do constitute some evidence, and in the absence of indications that they are unworthy of such trust, we may allow them to guide us.

EVALUATIONS HAVE ONLY DESCRIPTIVE COMPONENTS

Thus far I have argued that evaluations must have at least one assertoric or descriptive conjunct. I have not yet shown, however, that they might not have nonassertoric conjuncts as well. The statement "X is good" might really mean something like "I approve of X; do so as well."[11] This sentence as a whole could not be used as the antecedent of a conditional. If, however, only the descriptive conjunct appeared in the antecedent, but the whole sentence constituted another premise, a valid argument could be constructed. Thus:

> If X is good, I will buy X.
> X is good.
> Therefore, I will buy X.

could be translated as,

> If I approve of X, then I will buy X.
> I approve of X; do so as well.
> Therefore, I will buy X.

The validity of the argument does not depend upon the value of "Do so as well," and therefore does not assume a system of nonassertoric logic. Some form of nondescriptivism might yet be saved.

Two major problems stand in the way of such a project, however. (1) Either the descriptive component of the evaluation encorporates the full meaning of the evaluation or it does not. If it does, then there is no need for an additional nondescriptive component, and descriptivism is true. If it does not, then to translate "X is good" as "I approve of X" (or as some other indicative sentence) in the antecedent of the first premise in the above argument is not correct. When we say, "If X is good, then . . . " the phrase "X is good" certainly does not seem to mean something different from the same phrase used as the categorical sentence "X is good." Of course, when we only hypothesize that a thing is good, we don't express approval, or commend or prescribe it, but if the *capacity* to perform these functions were essential to the meaning of "X is good," this capacity must be represented in the mood of the antecedent of the conditional as well as in the categorical sentence. If representing X as prescribed is part of the meaning (the mood) of "X is good," then, when I say "If X is good, then . . ." part of what the antecedent does is to represent X's being prescribed. Grammatically, this can be done in the antecedent of a conditional only by describing the condition of X's being prescribed as "If I do prescribe X. . . ."But to *say that* X is or will be prescribed by me is not, for the reasons discussed earlier, the same thing as saying "I hereby prescribe X." If the argument given immediately above does include the condition of being prescribed in the antecedent of the first premise, it is invalid according to any logic now accepted. If it does not, then either X's being prescribed is not a part of the meaning of "X is good" or else the translated argument is not the same argument as the untranslated one. The same remarks may be made for any nondescriptive component whatever, for apart from these observations, it will be recalled from chapter 2 that the illocutionary force—i.e., the speech act performed by uttering a sentence—is not part of the meaning of that sentence. Thus that we *use* "X is good" to approve or commend X is not a part of the meaning of that sentence.

(2) Even if the argument "If I approve of X, I will buy X. I approve of X; do so as well. Therefore, I will buy X," is taken as a satisfactory translation of "If X is good, I will buy X. X is good. Therefore I will buy X" the validity of all arguments similarly translated will *not* be independent of the value of "Do so as well." For example,

The apples are good, and the strawberries are awful.
Therefore, the strawberries are awful.

translated as:

> I approve of the apples; do so as well; and I disapprove of
> the strawberries; do so as well.
> Therefore, I disapprove of the strawberries; do so as well.

can be valid only if, when each of the conjuncts in the premise
has a value analogous to truth, the conjuncts in the conclusion
both have values analogous to truth.

As I argued in the previous chapter, we do not yet have in
standard use a system of logic for which values of nonassertoric
sentences are given. When we do use nonassertoric sentences in
the inferences we draw, the premises and conclusions are assertoric sentences about these nonassertoric sentences. While nonassertoric logics which do not depend on this kind of metalanguage could be, and have been, developed, given suitable (assertoric) premises, criteria of validity, meaning-postulates, and so
forth, we do not have one in common use. For this reason, arguments which philosophers present as examples of nonassertoric
inference appear peculiar and stilted. This is not the case, however, with arguments which contain evaluations as premises or
conclusions. We have no trouble accepting these as valid. If they
are not really valid, the reason must be shown by the nondescriptivist.

If evaluations have a nondescriptive component, the burden of
proof is on those who claim that they do. They must tell us what
that component is and how it may be handled in arguments involving evaluations, or, if arguments involving evaluations are
not valid, they must explain why they appear to be. There have
been two major nondescriptivist types of theories: emotivist and
prescriptivist. Each has claimed that the fundamental part of the
meaning of evaluations is not an assertion, but some other type of
illocutionary act. I will discuss these theories in the next two
chapters, and hope to show their inadequacy. Unless I can do so,
nondescriptivists can refute my arguments by saying that since
evaluations are not assertions, arguments in which they appear
are not valid, as validity is currently conceived. They would still
need to account for their being generally recognized as valid, but
this might not be an insuperable obstacle.

5

Emotivism

The oldest of the nondescriptivist theories of the meaning of evaluative terms is emotivism. Here, moral and aesthetic judgments are expressions of a feeling or attitude held by the speaker. In chapter 1, we saw that the earliest forms of this theory, such as that of Ayer, had difficulties in accounting for the apparent rationality of evaluations. There is, however, one form of the theory which has been put forth in recent years and which has not been decisively put to rest. It is the view that there is a sort of attitude, e.g., approval, which is essential to positive evaluations, and a contrary attitude, e.g., disapproval, which constitutes the core of negative evaluations.[1] Unlike a feeling or emotion, an attitude is a stable, long-term range of reactions, which include both feelings and actions, toward the evaluated item. If I have a favorable attitude toward someone, for example, this will color my feelings, beliefs, and actions in a variety of ways, depending upon circumstances. For me to have this attitude, it is not necessary that I have any specific feeling or belief, or that I perform any particular action, so long as the pattern of my reactions satisfies some general form. If I disapprove of a kind of action, then I will tend to think less of persons who perform such acts, try not to perform those acts myself, and have unpleasant feelings when I contemplate their performance. These are all tendencies or dispositions, however, and no specific act or feeling is called forth in every case where one has an attitude of disapproval.

Moreover, according to the newer versions of emotivism, evaluations are expressions of attitudes, not toward particular objects, acts, and persons as such, but rather of attitudes toward them held in virtue of certain characteristics they possess. I approve of your stopping to help the motorist stranded on the interstate by virtue of the kindness and unselfishness you showed. Evaluations have an element of rationality, and this rationality is exhibited in my approving of any action to the extent that it shows kindness and unselfishness. Were I to favor your action, but not favor similar acts by others, my favor would be nonrational, a mere feeling, and not an *evaluation* at all.

According to emotivism, evaluations are a species of performative belonging to the genus of approvals and disapprovals, commendations and condemnations, grading and ranking. They are not assertions and are neither true nor false. In accordance with the notation I proposed in chapter 2, a speech act of evaluation would be analyzed, in the sophisticated emotivist theories, in something like the following manner. The propositional content ϕ designates a type of state of affairs in which some act, object, or person has a certain set of characteristics F. The mood τ of the evaluation is designated by some evaluative term E: for example, "good," "wrong," "beautiful," "brave," "unfair," etc. The indicator v of the illocutionary force of evaluating designates at the very least that the conditions of utterance are such that according to the conventions of the language the speaker is to be taken as intending his hearers to understand him to have a favorable or unfavorable attitude toward the act, object, or person evaluated and to have the attitude in virtue of the characteristics F exhibited by the item in question.

The relationship between F and E is that items which are F are items toward which the speaker expresses the attitude which he expresses toward those things to which he applies the term E. As a rule the term F does not appear in the evaluative sentence, but it is presupposed in that "X is E" implies "X has certain characteristics by virtue of which I (the speaker) have the attitude associated with things I call E," or "X has certain E-making characteristics," where "F" may be translated as "E-making characteristics."

It would seem that an evaluation has a value analogous to "true," according to a theory of the kind under discussion, when an attitude of the kind which is appropriate to the evaluative terms employed is expressed. These values might be defined in terms of satisfaction, of speaker-commitment, or of being-in-force. An approval or commendation would be *satisfied* when the item approved or commended becomes approved or commended as a result of the utterance of the performative. A speaker is *committed* to an approval or a commendation by virtue of making it, for the linguistic conventions are such that he is normally taken as intending his audience to understand him to be approving or commending, whether or not he does so intend. Evaluations are *in force* by virtue of their having been made in certain felicitous conditions.

Each of these values is applicable to evaluative sentences only if they are actually uttered in normal circumstances; that is, serious, non-joking, non-play-acting circumstances. The characteristics "satisfied," "speaker's being committed to," and "in force" are properties of speech acts rather than of sentences. We want, however, to be able to say that an evaluation has a value even when it is not actually uttered. Although not entirely satisfactory, we may, for our purposes, consider the truth analogue for evaluations as *termination* (compare chapter 3), rather than as a feature of the actual expression of an attitude; the evaluative sentence would be terminated when, if it had been uttered in felicitous circumstances, it would have been satisfied (or the speaker would have been committed to it, or it would have been in force, etc.) In short, an evaluation is terminated (analogous to true) if, had a person uttered it in normal circumstances, that person would have expressed the appropriate attitude.

This characterization of values for evaluations does not require that any speaker actually have the attitude in question, but only that this be the attitude he would convey. According to conventions of the language, he would be taken as intending others to understand him to have the attitude. If he does not have it, he is insincere; nevertheless, by uttering the sentence he did in the given circumstances, he used the conventions of the language to instill in his audience a belief that he has that attitude, even if he does not. The situation is similar to that of a person who makes a promise he does not intend to keep. His speech act follows certain conventions that normally arouse an expectation in his audience that he will perform the promised act. That it does makes his speech act a promise, even though he means to break it. Likewise, certain conventions normally convey attitudes; according to emotivism, evaluative expressions are among these conventional vehicles of expressing attitudes. Because they are conventions of the language, the audience normally understands the speaker to have the corresponding attitudes, whether or not he actually does.

As we saw in the last chapter, however, the emotivist runs into difficulties with defining negation and an analogue of falsity for evaluations. A sentence of the form "X is not-E" might be considered by him either an internal or an external negation of "X is E." If internal, it would, according to the theory, have to be the conveying of an attitude toward X which was contradictory or incompatible with the one associated with E. If external, it would have to be a denial that one was evaluating, or a refusal to evaluate. Such a denial or refusal would, perhaps, contextually imply an attitude, but it would not be the expression of an attitude. For example, "I'm not approving what he did" may suggest that I disapprove, or that I have no feeling one way or another, or even that I covertly approve, but that I do not want my approval on record. Which implications are present, however, depends upon the context of utterance, and they may be cancelled by explicit statements. For example, one might cancel the implication that one's refusal to approve shows disapproval by saying, "Of course, I don't disapprove of what he did, either."[2]

A refusal to express an attitude, or a denial that one is expressing one, is then not itself an expression of an attitude, but a different sort of speech act—either an assertion that one does not have the attitude in question, or a performative of refusing (to express the attitude). The negation of an evaluation, however, is far from being a refusal to evaluate or a denial that one is evaluating; it is itself an evaluation. "He is not a wicked man" and "That is not a great painting" *do* evaluate the person and the painting in question; they place the value of the item within a certain range of values by excluding the negated valuation. It appears, then, that "X is not-E" cannot be the external negation of "X is E."

There are also problems with interpreting "X is not-E" as an internal negation, i.e., as the expression of an attitude contradictory to or incompatible with the attitude associated with E. There is no one attitude which is the negation of an attitude of approval, commendation, or favoring, nor is there one which is the negation of disapproval, condemnation, or disfavoring. Not approving is not necessarily disapproving, nor is not disfavoring necessarily favoring. Not commending a thing includes indifference as well as condemnation, and the same may be said for the other attitudes as well.

One might think that just as favorable attitudes can run the gamut from mild liking to wild enthusiasm, so can nonfavorable attitudes run from indifference to extreme repugnance. Hence, if "X is good" expresses some favorable attitude or other, we might allow that "X is not good" expresses some attitude or other which excludes favorable attitudes. The difficulty with this approach is that merely not having a favorable attitude does not entail having any attitude whatever. To have an attitude is to take a position with respect to some item—to think about, feel toward, and act toward it in certain specific ways. Attitudes classified as being of a particular kind need not include the same reactions, or even any particular set of reactions, on the part of the person who has them. If, however, a person does not have *any* reactions (beliefs, feelings, or actions) falling into a certain circumscribed category, he cannot be said to have an *attitude* at all. Having an attitude toward something generally includes having a tendency to act in specific kinds of ways toward that thing. Even indifference—a tendency not to be affected by the thing to which one is indifferent—involves taking a position toward that thing, i.e., having certain beliefs about it. It differs from having no attitude, for indifference requires a person's fairly steady adherence to nonreaction. One cannot be indifferent to something one knows nothing about, or toward which one behaves erratically.

Simply denying a particular attitude does not, therefore, suffice to express any other attitude or even an alternation of attitudes. To deny having an attitude of hostility to Orientals is not to express any different attitude or one of a range of attitudes. Denying hostility toward Orientals is compatible with being friendly to, awed by, or indifferent to them as a class, but it is also compatible with having no attitude at all, for example, if one admittedly knew nothing about Orientals or was determined to treat each one on the basis of his characteristics as an individual and not as a member of a certain race. That a denial of a single attitude is *compatible with* a range of different attitudes is not to say that denial is an *expression of* any of those attitudes.

To consider something not good, according to an emotivist theory, must be to lack a favorable attitude, if it is to be the contradictory of having a favorable attitude. Since saying that something is not good, according to this view, is to express an attitude, then this lack of a favorable attitude must be an attitude in itself. The above considerations, however, indicate that lacking an attitude is not, by itself, to have an attitude at all, for it simply involves *not* having some specific and fairly well defined set of reactions toward that thing, without entailing that one does have some *other* specific and fairly well defined set of reactions toward it—the having of which constitutes the attitude.

Furthermore, one can consider an item not to be good and not take a favorable attitude toward it without thereby taking some other attitude toward the item. For example, after having studied a person's qualifications for a position, I can decide that he would not be a good choice without having decided whether he would be a bad or indifferent choice. I can thus not approve—and sincerely say that he is not good—without having taken any other attitude. By saying that he is not good, however, I *have* made an evaluation, but I have not expressed an attitude. At most, the emotivist can say that I have denied having an attitude of a certain sort. This sort of internal negation is different from the external negation of denying that one is *expressing* an attitude, and, furthermore, both denying having an attitude and denying that one is expressing an attitude can, it seems, only be accomplished by means of an assertion. To express a different attitude in terms of some nonassertoric performative is not the same kind of speech act as either kind of denial. Even the expression of a contrary attitude will not do. It is not a necessary condition of such a denial, since it goes beyond what is needed. As a result of these considerations, it does not appear possible that negations of evaluations, which are themselves evaluations, can be nonassertoric performatives expressing attitudes. Negations of evaluations deny evaluations, but no nonassertoric performative is suited to the task of denying an attitude—either denying that one has an attitude or denying that one is expressing an attitude. This is not to say that there cannot be internal and external negations of non-assertoric expressions of attitude; these cannot, however, perform the same linguistic tasks performed by negations of evaluations.

The above discussion has proceeded on the assumption that an attitude is fundamentally a set of feelings, desires, and tendencies to action and that they can be expressed by nonassertoric performatives. There is, however, reason to doubt this. Suppose, for example, that I admire Abraham Lincoln. My attitude toward him may involve, among other things, feelings of awe, desire to emulate him, interest in reading about or talking about him, and the belief that he possessed certain traits which I consider not only good, but uncommonly possessed at all or to the same degree. This belief is central to my attitude of admiration in a way in which feelings and actions are not. I might want to be like Lincoln in having his integrity, but I might also want to be as rich as a Rockefeller, yet not admire the Rockefellers because of their wealth. On the other hand, I admire Lincoln for his political wisdom, yet have not the least expectation of being able to emulate him in this virtue. Thus the desire to emulate is neither necessary nor sufficient for admiration. Reading and talking about Lincoln might be actions which would express my admiration, but I also read and talk about interesting villains. There is a difference, however, between the way I talk about Lincoln and the way in which I talk about persons whom I do not admire. I ascribe to him certain characteristics which I consider to be both good to have and to be rarely possessed. If I did not believe that Lincoln possessed these traits, or *some* traits both good and rare, I would not admire him. Furthermore, this belief seems sufficient for admiration to be present. Warm glows, desire to emulate, interest in knowing about a man are neither necessary nor sufficient for one to admire him. It seems, then, that having an attitude of admiration is nothing more or less than believing that the admired object has certain characteristics that are good to have, yet infrequently attained. If so, expressing admiration is purely and simply expressing these beliefs, and to express a belief is to make an assertion. If any attitude is characterized purely and simply by the holding of certain beliefs, then all expressions of that attitude are assertions, and if evaluations are expressions of this sort of attitude, then they, too, are assertions.

In an earlier paper, I argued as follows that this was the case.[3] Commendation or approval need not include liking for, pleasure in, or desire for the item approved. It does, however, involve a belief in the goodness of the item. If the speaker does not hold the evaluated act or object to be good in some sense, he does not approve of it, and he cannot sincerely commend it. There seems to be no other condition which is necessary to an act of commendation than its being an indication that the thing is good in some respect or other. Certainly there is no particular sensation, emotion, or act which necessarily characterizes commendations or approvals. Nor is there a set of sensations, emotions, or acts, some, but not all, of which are necessary for commendation or approval. Of course, we tend to like things we commend and desire the things we approve of. We need not, however, react in any one of these ways for a commendation or expression of approval to take place. There would seem, then, to be one and only one necessary condition for commending or expressing approval; namely, that the speaker indicate a belief in the goodness of the evaluated item.

Furthermore, this condition might also appear to be sufficient for such an act to have taken place. If I call you a good person, I have thereby expressed approval of your moral character. If I write a letter saying that you are well qualified to teach philosophy, I have expressed a belief in your goodness as a philosophy teacher and have thereby commended you. Expressions of positive attitudes such as liking or desire for a thing, or efforts to influence others to like or desire the thing—unaccompanied by an explicit or implicit declaration of belief in the goodness of the thing—are not commendations or expressions of approval.

It thus appears plausible to maintain that the only necessary condition and the only sufficient condition for an act of approval or commendation to take place is that someone designate the item in question as good in one respect or another. That the speaker believes the act or object or person to be good is not necessary, of course, but if he does not, he is being deceptive. That this is so suggests that approving and commending are nothing other than acts—verbal or nonverbal—which indicate the goodness of a thing. While it is possible to express beliefs nonverbally (by carrying an umbrella on a cloudy day, for example), or verbally, but nonassertorically ("My, haven't you grown?"), the normal vehicle of belief expression is an assertion. Nonassertoric expressions of belief are cancelable in the Gricean sense discussed in chapter 2.[4] Thus I can deny having expressed a particular belief by saying things like, "No, I don't think it is going to rain; I just like carrying this stylish umbrella," and "I really don't know whether you have grown or not; I was only asking." I cannot cancel assertions explicitly expressing beliefs, however, without contradicting them, although I can cancel beliefs expressed implicitly, or those which are contextually implied. Thus, if I say, "She is poor, but she is honest," I can deny that (I believe) there is any contrast between poverty and honesty, but not deny that she is poor, and still be consistent. Some expressions normally conveying approval may not be used as such on particular occasions, and these are consistent with a statement canceling the contextual implication of the speaker's belief in the goodness of the approved item. For example, "What an intelligent cat!" suggests approval, but the suggestion could be suppressed by "Of course, I don't think intelligence is a very good quality for a cat." Positive evaluations, however, expressed as sentences predicating qualities of items such as goodness, are not consistent with statements canceling approval or belief in the goodness (in some respect) of the approved item.

A person holding an emotivist theory might be content with this situation, which would allow him to maintain that belief in X's goodness was no more than approval of X. If, however, approval had, in turn, no emotional or action-inducing aspects, his position would not be demonstrably different from descriptivism. I have myself rejected the view that having a particular belief can be the only necessary and sufficient condition for having an attitude, including attitudes of approval, commendation, and their opposites. I still hold that there is no one kind of feeling about, or tendency to act with regard to, an object which it is necessary to have if one is to hold an attitude of a given kind toward that object, but that, on the other hand, certain beliefs about the object of an attitude are essential to having those attitudes. For example, if I admire a composer I may or may not buy records of his music or feel chills when listening to it, but I *must believe* that he is a skilled musician. I do think now, however, that some one or more of a *range* of feelings or tendencies to action are necessary for a given attitude to be present, and furthermore, that these feelings and tendencies fit a consistent pattern over a fairly extended period of time.

Suppose Larry were to say to Jess, "He is a very outgoing person." This might or might not be an expression of an attitude. If Larry admires outgoing people, his sentence might convey this admiration. If he greatly prefers introverts, the same words might be an expression of contempt for Jess. On the other hand, Larry may have no particular feelings one way or another for extroverts or for Jess by virtue of his being an extrovert. If so, Larry is not expressing an attitude. Under some circumstances we might say that his attitude to outgoing people was one of indifference; but this would be the case only if he had thought about extroversion, or was at least aware of it (even if not by name) as characterizing the behavior of some people, and had concluded that it did not much matter to him whether someone was an extrovert or not, and if his reaction to people was unaffected by whether or not they were outgoing. On the other hand, Larry might be positively affected by the outgoingness of one person, but repelled by that of another. How he would react would be dependent upon factors other than his perception of the other's extroversion; in such a case, he would have no reaction or pattern of reactions to the extroversion as such. If so, he does not have an attitude toward it or toward extroverted people, not even an attitude of indifference.

It seems, then, that if a person does not perceive a property as a distinct characteristic, or, if he does, his feelings and actions in response to it follow no consistent or recognizable pattern, he does not have an attitude toward that object. We cannot even call him indifferent, for indifference involves a deliberate nonpursuit, nonavoidance policy toward the object of one's indifference.

A bare belief does not, therefore, seem sufficient to be considered an attitude, and if this is so, the attitude of approval requires

Moral Language

more than a belief that the approved item is good. To approve of an object or act seems to require *both* a belief in its goodness and at the very least a desire to see realized either the specific item or good things generally, which desire might be expressed by any number of feelings or actions.

It seems improbable that any *sentence* can suffice to express an attitude. If some feeling or tendency to act is necessary for an attitude to be present, an assertion about a belief, no matter how essential to having the attitude the belief is, will not fully express the attitude. Nor could any nonassertoric sentence or expression accomplish that task. Since no *single* feeling, desire, or tendency to act need be a part of any given person's attitude, and since these same feelings, desires, and tendencies may constitute parts of many different attitudes, then those exclamations, imperatives, and expressions of wish or resolve which might encorporate such feelings, desires, and tendencies cannot serve to express fully a specific attitude. Such expressions as "Damn!"; "Would that I had his brains!"; and "Don't follow in her footsteps!" may be partial expressions of a great many different attitudes. We cannot even say that there is a typical attitude expressed by such sentences under a set of standard conditions.

If no single sentence can fully express an attitude, then neither can evaluations—be they assertoric or nonassertoric. Certainly, evaluations are used in partial expressions of attitudes, for among the beliefs that constitute attitudes are beliefs about the worth of the items toward which we have those attitudes. My believing that you are morally good may be part of an attitude of admiration, respect, affection, envy, fear, or even contempt, depending upon my other beliefs and the motives, feelings, and desires I have.

If no single sentence is a suitable vehicle for expressing an attitude, this explains why emotivists have trouble expressing negations of evaluations as attitudes. When any given sentence might be used to express any one of a large number of different attitudes, and only the context of utterance can indicate which, if any, of these attitudes the sentence expresses, the same is true of negations of those sentences. The attitude a sentence expresses seems, therefore, much more a part of its use on a particular oc-

106

casion than of its meaning. If so, then that (positive) evaluations express (among other things) attitudes of approval does not suffice to show that the approval-expressing function is a part of the meaning of evaluations.[5]

6

Prescriptivism

The second major type of nondescriptivist theory is the view that evaluations are essentially imperatives. They are sentences which are neither true nor false, but which prescribe actions or objects. The most fully developed analysis of this kind is that proposed by R. M. Hare, which I briefly described in chapter 1. According to his view, evaluations are universalized imperatives; instead of being addressed to one or more specific individuals, they are meant to apply to everyone. To say that it is wrong to cheat on examinations, unlike "Don't cheat on examinations!" is not a command promulgated to a specific, limited audience, but a prescribing of noncheating to all persons everywhere. "You ought not to cheat on examinations" is more like "Don't anyone ever cheat on examinations" than like "Don't cheat on examinations." For the most part, actions are not prescribed for all persons at all times. In these situations, according to Hare's theory, "Smith ought to rake his lawn," doesn't mean "Let everyone at all times rake his lawn!" but rather, "Let anyone in circumstances like Smith's rake his lawn!"

An important consequence of the universalizability of evaluative prescriptions is that they apply to the speaker as well as to everyone else. If I tell you that you ought not to cheat, I am, in a manner of speaking, telling everyone not to cheat, and "everyone" includes me. According to Hare, to accept a moral principle is to assent to the imperative, that is, to be willing to prescribe the action in question to anyone, including oneself. Prescribing for oneself involves being willing to act, and self-prescribing can be interpreted as an intention on the part of the person who holds the principle to act upon it. Accordingly, Hare draws the conclusion that unless a person *cannot* do so, he *will* act upon any moral principle which he accepts.

This raises a serious problem for Hare, which he fully recognizes.[1] If the acceptance of a moral principle entails acting upon it (unless prevented), then how do we explain moral weakness? The classic cases of moral weakness are those in which a person holds a moral principle but fails to do what it prescribes, even though, for all we can tell, he is able to do so. Consequently, I shall argue that prescriptivism, as Hare expounds it, entails that classic cases of moral weakness, as well as certain other phenomena of moral life, are impossible. Since these are not only possible but actual, they provide a strong argument for rejecting Hare's version of prescriptivism.

There are weaker versions of prescriptivism, which I shall consider later in this chapter, that do not have this undesirable consequence.

HARE'S STRONG PRESCRIPTIVISM

If it is true that action results from intentions, unless the agent is prevented by external circumstances from performing the intended act, and if prescribing an action for oneself is intending to perform it, then it seems that Hare is correct to hold the view that prescriptivism entails that an agent act upon the moral principles he holds, whenever the appropriate circumstances arise. That the theory does have this consequence is a fatal weakness, for it implies that we cannot fail to do what we ought to do except through the operation of external causes. Moral weakness and perversity would be impossible, for both phenomena are cases of failure to do what one believes one ought to do. In both, the agent thinks that he ought to do A and, for all we know, is able to do A, but nevertheless, he does not do A. Moral weakness differs from perversity in that the morally weak man has some desire, and often an intention which he subsequently abandons, to do A because A is right. This intention or desire is frequently absent in cases of perversity; however, most persons are perverse on occasion, even those who are generally conscientious. When one acts perversely, the desire to refrain from that act by virtue of its wrongness may be entirely absent, even when the agent usually wants to do the right thing.

Hare attempts to save prescriptivism by saying that moral

weakness and perversity, as I have characterized them above, do not exist. What we call cases of moral weakness, he says, fall into one of two categories. Either the subject does not really believe that he ought to do A, although he may deceive himself into thinking he does, or he is sincere, but unable to do A. Perversity, on the other hand, is not a person's going against what *he* believes he ought to do, but against a moral rule which others expect him to follow, but which he does not adopt himself.

Each of the above fails. First let us consider the case where the subject believes that he accepts the principle that he ought to do A, but does not really accept that principle. Since, according to this analysis, holding a moral principle is assenting to it, committing oneself to act on it, or choosing to act on it, to believe falsely that one holds that one ought to do A is like thinking falsely that one has chosen or decided to do A. A false belief of this sort is exposed when one changes one's mind at or before the time when doing A is called for. But choosing, deciding, or intending to do A always involves fitting doing it into any future plans. Thinking that one has chosen seems inseparable from choosing. While the chosen act A might also be describable by B, and the agents unaware of the fact, in fitting the act *as* A into his plans, he must know he has chosen A. On the other hand, we can stop intending to perform some act; we can change our minds and choose differently. I can decide or intend to own up to a mistake when I next see my boss—and be said at that point to hold that I ought to own up then—yet when I do next see my boss decide *not* to own up at that time. I have then, if Hare is right, changed my mind about what I ought to do by abandoning my original intention.

Should I act in this manner, I have certainly been weak-willed. I have vacillated in my intentions; instead of acting upon my original decision, I have abandoned it as a result of being swayed by considerations (fear, pride) other than those which led me to intend to confess in the first place. Such behavior would ordinarily be considered as *morally* weak as well, assuming that I had decided to own up to my mistake on the grounds that it was morally right to do so, but that the desire to do right was not strong enough to outweigh my other inclinations.

This view of my behavior is not, however, open to Hare. He

can agree that by my indecisiveness I have been weak of will, but not that my weakness is a *moral* failing. For on his view in choosing *not* to confess, I have rejected assent to the prescription to confess and therefore do not hold that I ought to confess—at least I do not hold this when I actually see my boss. If so, then it is not the case that I ought to confess then, and my not doing so is not a moral failure.

The fact is, however, that I and others would rightly accuse me of having been morally at fault. That I changed my mind about confessing did not cancel my obligation to do so. Being committed to a moral principle or belief entails not only acting on it, but considering it to be *worthy* of being acted upon. The guilt and blame attached to failing to act on a principle is a consequence of our belief that that principle is worthy of being acted upon.

The morally weak person does feel guilty when he does not live up to the principles he thinks he holds—not because he does *not* hold the moral principle, but precisely because he thinks he *does*. The belief that we are committed to a moral principle has two components: first, that we will act on the principle; and second, that the principle is worthy of being acted upon. One's disappointment in oneself on discovering that the first belief is false is dependent on one's still holding to the truth of the second.

If a person finds he does not act to get something that he thought he wanted and hence does not want it, or at least does not want it very much, he does not ordinarily feel guilt or disappointment in himself, unless he thinks he *ought* to want the thing. In this case, he may reproach himself, because he believes that his character is defective in having such weak motivation for what he ought to desire. For example, suppose that a man, under the prodding of his wife, comes to think that he wants a promotion to an administrative position and that he ought to want it for the good of his family. Yet he fails to do some of the things which would enable him to get this promotion. Realizing that he does not in fact want the job, he might accuse himself of moral weakness, but once he comes to realize that he is not obliged to take it for his family's welfare, he can abandon these self-accusations.

To suppose that a person suffers from moral weakness, we must suppose that he fails to act in accordance with principles which *he believes* worthy of being followed. Thus, if the person in question does not really hold principle P, then, even though he thinks he is committed to P, we cannot accurately accuse him of moral weakness, even though he may accuse himself of this fault. One may, of course, be ashamed of an inability to decide what principles are worthy of being acted upon. This is indeed a kind of weakness, but not a moral one.

There is still another problem with Hare's analysis. When a person realizes that he has acted in a morally weak manner, he thinks he has done something morally wrong. Because he holds "I ought to have done A" and "I did not do A," he concludes, "I was wrong not to do A." If Hare is right, however, the morally weak man is not justified in drawing this conclusion because his first premise, namely, "I ought to have done A," is false, or rather what corresponds to a truth value of "false" in imperatives. Only if he actually held that he ought to do A, that is, had prescribed A to himself and to anyone else in the same circumstances, would it be wrong for him not to do A. Naturally, if he believed that he held the principle in question he would believe that he had done wrong. But if, after further failures, he came to realize that he did not hold the principle after all, he would no longer think he had done wrong.

Consequently, if Hare were right, situations like the following would occur. X believes falsely that he holds the principle P which requires that he do A_1 under conditions C_1, A_2 under C_2, . . . A_n under C_n. In C_k, however, X fails to do A_k. He feels that he has been weak and morally at fault because of his belief that he holds, i.e., is committed to, P. As time goes on, however, X fails on a number of occasions to do acts of type A under conditions of type C. If Hare were right, then, if X were faced with this evidence of his lack of commitment, he would conclude that he does not hold P after all. Once he were to realize that he does not hold P, he would take back the judgments that he has been morally unworthy and would no longer blame himself.

This is not the usual pattern, however. When X discovers that he consistently fails to act on P he concludes neither that he does not believe that he ought to have acted on P nor that he is no longer worthy of censure. Rather, he thinks that his offenses have been multiplied and that he is more than ever weak and morally inept. Of course, there are cases in which a person would not draw this conclusion. He might, when having realized that he had repeatedly failed to act on P, relinquish P. A young woman with strict upbringing in sexual matters might, after a number of falls from virtue, decide that it was not wrong, after all, to engage in extramarital intercourse. Whether she would be deceiving herself or not in this case does not matter here. The point is that she would differ from another woman who still believed that her promiscuity was wrong, although she was not prepared to change her ways. If Hare were right, there would be no difference between these women. But it seems clear that there is a difference; namely, that the one woman believes that the principle which she has failed to act upon and to which she cannot be said to be committed, is still a principle which is *worthy* of her commitment, that is, one she ought to act upon, while the other woman does not believe this.

In other words we recognize a distinction between being committed to a moral principle, i.e., acting, at least most of the time, in accordance with it, and believing that the principle is worthy of commitment, i.e., that we ought to act on it, that it is morally right to act on it and wrong not to do so. Hare must maintain that this is a false distinction, despite the fact that it is a common feature of the way we talk about morals.[2]

He might try to explain away the distinction by saying that the only way we can be said to believe that p is true is that we act as if p were true, that action is the sole criterion of belief. A person cannot believe that it will not rain if he leaves the house with raincoat, boots, and umbrella. Likewise, we cannot believe in or hold a moral principle unless we are willing to act on that principle. But this ploy will not work. There are many ways in which we can act in accordance with a belief, and persons holding the same belief may act in various ways, even though their circumstances do not differ markedly. One person may believe that it will rain, and, as a result, not leave the house without being fully prepared. Another may decide that he doesn't mind getting wet as much as he minds lugging his umbrella about all day. Still another may not go out at all. Likewise with moral beliefs; some may act scrupulously to do what they think they ought. Others may do so as a rule, but occasionally let other considerations interfere. Different people may give different weight to different moral principles and so, even though they both believe that both P_1 and P_2 are legitimate principles, one will act in accord with P_1 and the other with P_2 in situations where P_1 and P_2 conflict—even in situations where they believe both principles are equally worthy of being acted upon. Still others may have no compunction whatever about acting immorally, even though they believe that some moral principles ought to be followed.

Differences in how we choose to act upon our beliefs depend upon differences in our desires. Likewise, differences in our degree of desire for morally right action—our commitment to it—are partly responsible for the differences in the ways in which we act upon our moral beliefs. A, B, and C may act in different ways upon a common belief that it will rain today because of the difference in the degree to which they fear getting wet. They may also act differently upon their belief that they ought not to cheat on their income tax returns, depending upon their degree of commitment to morally right action, as well as upon their differing financial circumstances.

What evidence could we have for saying that a person held a moral principle, even though he did not act on it? There are a number of possibilities. For one thing, a person may feel ashamed of himself when he fails to act on a given principle. He may show approval of those who do act upon it, and disapproval of those who do not. He may deceive himself into believing that he really was acting on the principle in question or that, in the particular instance, this principle was outweighed by another, or that his own circumstances provided an exception. He might even admit that, while he ought to follow the principle, he just was not up to it on the occasion in question.

I conclude, then, that cases of moral weakness are not instances of a person's believing that he holds a particular moral principle which in fact he does not hold. Rather, moral weakness occurs only when the agent *does* believe that he ought to follow the principle which he has violated. Hare, of course, does not maintain that all cases of moral weakness are those in which the agent thinks wrongly that he holds the principle which he violates. He says that other instances of so-called moral weakness occur when a person does hold the moral principle he violates, but is *unable* to act upon it. In such cases, Hare says, it is not strictly true that the agent ought to do the act in question. His reasoning is that because "ought" implies "can" it is not true that one who cannot do A ought to do A. Therefore, we do not have genuine cases of moral weakness when X cannot do A, yet believes that he ought to do A—at least, these are not cases of a person's failing to do as he ought.

No doubt all would agree that if I have promised to meet you for lunch and get hit by a truck on the way, thereby failing to keep the engagement, it would not have been possible for me to do so and I am not to blame for the failure. There is no question of moral weakness here. There are other cases, however, in which it is not obvious that the agent could not have done what he believes he ought to have done, despite the fact that it might have been hard for him to have done so. Such situations are typical of what is usually considered moral weakness. If I am afraid of crowds, I may not bring myself to enter the restaurant at which I have promised to meet you. While it may be possible that there are never any cases in which a person is able to act on a principle he holds and still fails to do so, this has yet to be proven. We do not blame or think morally weak those persons who *obviously* cannot act in accordance with their principles on certain occasions. We blame them only when, for all we *know*, they are able to act so. Such situations, in fact, occur often. If the agent and those who observe him see no reason why he cannot do as his principle bids, then what reason, we may ask, does Hare have for saying that the agent was unable to act so?

He might espouse a form of determinism, incompatible with any kind of freedom of action, and maintain that no one could have acted differently from the way in which he did act because the antecedent conditions causally necessitated his act. This view, together with the doctrine that "ought" implies "can," would enable him to draw the conclusion that no one does anything he ought not to do.

It is not clear that Hare wants to accept this conclusion, and he certainly does not argue for it. Unless he is prepared to show that we are *never* morally responsible, he needs to show what the difference is between acts we could *not* have have avoided and those for which we *are* responsible. It does seem that of all those actions in which we believe that we could have behaved differently, cases of moral weakness provide some of the most typical examples. Since we do hold ourselves blameworthy and responsible for morally weak actions, the burden of proof is on Hare to show that we are not. Where a person tells a lie to preserve the image he presents to others, we suppose that, if he really wanted to be truthful, he could have avoided the lie. If he is morally weak he has *some* desire to do what he ought to do. This desire is weak, however, in the sense that contrary desires easily overcome it. If there are any cases in which a person is free to behave differently, this kind is among them. We are more hesitant to conclude that an agent is free to choose in cases of great temptation like that to which a heroin addict is subject. But where temptation is relatively small, we do judge that had the agent a stronger desire to do what was right, he would have done the right thing. We blame him for not having a stronger will to do what is right, for if anyone is ever capable of acting differently from the way he in fact did, these are situations where he could do so.

Of course, Hare has a place for cases of this sort; these, he says, are situations in which the agent does not really believe that he ought to do the act in question. Therefore, he will not prescribe it for himself. But, as we have seen already, Hare's analysis would not allow us to call these typical cases of moral weakness moral weakness at all. For if he were right, the agent would not believe that he was wrong not to do A, or that he ought to do A, and hence his not doing A is not immoral.

In short, Hare supposes that cases which are called cases of moral weakness are either situations in which the agent did not really hold that he ought to do A or situations in which he was unable to do A. But the typical cases of moral weakness do not fall into either of these categories. In these cases, the agent is both able to do A (assuming that anyone is ever able to do otherwise than he did) and believes that he ought to do A. Unless Hare can provide observational criteria for showing that one or the other does not apply in each so-called case of moral weakness, we are under no obligation to accept his analysis. In most cases of moral weakness, on the contrary, we have evidence that the agent did believe he ought to do A, and that, had he wanted to do A as much as he had wanted to do the alternatives to A, he would have been able to do A. Specifically, we can see that his temptations were no greater than ordinary ones and that he suffers remorse, or that he does A-like acts as a rule, or that he admires them in others. Hare has clearly failed to support his account of moral weakness adequately.

The other phenomenon of moral life which Hare tries to explain away is that of perversity. The perverse person is one who knows or believes that an act is one he ought to perform, but, despite this knowledge, chooses not to perform that act. According to a prescriptivist account, perversity is impossible, since holding a moral belief entails prescribing it for oneself, intending to do it, under given conditions. Hare attempts to throw out perversity by saying that those whom we call perverse are acting, not against their own moral principles, but against those of others—family, caste, or nation. Should the perverse man *say* "I ought to do A, but I won't," he is using "ought" in a different sense from the usual. This term Hare designates as " 'ought' ": if X "ought" to do A, that means that some group to which X belongs considers that X is obliged to do A; it may be that he really ought to do A as well, but it need not. It is easy to see why Hare needs another sense of "ought." Without it, prescriptivism is directly refuted by an all-pervasive moral phenomenon.

The best way of refuting Hare's claim seems to be to point out cases of perversity; cases in which the agent recognizes a moral obligation, which, for all we know, he is able to carry out, but which he simply does not fulfill. There are few people for whom moral reasons always and in every instance outweigh every other consideration. The reader may ask himself if he *never* steps on grass that sports a "Keep Off" notice; if he *never* runs his air conditioner during peak hours; if he *never* drops a bit of trash on the street. Pecadilloes of this sort are innumerable, and it is unlikely that there is anyone who is never guilty of them. This by no means implies that most of us do not believe that we ought to refrain from such actions.

Perversity differs from moral weakness primarily in that the latter is a kind of weakness, while the former need not be. Clearly, moral weakness differs, in turn, from a number of other forms of weakness. Where a person is unable to do what he believes he ought, he may be physically or psychologically weak, but not morally weak. If he does not know where his commitments lie, this is an intellectual rather than a moral weakness; he has failed to know himself. If he vacillates in his commitments he is indecisive and weak-willed, but not necessarily morally blameworthy.

Moral weakness may reinforce or be reinforced by those other defects of the personality, but it is not identical with them. For example, my moral weakness may be partly responsible for my not examining myself to see just what I do believe or to find out what are my psychological handicaps so that I may overcome them. Moral weakness proper, however, is a weakness of the will to do what is right. Ordinarily, the morally weak man *will* do what he thinks is right, but when confronted with a choice between an act which is wrong, but attractive for other reasons, and one which is right, but unpalatable, he finds his desire to do right outweighed by his other desires. This weakness may manifest itself in self-deception. The morally weak man, because of his wish both not to do what happens to be the right thing and to absolve himself of blame, may construct a case for the position that what he actually did was in fact morally correct. If successful, he will convince himself that he acted rightly.

In moral weakness there is some desire, no matter how puny, and often a prior intention, to do what is right in the situation in question. In a case of perversity, the agent may have a general desire to do what is right, but in the situation in question, he may have no desire whatever to do the right thing, and at no point does he intend to do it. The vacillation characteristic of moral weakness, and of weakness of will generally, is absent in perversity. If I am morally weak, I will feel guilty about what I have done; if I am perverse I may not. But in both moral weakness and in perversity, moral considerations have been overriden by contra-moral considerations. In both cases, we have a culpably small motivation to do what is right, and for this reason, both moral weakness and perversity are considered blameworthy.

BEHAVIORAL NORMS, MORALITIES, AND THE MORALLY RIGHT

While Hare has not succeeded in showing that what one ought to do is what one prescribes for oneself, he has still brought out a distinction between two senses of "moral" which has been noted by a number of other writers[3]; namely, that between social norms—those which prescribe the actions our fellows expect of us—and our own ideals and values—those principles which actually guide our behavior and which are overriding for us. In cases of conflict the question arises as to which of the two moralities one really ought to follow. Should we always abide by the social norms or always abide by our personal values? Is either of these the "true" morality, or is there some third standard to which we can appeal to adjudicate the issue?

The question has arisen as to whether it is ever possible to specify what a morality (in either sense) is, apart from some answer to the question of what is really morally right. In this section, following Frankena,[4] I want to distinguish between three concepts (namely, behavioral norms, moralities, and what is morally right) in such a way as to show that each is independent of the other, although all three are sometimes called "morality." While what I say here should not rule out the possibility that what is in fact morally right might be identical with personal behavioral norms or with a social moral code, it should show that what is morally right is not identical in meaning with either.

A *behavioral norm* is any standard which guides the conduct of a set of persons. The behavioral norms of an individual are those which actually guide his action and which express his values. A person who is ruled by F values is one for whom F reasons typically override others. If I sacrifice everything for an artistic career, up to and including leaving my children to fend for themselves, then I have committed myself wholly to artistic values. The dedicated Nazi has given himself to Nazi values. One's values may be good or bad in a moral sense, and living up to them may be either morally right or morally wrong. Furthermore, a set of values—if it governs behavior not directly affecting sentient beings—need not constitute a *morality*.

A morality is not concerned with all action as such, but only with action as it affects sentient beings. A morality is a set of beliefs or rules which stipulates the ways in which it is good or bad, right or wrong, to treat others and even oneself. A person's morality is that set of beliefs and rules of this kind which he accepts. This characterization of what *a* morality is in no way prejudges the question of *which* sets of beliefs and rules constitute good, correct, or true moralities. *Any* such set counts as *a* morality; the only requirement is that the beliefs and rules be concerned with the effects of one's actions upon persons and perhaps upon other sentient beings.

This stipulation may not seem sufficient, however. While an artist's activities and those of an industrialist are primarily concerned with nonhuman material, other not specifically *moral* activities *are* concerned with effects of actions on persons. A dentist's work is done upon people, but it is not obviously a concern of morality. Whether or not Dr. Payne should extract Mrs. Smith's wisdom tooth seems to be a medical question rather than a moral one. Closer examination, however, reveals that it is at least partly a moral issue. Granted that the answer to the question "Will the removal of Mrs. Smith's wisdom tooth best promote her dental health?" has nothing to do with morality, that of whether Dr. Payne *ought* to remove it does. That he should do what best promotes the health of his patient, rather than what will bring him the most money or least inconvenience, *is* a moral judgment.

In all of our activities we must make judgments about what effects our actions will have. By themselves, these are not moral judgments, evaluations, or action guides. When we decide we ought to perform an act, we have made a *practical* judgment, but not necessarily a moral one. It is moral only if we explicitly take into account the moral beliefs and rules which we accept—those concerned with good or bad, right or wrong, ways of treating people generally. Even if I have not made a moral judgment about what I do, my acting in accordance with any practical judgment may be considered morally good, morally wrong, or morally indifferent by the moral standards of anyone, if the act has some good or bad effect on some person or persons. This is not to prejudge the question of what effects *are* good or bad. According to standards held by some, the moral quality of the act is not even dependent on the consequences of the act. If, however, an act has any moral quality, it must affect someone.

Our moral standards are those which we accept as rightfully governing our actions affecting people. As shown above we may or may not choose to act in accordance with them. At times all of us let concerns other than the desire to do what is morally right take precedence over the moral concerns we have. Some persons do so consistently; those who do have a code of behavior which values something else more highly than the right and good treatment of human beings. The acquisition of wealth, the pursuit of knowledge, the establishment of a particular political system, may all take precedence over moral action. When this happens, the agent has a set of values which assigns a relatively low place to morality. But these values and rules of behavior do not constitute the agent's *morality*. No doubt he *has* a morality—beliefs and rules which he thinks order the way in which he ought to treat others and which, moreover, he usually follows. He simply does not abide by these tenets when they enjoin action which conflicts with what concerns him more deeply. Everyone has *a* morality—with the exception of infants, mental defectives, and (perhaps) psychopaths. People's moralities differ in what behavior they enjoin; some are, I think, more truly moral, or right, than others. Furthermore, people differ in the extent to which their morality—whatever its content—governs their behavior.

Weak Prescriptivism

Frankena has suggested that one can obtain a tenable imperativist view by altering the positions that holding an action A to be right is to prescribe it, and that for a principle to be a moral principle it must be overriding.[5] We might say that holding an action to be right involves only some desire or inclination to perform it. The phenomena of weakness of will and perversity would not present a difficulty for such a theory, for the desire to do the act believed right might be overridden by some nonmoral desire, without our being forced to conclude that the agent did not believe the act in question to be right.

Frankena's view is not subjectivism; "X ought to do A" does not mean simply "The speaker desires that if he were in circumstances similar to those of X, he would do A." This would be a form of descriptivism.[6] Rather the inclination to do A must be expressed in the moral judgment as a sentence in the imperative (or perhaps some other performative) mood; for example, "Let me do A." In addition to this nonassertoric component, Frankena also holds that right actions are partially definable as those acts which would be performed by someone who takes the moral point of view—a person who is completely dispassionate and impartial and desires the good of everyone alike. Consequently, according to the analysis he suggests, "X ought to do A" would mean "If in X's circumstances, any person taking the moral point of view would do A, and whenever *I* am in X's circumstances, let *me* do A."

While avoiding one of the most serious problems faced by the stronger versions of prescriptivism, Frankena's view shares with both precriptivism and emotivism the difficulty of formulating negations of evaluative judgments. To say, "It is not the case that X ought to do A," as opposed to "X ought not to do A," is not connected with any particular desire. On the above analysis, this sentence would be "Either it is not the case that if in X's circumstances, a person taking the moral point of view would do A, or not-(if in X's circumstances, let me do A)." The problem lies, as in other theories discussed, with interpreting "Not-(if in X's circumstances, let me do A)." It does not mean, "If . . . let me do not-A," but under any other interpretation, it ceases to be an imperative, but rather becomes an assertion that one is not issuing an imperative, or, perhaps, in this case, that one does not have the desire to do A when in X's circumstances. That one does not have a desire of some particular sort does not entail the having of any *other* desire. Thus the negation of an evaluation is not the expression of a desire, nor is it an imperative or a performative, but it *is* an evaluation. The obvious conclusion from this, together with the other arguments of the last three chapters, is that evaluations are not—in whole or in part—sentences which are nonindicative, nonassertoric, or nondescriptive.

If my arguments up to this point have been sound, evaluations are, therefore, indicative sentences which are either true or false. This successful defense of my conclusion would, however, be an empty victory, unless there was some way of knowing how to determine the truth or falsity of evaluations. It is to this problem that I now turn.

7

Fundamental Criteria

If I am right in contending that evaluations are statements that are either true or false, then the obvious question to be answered is how we decide whether a given evaluation is true. In this chapter I shall consider the methods by which, given the truth of descriptivism, the truth conditions of moral judgments may be determined.[1] I think the methods might be extended to other kinds of evaluations, but will not defend that view here. I shall argue that the fundamental criteria for the application of moral terms may be discovered by an examination of the process of evaluative argumentation and of the results of that process.

When we engage in moral arguments, we justify specific judgments by appealing to the fact that the things or acts being evaluated satisfy the criteria we accept of goodness, rightness, etc. I have argued in the earlier chapters that a statement to the effect that an item satisfies these criteria constitutes a set of conditions for the truth of a judgment that a thing is good or an action right. Thus, if F represents the criteria for goodness, then "X is good" is true when X is F. These conditions may be both necessary and sufficient, but it is also possible that moral terms are not fully characterizable by a set of necessary and sufficient conditions for their application.

Whether or not F is a complete set of necessary and sufficient truth conditions for "X is good," it does not follow that "X is good" means "X is F." For one thing, being F must be the *conventionally recognized* truth condition for a thing's being good if "good" is to mean F. And meaning may well comprise more than such a set of truth conditions—a possibility mentioned in chapter 2 (see footnote 22). Besides, the meaning of a moral judgment consists not only of its propositional content (the recognized truth conditions), but also of its mood, which I have tried to show is indicative. In this chapter and the next I shall discuss the way in which the conventionally recognized truth conditions of moral judgments may be determined. If such a method yields a set of truth conditions, then moral knowledge is possible, for we have criteria for determining what is right or wrong.

THE METHOD OF DETERMINING CRITERIA

When people attempt to justify an action as right (morally or otherwise), they generally give as a reason for their claim that the action is of a certain kind. The basic form of such arguments is the following.

(1) All acts of kind F are right.
Act A is of kind F.
Therefore, act A is right.

Other moral terms may be substituted for "right," of course, and in actual practice one or the other of the premises is usually left unstated because it was not questioned by any party to the argument.

When the dispute concerns not whether some particular action is right, wrong, etc., but rather whether a given *kind* of act is right, the argument takes the form of showing that that kind of act is right, because such acts have a further characteristic which marks them off as having a particular moral quality. This sort of argument has the following form.

(2) All acts of kind G are right.
All acts of kind F are acts of kind G.
Therefore, all acts of kind F are right.

In other words, the disputants appeal to a further criterion of rightness; namely, G, in virtue of which F acts are right.

Frequently the parties to the dispute do not wish to claim that the act or type of act in question is right absolutely and without qualification, but only that it is right, other things being equal. If so, their arguments take one of the following forms:

(1a) All acts of kind F are right, *ceteris paribus*.
Act A is of kind F.
Therefore, act A is right, *ceteris paribus*.

(2a) All acts of kind G are right, *ceteris paribus*.
All acts of kind F are acts of kind G.
Therefore, all acts of kind F are right, *ceteris paribus*.

In actual situations, argument will stop when it is agreed that the act in question is of a certain kind and that acts of that kind are right, wrong, or indifferent—either absolutely or when other moral considerations are not relevant.

Now, every person holds universal moral judgments which express those criteria which, for him at least, are fundamental. Let such a criterion be F_n. Then, if X argues that an act or kind of act A is right, because it is F_n, and Y still cannot agree that A is right, even though he agrees that it is F_n, then X will not appeal to some criterion F_{n+1}, such that X holds that F_ns are right *because* they are F_{n+1}. He might appeal to a subsidiary criterion, F_{n-k}, which he thinks might be convincing to Y, or, perhaps, he might respond to Y with "If F_ns aren't right, I don't know what is." If he makes such an answer, he is claiming not to be able to justify his reasoning by further criteria, and his reaction can be explained by the fact that he has come down to the fundamental moral beliefs or commitments he consciously holds. He can at the time think of no further reason for holding F_ns to be right. There may be still more fundamental beliefs underlying these principles, and, if X is so motivated, he may uncover these by an analysis of his reasons for holding F_ns to be right. If pressed far enough, however, we all reach a point at which we can argue no further. To reject certain beliefs would cast doubt upon the whole moral code we accept and leave us unsure of what, if anything, could be called "good," "right," etc.

Such beliefs are principles incorporating the truth conditions for moral judgments that we recognize—explicitly or implicitly. They may be expressed as universal moral judgments stating that acts of a certain kind are right, or right, *ceteris paribus*. They may, furthermore, serve as major premises in arguments whose minor premises assert that the act is of the kind in question and whose conclusions assert that a given act, or kind of act, is right.

I shall argue that the fundamental criteria of moral rightness, goodness, etc., which are conventionally recognized by those who use moral language, can be discovered through critical analysis by well-informed and careful thinkers of the way in which evaluative terms are used, and I intend to propose such a set as a definition of "X ought to do A" in a subsequent book. For now I wish to consider what would characterize a set of fundamental criteria for the application of evaluative terms.

Criteria of the kind in question may best be discovered by means of examining moral arguments, for these criteria are expressed in the reasons given in defense or criticism of specific moral judgments. By means of this procedure, we may determine whether there are any F_ns which are the basic criteria most generally used. It does not follow, however, that the criteria most generally used constitute a set of necessary and sufficient conditions for the truth of moral judgments.

But if the criteria actually employed are not the truth conditions, then on what grounds can it be decided whether any criterion constitutes these conditions? Furthermore, given criteria which do constitute a set of necessary and sufficient conditions, on what grounds do we decide whether they are conventionally recognized and a part of the meaning of moral expressions? Suppose that there is a set of criteria $F_1, F_2 \ldots F_n$, such that for any i, an act which is F_i is judged to be right, by some or by all, by virtue of its being F_{i+1}. Suppose that for each criterion in the series there are some persons who find that criterion basic. It does not follow either that each of these criteria is fundamental or that none is.

Let us consider two F_is, F_k and F_{k-1}, such that one group of people, S, takes F_k to be the fundamental criterion of moral rightness, while another group, S', takes F_{k-1} to be the fundamental criterion. In general, if objects to which the term T applies have two properties, F_k and F_{k-1}, then F_k is the more fundamental criterion, for the reasons that follow. People often do not fully comprehend the grounds upon which their judgments—moral or otherwise—are justified. A person might, for example, believe that people ought to be honest and that honesty is one of the fundamental criteria of right action. He might never have tried to justify this belief in terms of some broader criterion, such as that of utility. Yet if someone were to suggest that he could do this, he might very well agree and adopt utility rather than honesty as a fundamental criterion of moral rightness, especially if he could see no way of justifying utility in terms of honesty.

The situation is similar in the sciences. Prior to the development of the atomic theory, the elements were defined in terms of various physical and chemical properties which they exhibited. Once the atomic structure of these elements was understood, however, and it was clear that their physical and chemical properties were direct consequences of the number of electrons and protons they had, the elements came to be defined by this number; that is, the atomic number. Thus, chlorine is defined, not as a green, poisonous, water-soluble gas which replaces bromine and is replaced by fluorine in salts, but rather as the element with atomic number seventeen, for the atomic number specifies the electron structure of chlorine, which in turn accounts for all these properties.

In general, if objects to which the term T can be applied have the properties F_k and F_{k-1}, then F_k is the more fundamental criterion for the application of T, if the following conditions hold. (1) All objects which are F_{k-1} are F_k, whenever T applies to them. (2) That an item is F_k is actually cited as a reason for considering it to be T. (3) There is no further property F_{k+1} such that an F_k item's being F_{k+1} is generally accepted as a reason for believing that T applies to that item. Any F_k that satisfies (1)–(3) and which may therefore be considered a fundamental criterion for the application of some term T, I shall designate by F_n. Any such F_n is a conventionally recognized truth condition for the sentence "X is T," when "X is T if and only if X is F_n" is not only undisputed, but also when some person who used T in such a way as to suggest the falsity of "X is T if and only if X is F_n" would not be understood to be referring to the same items that others who used T refer to.

An F_n need not be a single property which is a necessary and sufficient condition for the application of T. It may be; for example, featheredness is the one necessary and sufficient condition for an animal's being a bird. On the other hand, F_n may be a conjunction of several properties (i.e., $_1F_n \cdot {}_2F_n \cdot \ldots \cdot {}_mF_n$), where this conjunction is a necessary and sufficient condition for the application of T. For many terms there is no set of necessary and sufficient conditions. There are borderline cases which cannot be decided on the basis of the available criteria, even though these criteria are fundamental. Let us consider Wittgenstein's famous example of "game."[2] There are several fundamental criteria by which we determine whether an activity is a game, for example, the existence of rules, the notion of winning or losing, competition. These criteria are undoubtedly sufficient, taken conjointly, for an activity which satisfies them to be called a game. No one of them is necessary, however. On the other hand, if none of these criteria applies, then we would hardly classify the activity as a game. If a given set of criteria for a term T is fundamental, then any item which satisfies all of them is a T, and any which satisfies none is not a T. In other words, the conjunction of all the fundamental criteria is sufficient and some disjunction of them necessary for the application of the term. For the sake of simplicity, I shall in what follows let the term F_n stand for sets of fundamental criteria $_1F_n, {}_2F_n \ldots {}_kF_n$, such that $_1F_n \cdot {}_2F_n \cdot \ldots \cdot {}_kF_n$ is a sufficient condition for the application of T and $_1F_n v_2 F_n v \ldots v_k F_n$ is a necessary condition. This set, may, of course, have only one member. It may also have several members, of which $_1F_n \cdot {}_2F_n \cdot \ldots \cdot {}_kF_n$ is a necessary, as well as a sufficient condition.

Let us suppose that we discover that a certain set of criteria is employed by those who have reflected upon their moral beliefs and who are knowledgeable of the situations in which they apply them. There may be some who do not adopt these criteria. Have we any right to reject their opinions as less valid than the opinion of the educated moral thinker? I think we have, for the reasons which follow.

In order to see what these reasons are, we must consider what will count as confirmation or disconfirmation of a theory of what the fundamental criteria for the rightness of an act will be. It is, I think, that the proposed criteria can be expressed in terms of fundamental principles which may be used to justify all well-established moral principles. By justification I mean here that, given the fundamental principles and the relevant facts about the circumstances of those who adopt a particular principle, we may deduce that they ought to act in accordance with that subsidiary principle.

For example, consider the rule that torturing people for fun is wrong. Suppose we have as a fundamental criterion of moral rightness that we ought to increase the happiness of all persons except when increasing the happiness of some is incompatible with a like degree of happiness for others. Assuming that torture results in extreme decreases in happiness, making the tortured far worse off than the torturer, it follows that torturing for fun *is* wrong.

While the manner of deduction by which the process of justification occurs is fairly obvious, something of the complexity of such justifications can be seen by the example given. This complexity is the primary reason for most disagreement on moral matters.

What is a well-established moral belief, and why should these and not non-well-established beliefs be chosen as the data to test the proposed criteria? A well-established belief, moral or non-moral, is one which has withstood a significant amount of criticism. Criticism of a belief occurs when arguments are given against holding it. Generally these are designed to show that the belief is false and that the reasons for holding it are inadequate. In the case of moral beliefs, the arguments often take the forms (1) and (2) or (2a) above. When people come in contact with others whose moral beliefs differ from their own, such discussion takes place frequently. As a result of these discussions many people change their views about whether certain sorts of acts are right. A well-established moral belief is one which has tended not to be given up. Such beliefs are usually widespread among varied societies, but they need not be. Under very unusual circumstances, it is possible that acts of a kind that are normally wrong or at least indifferent may be right. Other beliefs may be widespread but not well-established. If no one has questioned it and no arguments have been proposed in its favor, it may be true, but it has not been tested in the manner necessary for it to become well-established. Various practices have been considered morally acceptable, or even obligatory, in many parts of the world, but when those who adopted them came in contact with other peoples, they tended to give them up. When this happens to a moral belief or any other, we may consider it not well-established, for in such a situation the belief has succumbed to criticism.

It should be noted at once that being well-established never guarantees the truth of any belief, moral or otherwise. Nor does failure to withstand criticism give us a sure indication of the falsity of any belief. The practice of slavery and the belief in its moral acceptability continued for centuries, despite critical examination of the institution by many persons. A person living in the Roman Empire in the third century A.D. might with justice have considered the belief in slavery's rightness to be well-established. On the other hand, there have always been complaints that the old moral standards of the society have been abandoned by the young who criticize them. Undoubtedly, some of these standards were reflective of true moral beliefs, even though they did not stand up to their critics.

Justification of the Method of Determining Criteria

Why, then, should well-established moral beliefs hold a place of such importance? A well-established belief is one which is widely accepted as being true, in part because of the arguments given in answer to criticism. The arguments in favor of applying any term T to a given item center around showing that the item satisfies the criteria for the application of T, i.e., the F_1, F_2 . . . F_n. If the arguments are valid and the premises true, the belief is true. If the arguments are accepted as sound, the beliefs will be accepted. These arguments count as evidence in favor of the belief. Presumably, the more evidence we have for the belief the more likely it is to be true. The more evidence we have that a given item satisfies the criteria for the application of T, the more likely it is that T *does* apply in this case. The more evidence in the form of arguments in favor of applying T that is brought together, the more well-established is the view that T is applicable to the items in question, and the more likely it is that that belief is true.

When beliefs are questioned, people are stimulated to look for evidence for or against them. Such evidence as they find will be evidence, and be recognized as such, because it tends to show whether the criteria for the application of the key terms in the statements of the belief are satisfied. Hence a belief which has stood up to doubt and criticism will be one for which evidence has been sought. If the belief has been retained in spite of criticism, we can assume that evidence has been found that shows the belief is acceptable, and that this is so because the evidence has tended to show that the criteria in question have been satisfied. This implies some kind of awareness on the part of those who have engaged in the argument of what counts as a criterion. The parties to the dispute may not have formulated these criteria explicitly. Yet if they are to reach agreement they must have some common understanding of what these are. A belief becomes well-established when, and only when, it is agreed upon by a substantial number of people, at least partly as a result of arguments given in the course of defending it against critics. Such agreement is not possible when there is no agreement about the criteria for the application of the terms in question. It is this sort of agreement which establishes which truth conditions are conventionally recognized, in that sense of "conventionally recognized" which I spelled out in chapter 2.

Well-established beliefs are, then, more likely to be true than those which are not well-established. That there are such beliefs also provides evidence that there are criteria for the application of the terms in which they are stated which are—implicitly or explicitly—accepted by those who have argued about the belief. By examining these arguments it is possible, moreover, to discover what these criteria are. If someone argues that apteryxes were birds, while pterodactyls were not, on the grounds that the former, but not the latter, had feathers, this clearly suggests that being feathered is a criterion for something's being a bird.

Often we are in doubt as to what the criteria for the application of a term are. This need not be due to the term's being indefinable or vague, although it may be. Most of us, when asked what a term means, do not have a pat definition ready to give. Often we must stop and think a bit. In our thinking we consider the contexts in which we have seen the term used, and whether we could use it correctly in other contexts. Here we are using for our data true sentences in which the term is used in order to discover what are the criteria for the use of that term. We employ this kind of procedure frequently to analyze many philosophical terms, nonmoral as well as moral; for example, "knowledge," "cause," and "mental."[3] Similar considerations may be used to analyze evaluative terms as well.

If descriptivism is true, there are conditions which must be fulfilled if an evaluation is to be true. These are fulfilled if, and only if, the terms in which the evaluation is stated correctly apply to the evaluated item. These terms apply if, and only if, the items satisfy the criteria for the application of the term. Unless descriptivism is false—a possibility which I am ignoring in this chapter—satisfaction of these criteria suffices to show the truth of the evaluations in which the terms are used. What the criteria are may be discovered by analyzing the arguments in favor of well-established beliefs. Wherever a moral belief is well-established, there is some agreement as to what criteria must be satisfied for certain kinds of actions to be right. We find out what these criteria are by seeing what premises are used in the arguments presented in favor of those beliefs.

Once we think we know which criteria are fundamental for the application of any term, moral or nonmoral, we may test the hypothesis in the following manner. If we propose that F_n is the fundamental criterion (or a set thereof) for the application of T, we may find this hypothesis confirmed if, given particular circumstances, we may deduce some well-established belief from a statement that F_n is a fundamental criterion for T. Let P be "All F_ns are T," Q be "X is F_n," and R be "X is T." Then, given the truth of Q and R, we have some confirmation for P, just as we would if P were a scientific hypothesis, Q a statement of experimental conditions, and R a statement of the data obtained. Confirmation of P is obtained only if P is consistent and R true. For our data, therefore, we wish to choose what is most likely to be true. These will be the data which can best withstand criticism. If we are testing a theory about the fundamental criteria for the use of a term, we want our data, i.e., the examples of the actual use of the term, to be statements which are well-established. We desire this because we want the data to be correct and statements which are well-established are more likely to be true than those which are not.

What has been said above about terms in general applies equally to moral terms. A theory about the fundamental criteria for the application of such terms can best receive confirmation or disconfirmation from well-established moral beliefs. People disagree and argue about moral matters as much or more then they do about nonmoral matters. Those cases in which some sort of consensus has been reached and where a moral belief is well-established are interesting since they shed light upon what are the actual criteria used in making moral judgments. Presumably, moral judgments become well-established through meeting the requirements set by whatever criteria are used. If there are well-established moral beliefs which cannot be accounted for by a proposed set of criteria, then this is an indication that that set of criteria is not sufficient, and that there must be other fundamental criteria which are used in making moral judgments. On the other hand, if this set of criteria serves to justify or show to be morally right, acts and institutions which are generally believed wrong, this indicates that some one or more of the supposed criteria are not true criteria of moral rightness. It is, of course, possible that the criteria are not at fault, but that the beliefs are. Some institutions were thought morally acceptable for ages, only to come to be believed morally reprehensible. Undoubtedly some of our present-day beliefs, although heretofore well-established, will also be rejected after critical examination by future generations. Still others that have not yet even been dreamed of may become well-established in years to come.

Rawls has suggested that we may revise some of our moral beliefs in such a way as to make them accord with a proposed set of criteria, in addition to using the converse procedure.[4] What we are looking for, he says, is a coherent system. I agree that fitting into a coherent system of broad principles and specific rules is a

necessary condition for the adequacy of a proposed set of fundamental criteria, but it is not sufficient. Rawls, too, recognizes
this, for he says that the beliefs we may alter to fit the proposed
criteria are those about which we feel unsure. Such beliefs would
correspond to those I would call not well-established. Sometimes
we feel unsure about a belief because its defenders have not supplied convincing arguments in its favor. In such cases we ought
to feel unsure, and not consider such beliefs as reliable data for
or against any set of proposed fundamental criteria. If we have a
set of fundamental criteria which appears generally adequate, we
probably should revise those beliefs which conflict with it when
they are not well-established. However, those beliefs about which
we do feel conviction, at least partly because of their having been
well defended against critics, should not be given up merely because they do not fit into a proposed system, even when that system seems otherwise satisfactory. That they do not is rather an
indication of the inadequacy of the system. A scientist will suspect his data rather than a theory when the theory explains much
and the validity of the data is questionable, but once there is no
reason to doubt the experimental results apart from their failure to
fit his theory, he must at least seriously reconsider the theory.

The above considerations clearly show that whether a proposed
set of fundamental criteria for moral rightness is adequate cannot
be determined with certainty. The best that one can hope to show
is that a significantly large proportion of those moral practices
now considered well-established are explicable by the proposed
criteria and that the proposed set does not entail the falsity of any
well-established beliefs. I will suggest here a method for finding
out whether there are any such fundamental criteria; in the next
chapter I will argue briefly that the available evidence suggests
that there are fundamental criteria and that these are of a certain
sort. The task of *proving* these conclusions cannot be completed,
however, for new evidence may be discovered at any time, and
even a detailed specification of current criteria is beyond the
scope of this book.

Suppose that moral beliefs and institutions change so radically
that the criteria by which they can be justified differ greatly from
the criteria upon which the earlier beliefs were based. Do we say

in this case that the concept of moral rightness has changed, or that the concept includes both sets of criteria and that any analysis based on only one of them is inadequate?

If the set of all criteria for the application of any term T contains members which are mutually contradictory, or which lead to mutually contradictory judgments under the same conditions, we may suppose, unless this is a peculiarity of usage by some relatively small proportion of those using T, that there are at least two concepts of T—T_1, T_2 . . . T_n. If T_1 occurs during some period of time Δt_1 different from Δt_2 in which T_2 occurs, then we may say that the meaning of T has changed between Δt_1 and Δt_2. If, on the other hand, T_1 is used concurrently with T_2, we may suppose either (a) that T has two or more senses or meanings, or (b) that there is no demonstrable set of criteria governing the use of T, which is the same for all users of the term. We would consider (a) to be the case if T_1 and T_2 occurred in separate contexts. If, however, T_1 and T_2 were used in the same contexts, we would suppose that (b) held.

An example of (a) is the verb "to know." That there are two senses are indicated by the peculiarity of such a sentence as "I know John and five is the square root of twenty-five." Another good indication that "know" has more than one sense is that the two different senses have different synonyms in the same language and different translations in foreign languages (French and German, for example).[5] Examples of terms of which (b) is true may be found in the jargon of various political groups, for example, "colonialism" as used by the Left and "socialism" as used by the Right. Both terms have fairly precise meanings, but when adopted by persons with ideological axes to grind, they have, for all practical purposes, become different terms. When this occurs, the term ceases to have its original meaning and becomes very nearly nothing but an instrument of abuse. An even clearer example is that of the word "dum-dum" as it was used by my daughter at the age of two. She had no notion of what it meant, but used it only to infuriate her brother. Were her employment of this elevating phrase to become standard, "dum-dum" would be a perfect example of situation (b). There would be no set criteria for its use—at least none which could be said to constitute the meaning of the term. This may also be the case when the original concept is incoherent. All in all, then, we have a means for determining: (1) whether the meaning of a term has changed over time; (2) whether a term has more than one sense; and (3) whether there is no set of criteria which determines that a term applies in a given case for all speakers of the language.

Suppose, however, that we have a proposed set of criteria which is accepted by most persons, but rejected by a few. Are we justified in maintaining that the minority is wrong: that its members do not fully grasp the meaning of the terms in question? The following considerations do, I think, support an affirmative answer.

Moral beliefs may be held for many reasons, both good and bad. They may be comforting. They may incorporate what we have always been taught, and be held simply from habit. We may be afraid to depart from them in word or deed. We may believe that a loving God wants us to put them into practice. We may believe that some kind of action is right because its being performed keeps us in a position of supremacy. On the other hand, we may hold the beliefs because they are expressions of, or entailed by, what it means to act rightly. If there are any ultimate criteria which are truth conditions for statements asserting the rightness of actions, then we would expect them to be cited as reasons for holding a moral belief, at least in a large proportion of arguments. We have seen above why this is so. A good reason for holding a moral belief is that it satisfies these criteria. A bad reason is one which is contrary to or unrelated to the criteria. Sometimes people's motives for wanting a moral belief to be true and accepted will make them deceive themselves into thinking that certain actions satisfy the criteria for moral rightness when they do not. When they argue for the rightness of such actions, their arguments will be faulty in ways which can be detected by more impartial persons.

In this way, when beliefs—moral or otherwise—are questioned, irrational motives for holding them tend to be rejected, while good reasons are generally accepted. This is true, at least in situations where free inquiry into the matter is possible. When societies in which different moral opinions are held come in contact with each other, the members of these societies will undoubt-edly look critically upon some of the beliefs professed or prac-ticed by the members of the others. Some of these principles, however, they may admire and follow, even when this involves rejecting some of their former beliefs. If members of the two cul-tures have opportunities to discuss moral issues and to defend or criticize the views in question, they will tend to reject views for which good reasons cannot be given and retain those which with-stand criticism.

Moral beliefs are well-established because good reasons—at least reasons convincing to the parties to the arguments—have been brought forward in their support. It is, of course, perhaps the case that there may be good reasons for holding moral views even though there are no ultimate criteria which define rightness. Hare's theory is typical of this line of thinking. Still, I think we may say that *if* there are any ultimate criteria, they will be found to explain those moral beliefs that are well-established. If there are no such ultimate criteria, then any proposed set will fail to explain at least some significant number of well-established be-liefs.

It might be helpful at this point to indicate a few practices that have been rejected as a result of the mutual contact of different cultures and to discuss one of the difficulties which may be met in determining whether or not a given moral belief is well-estab-lished or has been disestablished; that is, rejected as false. Among the customs which have been found in relatively isolated socie-ties, but which have been given up as morally wrong after exten-sive contact with other peoples, are cannibalism, female circum-cision, human sacrifice, headhunting, and binding the feet of little girls. For the most part, belief in the moral permissibility of such actions has been discarded in the areas in which they were once performed. It may be argued, however, that these beliefs have been rejected for reasons that do not count as good. The people who engaged in these practices have been coerced into abolishing them, and the belief that they were wrong inculcated, not ratio-nally, but through fear of punishment, or perhaps by more subtle means. For example, the natives might be told that there was a god who punished the performance, or rewarded the nonperformance of practice P. Because of their desire to gain the favor of this deity, they would give up P, and through some process of self-deception convince themselves that the reasons they once had for engaging in P were bad ones.

This sort of situation has undoubtedly occurred many times. If the sole factors involved in the change of moral opinion by the society in question can be traced directly to coercion, then the belief has surely not been disestablished thereby. On the other hand, if the source of coercion has been removed and the belief is not reinstated, then we may consider that belief to have been rejected as false by most of that society. Where sanctions against some practice which was once followed are removed, we normally expect the practice to be resumed. Whatever satisfactions people once gained from them will tempt those persons to engage in them again, once these satisfactions are no longer outweighed by the prospect of punishment. It is true that the effect of former sanctions often lingers in the form of inhibitions and taboos. Yet people frequently overcome or defy these obstacles, and when others see that no dreadful consequences occur, they tend to follow the example of the daring.

One way in which irrational fears and inhibitions can be exposed is through the process of argument. When a person is called upon to defend his moral beliefs and fails to persuade others to accept them, he often relinquishes them himself. Even when he does not, the weaknesses are perceived by others who are less committed than he. In this way rational discussion among those who disagree on moral matters leads to the rejection of some beliefs and the establishment of others, i.e., their being accepted as true, partly because the arguments in their favor appear cogent. Where rational discussion of moral questions has not occurred, few beliefs can be considered well-established. Those held by persons in such societies do not, therefore, provide good evidence for accepting any particular set of criteria for the application of the moral terms in question.

It is, of course, always possible that, although we think we are arguing rationally, using true criteria for moral rightness, we are in fact blinded by custom or special interest, and, further, that potential critics are likewise blinded. It seems unlikely, however, that all persons are and always will be hampered by precisely the same prejudices. When different persons with different biases meet in argument, they must look to still different criteria to resolve their differences and these, being more universal, have a greater likelihood of being valid.

The method I have outlined for determining what are the fundamental criteria of moral rightness may appear viciously circular. In order to know what criteria are used, we must know that they are incorporated in premises of sound moral arguments, from which well-established moral beliefs may be derived. But we cannot know that an argument is sound unless we know that its premises are true: in this case, that they express the truth conditions, or fundamental criteria conventionally recognized, for moral judgments. If we know that the conclusion of an argument—in this case, a particular moral judgment—is true, this gives us an inductive reason for supposing that the premises are true. But we cannot know whether the conclusions are true unless we know that the arguments are sound.

I admit that the method proposed here of discovering fundamental criteria is a rough one. It is based, however, on two considerations which can, I think, refute the charge of circularity. The first is that there can be a set of fundamental criteria for the truth of moral judgments only if moral language is actually used in accordance with those rules. To claim that there are truth conditions for the employment of an expression, yet deny that these are reflected in the way that we use the expression, makes no sense. If there are any fundamental criteria for moral rightness, then mature speakers of a given language will use terms for moral rightness in accordance with those criteria. They will follow these rules in moral arguments as well, especially since they are being challenged to defend their judgments. They can defend these judgments only by showing that the terms in question apply just because they satisfy the truth conditions. It may well be that in morals, as well as in other areas of inquiry, these truth conditions and criteria have not been explicitly formulated by those who use moral terms. Yet this does not entail the speakers' total unawareness of what these are.[6]

The second consideration is that over a period of time fallacious arguments and those with false premises tend to be rejected, while good arguments stand up. By the first presupposition, true and false premises will generally be recognized as such, even if the debaters are unable to formulate them. Therefore, those positions—moral or otherwise—supported only by bad arguments tend to be abandoned. Of course, this does not invariably happen, and it is this element of irrationality that leads to uncertainty as to what the fundamental criteria of moral rightness are.

8

Some Objections to Descriptivism

In the foregoing chapters I have argued that evaluations are assertions—descriptive statements which are either true or false—primarily because they have the grammatical and logical features of this kind of sentence rather than those of such nonassertoric sentences as imperatives and explicit performatives. Many assertoric or indicative sentences, however, do not convey knowledge, since we have no way of determining whether they are true or false. Often this is a consequence of there being no set of stable criteria for the application of certain of their terms. In such cases we have no way of determining the truth conditions of the sentences in question, nor any way of discovering whether they are true or false. In the last chapter I spelled out a method of discovering whether there are such criteria for the application of moral terms, and, if so, what these are. The use of this method to analyze these criteria is a task upon which I am still at work.

Some objections can be and have been made against the possibility of succeeding in such a project, and it is these objections which I shall consider in this final chapter. They are (1) that there has been so much debate even among moral philosophers as to the meaning of ethical terms that we can hardly expect to find a stable set of criteria for any of them; (2) that there can, for various reasons, be no analytic evaluations; (3) that we can understand evaluative expressions without knowing descriptive criteria for their use; and (4) that a descriptivist analysis of moral terms cannot provide us with reasons for acting morally.

DISAGREEMENTS AMONG MORAL PHILOSOPHERS

One weapon with which Moore attacks the so-called naturalistic fallacy is the fact that agreement has never been reached on the definitions of evaluative terms.[1] Philosophers have proposed a large number of analyses of "good," "ought," etc., which have been disputed for centuries. When anyone, therefore, proposes a new analysis, he is at once confronted with the questions, "Why should you think that you are right, while all the rest are wrong? What right do you have to think that you have avoided the same kinds of mistakes of which the greatest philosophers have been guilty?"

These are questions to make one pause, but they may equally well be asked of those who are working in areas of philosophy other than value theory. In ethics, as well as in other philosophical disciplines, the proper response to such questions is to give an indication of why the problem has eluded solution. Ways of doing this are to point out that the wrong questions have been asked, or that different questions have been confused with one another, or that there is some new feature of the subject matter, hitherto un-detected, which throws new light on the problem.

One of the appeals of nondescriptivism has been that it gives such an explanation of the failure of the great ethicists of the past to reach agreement—namely, the central position of the illocu-tionary function of evaluations, and the tenet that factual agree-ment need not lead to agreement in moral judgment. If some such function is central, then the descriptive elements are not what primarily determine their meaning, and attempts to define evalu-ative expressions in terms of descriptive predicates are miscon-ceived from the start. If I am to reject this sort of explanation, it is incumbent upon me to give another account of why moral phi-losophers have thus far failed to reach agreement on the proper analysis of moral terms.

A plausible explanation is the complexity of the terms in ques-tion. It would be naïve to suppose that "good" can be simply defined as "pleasant" or "functioning properly." But that it cannot be so simply analyzed does not necessitate the conclusion that it cannot be analyzed descriptively at all. One might object that complex though the matter is, we should expect that philosophers would have unraveled it after twenty-five centuries. I do not see, however, that this is a convincing argument against the possibility of a satisfactory descriptive account of moral language. Philoso-phers are still arguing about the analysis of many *non*evaluative expressions. That agreement as to their meaning has not yet been reached has not led us to suppose that definitions of the terms are impossible or that statements containing them are not statements of fact.

One reason why agreement has not been reached as to the proper analysis of many philosophical terms—both moral and nonmoral—has been disagreement over what a proper analysis would involve. Until comparatively recently, it has not been generally thought part of a philosopher's task to explain the way in which the terms with which he is concerned are actually used. Indeed, the complexity of the ways in which these terms are employed was often thought in the past to be indicative of confused thinking on the part of "the vulgar." What the philosopher was supposed to do, it was believed, was to assign a clear, pristine sense to these old terms—much in the way that scientists go about standardizing their terminology—to make them technical terms in a new, scientific, systematic vocabulary, which would permit the construction of a true metaphysical, epistemological, or moral system.

Sometimes procedures of this sort have been immensely fruitful. In the physical sciences, such terms as "force," "energy," and "momentum" bear little relationship to the same words used in nonscientific discourse. By using such terms in a precise, clearly defined way, scientists have been able to construct exact and testable theories. In philosophy, however, the results of redefining procedures have been less happy, and in moral philosophy they have been disastrous. The main reason for this is that philosophical theories have been proposed to provide answers to questions which are expressed in our everyday language. If the terms are redefined, then whatever solution may be given will be stated in the new language, and, unless this can be retranslated into ordinary terms, the answers given will not be answers to the questions raised. Nobody supposes, for example, that the momentum of an object, as calculated by the product of its mass and its velocity, is the same thing as the momentum of a political campaign. But moral philosophers have purported to tell us what things are good and what we ought to do, as if they meant the same thing we do by these expressions. When they do not mean the same thing, the resulting confusion is understandable.

In this century, of course, philosophers of the analytic tradition have been concerned to pay attention to ordinary language and to use terms as nearly as possible in the sense that they have in everyday speech. When Moore published *Principia Ethica*, this attitude had not yet prevailed. Since that time, more attention has been paid to finding nondescriptivist accounts of moral language, because descriptivism has, as a result of Moore's work and that of others, largely fallen into disrepute. My contention is that, since the time that moral philosophers have generally recognized the need to analyze the actual use of such terms as "right" and "good," there have been only a few attempts to give a descriptivist account of their meaning. For this reason, it is not surprising that a thoroughly adequate analysis of this sort has yet to be proposed.

Just what particular misconceptions have philosophers had which have led them to faulty analyses of moral terms? Or what misunderstanding may we have had of just what they were doing? I will consider below the ways in which three philosophers—Spinoza, Kierkegaard, and Nietzsche—arrived at moral beliefs which differ widely from what philosophers of the mainstream and people generally take to be true. I hope to show that the disagreement rests largely upon the fact that they conceived their task differently from that presently accepted by moral philosophers, rather than in actual differences in the analysis of the meanings of moral terms.

Spinoza

Spinoza is an egoist, holding that the right act is that which is in the interests of the agent, or what enables him best to preserve his own being.[2] This is at odds with what people generally think of as moral rightness. While it is possible that, at least most of the time, what we do in our own interest is morally acceptable, if not morally praiseworthy, this is hardly what we *mean* by moral rightness. But Spinoza is not attempting to analyze what the ordinary man means by moral rightness. What he eventually recommends that we do virtually coincides with well-established moral beliefs; we are to be just, benevolent, and honorable (even when this necessitates the sacrifice of one's own life). He recommends such action, however, not because it follows from what is meant by "moral rightness," but rather because this is what he claims that reason demands. It is noteworthy that Spinoza seldom uses the term "ought," but rather says that the *wise man* does thus and so. This may—although here I am only conjecturing—have been an expression of his awareness that he was doing something other than analyze what people usually mean when they use ought expressions.

Spinoza arrives at his conclusions as follows. First of all, he maintains that the endeavor of an object to preserve its own being, the essence of that object, and its virtue or power, are all equivalent. This endeavor, or *conatus*, is, moreover, the source of all desire. The reasoning by which Spinoza arrives at this astonishing thesis is rather involved and does not directly concern us here. But if it were true, both psychological and ethical egoism would be established in one fell swoop. If all desire can be traced back to the desire to preserve one's own being, that is, if it is for the sake of this that we desire anything at all; then, in fact, we really do not have any non-self-regarding desires. If all virtue, which, presumably—as it does for Spinoza—includes moral virtue, is our power to preserve ourselves, then nothing is virtuous or morally right which does not lead to this end. This virtue is not, however, *equivalent* to moral virtue, but is much more akin to the Aristotelean concept of general excellence. Of course, for Spinoza, rationality and understanding are the highest expressions of virtue or human essence. And, if our only desires are ultimately self-regarding, the only rational (in one sense of the term) way to act may well be self-interestedly. To act in any other way is to be irrational, since this is what prevents us from attaining the ends we actually have. And behaving irrationally is contrary to virtue. Acting self-interestedly is, for Spinoza, to attain the greatest degree of understanding. The pursuit and achievement of this does not, he says, involve us in conflict with others; indeed it is to our advantage to have others achieve it also. Thus we have nothing to gain by hurting anyone else and much to gain by helping others. In this way, he says, the wise or rational man will behave; this is the most effective means for preserving his own being, the desire for which is, ultimately, the only desire anyone has.

We can see that what Spinoza has done is not to show how "moral virtue" and "right action" are actually used, but rather to give a justification for morality. Morality is justified, he argues, because it is rational, although what is rational can only be what is in our interest, since preserving our being is the only end we have. For Spinoza, as for many others, morality is not something to be pursued for its own sake, but is worth pursuing only on other grounds, such grounds usually being those of rationality or self-interest.

For over two thousand years, the justification of morality on some other grounds has been held by many to be necessary. For if morality is irrational, then surely we, as philosophers, will have no professional interest in it. Whether or not we decide to be concerned with being moral or with moral questions would have no more to do with our work than does our liking for sports, gardening, or mystery novels. And if it is not in the interest of the agent to be moral, then how can we expect people generally to be motivated to act morally?

Now it may be—and this is one of the hopes of nondescriptivism—that the answer to the question of what morality is will also provide the answer to the question of how we are motivated to be moral. If, for example, what we think to be right should be what we prescribe for ourselves, or intend to do, then we are *ipso facto* motivated to be moral. However, even if both questions may receive the same answer, we are not entitled to confuse them with each other.

Kierkegaard

Kierkegaard has been taken as saying that we sometimes ought to do what it is not morally right to do. In his famous discussion of the story of Abraham's taking Isaac to the mountain to be sacrificed, he indicates that Abraham was justified in being prepared to sacrifice his son.[3] Morally speaking, this would be wrong; as Kierkegaard says himself, Abraham was a would-be murderer. But God commanded this deed, and, because of Abraham's faith in God, he was justified, indeed *right*, to carry it through. There are times, Kierkegaard says, when the individual has the right to, and ought to, do what it is in general wrong for anyone to do. This position certainly seems at variance with common belief, according to which the transgression of a moral rule is always wrong, unless this is necessary to satisfy another moral principle which takes precedence over it. The only occasions, however, upon which Kierkegaard thinks one is justified in acting contrary to moral principles is when one must do so to perform an act of faith. For this reason and for the following, the difference is not so great as it appears at first.

Kierkegaard insists that the man who acts against moral laws to do what God commands is in mortal danger, and is rightly in a state of dread. He could be wrong in believing that the thing he has done was really commanded by God. The faith of such a man, as Kierkegaard says, consists of his trust that God will provide, despite all appearances to the contrary. A central part of Christian faith is the belief that God loves everyone, so that he will not command anything that will be ultimately detrimental to any human being. He might demand an action of a kind which normally produces harm, but since God is good, nothing he asks of us will really bring evil. The man of faith believes that the evil which seems the inevitable consequence of the act he believes God to have commanded will not come to pass. Thus we are justified and right to do what God wants us to do, even when it violates moral principles by which we are normally bound. If we act as a loving God has commanded, we cannot do wrong—morally or otherwise. While the act may violate certain moral rules, it will in the end fulfill the purpose of a God who loves all. Thus, it would not be wrong, even though it might appear so by all the tests we can apply. Consequently, I do not think Kierkegaard's view of what is right and what ought to be done, or his understanding of what these terms mean, differs greatly from well-established moral opinion. It appears doubtful at least that Kierkegaard holds that moral reasons ought sometimes to be overridden, even by religious considerations. For religious faith itself, and obedience to God's commands, is justifiable on the grounds that God's will is righteous—morally good. Therefore, to do the will of God is to act upon the best of moral reasons.

Some Objections to Descriptivism

Nietzsche

Nietzsche is another philosopher whose moral views appear to diverge widely from those of most persons. Equality and democracy he despises as devices that allow the incompetent and base to hold back the talented and strong. Those with real power, he maintains, have the right to do as they will with the majority of mankind, for the latter are slaves by nature, and it is right that others should be their masters.

When Nietzsche talks about what ought and ought not to be done, what is right or good, etc., he uses these terms in two different ways. He has a tongue-in-cheek use, where what is good or right is what the masses hold to be good or right. Here he is speaking of the slave-morality, which he vehemently rejects. In the title of his book, *Beyond Good and Evil*, "good" and "evil" are being used in this way. At other times, however, he uses these terms to characterize what he himself believes to be good or evil.[4]

Much of what Nietzsche says is not contrary to commonly propounded moral beliefs. When he inveighs against equality, he often seems to say only that to insist upon dragging down those capable of a high degree of fulfillment solely for the sake of equality with those who are incapable of such fulfillment is clearly wrong. Most moralists would agree with this.

We must admit, however, that Nietzsche also advocates views that are totally at odds with what most people accept. In order to see what answer one could give to a Nietzschean, we must consider more closely the nature of the divergence. Generally, Nietzsche parts company from enlightened modern moralists in his virtual advocacy of slavery for the greater part of the human race. The mass of humanity ought to exist for the benefit of the natural masters, he tells us. They have no rights against the masters, and the latter have no duties toward the slaves. The masters may choose to be kind or helpful; indeed the better they are the more they will tend to be so. But they have a right to treat the slaves as they please. This relationship is much like that which most people think ought to hold between people and animals— that it is shameful to mistreat animals and good to be kind to them, but that we often have a right to benefit at their expense. Indeed this is what Nietzsche seems to be advocating: that only some human beings be treated as persons. Only some, he clearly thinks, are capable of acting in the highest way, morally speaking. Only superior people can be expected to tell the truth, keep promises, etc., and only such people are worth having honorable relationships with. The rest of mankind are little better than animals and should be treated as such.

Two sorts of disagreements in ethics may be distinguished: namely, disagreements about how one ought to treat persons, and disagreements about who is to count as a person. Nietzsche differs from most on the second question, but not the first. Whatever else a person may be, he is a being who has the right to be treated in accordance with moral principles and whose interests must be considered. As a rule, we today think that all, and only, humans qualify as persons, but this need not be the case. Gods, angels, intelligent creatures from other planets, or even machines might conceivably have or receive the status of persons. On the other hand, large groups of human beings have often not been considered as persons by other groups. Attempts to justify this lack of moral consideration have usually been grounded upon assertions to the effect that the oppressed group is inferior in certain ways and that its members are thus not quite human. One moral question of great concern at the present time—that of whether abortions are justified—depends largely for its solution upon ascertaining the boundaries of personhood. If a fetus is a person, then abortions are murders; if not, then abortions are, if not permissible, at least a far less grave offense than murder.

Nietzsche seems to think that the larger part of mankind does not consist of persons, or at least that their interests are not to be considered on a par with those who *do* count as persons—the natural aristocracy. The difference between the latter and the mass of mankind is represented by him very much as a difference between two species of creature. As a rule, whether to consider an individual as a person is thought to depend upon his rationality and his ability to act morally, or, generally, to understand and act upon laws and principles. That one or more individuals are not persons is usually argued on the grounds that they lack such capacities, and Nietzsche evidently thinks that most humans do lack them.

Those who attempt to justify the suppression and exploitation of one group—a race, a nation, or a class—by another, generally argue that the former lacks these capacities for rational and moral behavior and hence does not merit full moral consideration, or personhood. Most such prejudiced people are not, of course, so reflective as to work out a theory to justify their oppression. I am not, however, immediately concerned here with how people behave or with their motives, but rather with the way in which they attempt to justify their practices.

I have tried to show that the views of several moral philosophers, which seem to differ radically from most, are not so divergent as they first appear, at least in so far as the *meaning* of moral terms is concerned.

ANALYTIC EVALUATIONS

Nakhnikian proposes a general argument to the effect that no evaluation—no judgment that some object or act is good or bad, right or wrong—can be a definition or an analytic statement.[5] No definition can be an evaluation because definitions and evaluations have different functions altogether. Definitions are relative to languages; that is, they stipulate that in order to speak correctly in a given language, we must use each of the equated expressions in accordance with the same rules. The term "bachelor" is used according to the same rules which govern the use of "unmarried man." Evaluations, however, require or prohibit certain actions. Nakhnikian concludes from this that no definition, and certainly no definition or analysis of a moral expression, can itself be a moral assertion. There can be analytic moral statements, e.g., "All wrongful killings are wrong," but these are not genuine evaluations because they do not specify any independently characterized action or object of which it is said that it ought or ought not to be done, or that it has or has not merit or worth.

Nakhnikian seems to be saying something like the following: definitions differ from evaluations in a manner comparable to the difference between definitions and factual statements. When we utter a definition we do not state a fact or tell anyone anything about the world. The sentence "'Bird' means 'animal with feathers'" tells us nothing about nature, but only informs us of the way certain terms are used. Nakhnikian holds that the same dichotomy exists between evaluations and definitions of evaluative terms.

It is not obvious, however, that we need to accept the view that *analytic statements* cannot be used to tell us about the world, even if *definitions* cannot be. If I tell a child that birds have feathers, I have given him a piece of information quite on a par with the information that birds lay eggs. I am telling him that any bird he may run across will have feathers, just as in the latter sentence I am telling him that any female bird will, under appropriate circumstances, lay eggs. What I am doing in both cases is to tell the child something which is true of all birds. Yet given the present system of classification, "Birds have feathers" is analytic, while "Birds lay eggs" is not. I might, of course, tell the child that not only do all and only birds have feathers, but that this is what we mean by "bird," namely, an animal having feathers. When I say *this*, I have *defined* "bird" for him. But in doing so I have said something in addition to telling him that birds have feathers; I have told him that featheredness is a criterion accepted by the conventions of our language (and of biologists) for something's being a bird.

While a definition is a rule of language, describing the conventions which govern the use of certain terms, this is not the case with statements that are true *by* definition, i.e., analytic statements. That sentences like "Birds have feathers," "Bachelors are unmarried," "The momentum of a body is the product of its mass and its velocity," are analytic, or true by definition, is not something conveyed by the sentences themselves. Like "Most birds fly," "Some bachelors are dissolute," and "Momentum is conserved in every physical change," all of which are synthetic, they present some information about the world, not about language. We must be told that the first set of sentences is analytic by some other, metalinguistic, sentence about the meanings of the words in question; for example, "All and only those creatures which have feathers are, by definition, birds," "The word 'bachelor' means 'unmarried man,'" and "It is one of the definitions of mechanics that momentum is equal to the product of mass and velocity." These may all be translated into statements with the following form: "The sentence p is true by definition" (or, depending upon one's pet theories, " . . . by virtue of the meaning of its terms," " . . . in all possible worlds," " . . . by the linguistic conventions adopted in language L"). It is these statements which are *about the language*—the metalinguistic statements asserting that p is true by virtue of the meanings of its terms. The statement p itself is *not* a statement about the language—be it analytic or synthetic. As a result, we cannot distinguish between analytic and synthetic (evaluative or nonevaluative) statements on the basis that only one is about a language.

Nakhnikian maintains, however, that analytic sentences in general—and not merely definitions—cannot be genuine evaluations. He presents the argument first given by Moore, which I considered in chapter 1, that the reasons we use to support our evaluations—the good- or bad-making characteristics of the evaluated item—cannot be defining characteristics of the evaluative terms in question. If "X is good" means "X is F," then to say "X is good because X is F" is simply to say "X is good because X is good." But if this argument is to go through, we must suppose that it holds for nonevaluative definitions as well as evaluative ones. We would have to admit that my justifying the statement "This animal is a mammal" by pointing out that it nurses its young is no justification at all, because it is as uninformative as "This animal is a mammal because it is a mammal." Citing the fact that the creature nurses its young is, on the contrary, one of the very *best* ways of showing that it is a mammal. Presumably, doing so would be pointless if my hearer knew both that the animal nursed its young and that all and only those which do so are mammals. But he might very well not know the former and perhaps not the latter either, in which case my justification *would* be informative.

In the case of nonevaluative terms, these remarks seem obvious. Why should they not apply equally well to evaluative predicates? A possible clue as to Nakhnikian's reason for supposing this is his remark toward the end of the paper that if doing one's duty is defined as contributing to the welfare of the community, then to try to persuade someone that it is his duty to do A by pointing out that doing A would contribute to the welfare of the community would be fruitless, for this would simply be to say that doing his duty would be doing his duty.

If it were the case that "duty" actually did mean "contributing to the welfare of the community," then citing the fact that A would contribute to the welfare of the community as a reason for its being someone's duty to do A would be reasonable only if the hearer did not know the meaning of the term "duty." In general, however, our knowledge of meaning does not consist of having at our fingertips exact synonyms for the terms in question (like "unmarried man" for "bachelor"). Only when one has made a special study of philosophy or of some discipline containing a number of technical terms is one likely to make a distinction between what is true by definition and what is simply true. One knows—at least roughly—the meaning of a term T if one accepts as true the sentences that fix the reference of T. When one has this rough knowledge, then to have some other person cite the fact that X is F as a reason for the truth of "X is T"—even where F could be a defining characteristic of T's, is analytically related to "T," and fixes the reference of "T"—does not strike one as odd or insulting.

Nakhnikian might try to argue that no analytic sentence is informative, since we have no way of distinguishing the thing defined except by means of showing that the defining terms apply to it. If a person does not already know what the terms in a sentence mean, the sentence can convey no information, and analytic sentences convey nothing but what the constituent terms mean. For example, he might say that we have no way of picking out birds except by their featheredness. We may say that birds have feathers, but this is of no use to someone who does not already know that this is true, for if he does not, how will he be able to distinguish birds from other creatures? This objection fails, however, for we *do* have ways of picking out birds independently of their featheredness. They fly, lay eggs, sing, and so forth, and while no one of these characteristics holds of all and only birds, together they enable us to specify the class in a very precise manner. This is not true of all analytic statements, for example, "All bachelors are unmarried men." There are no general characteristics of bachelors which serve to distinguish them, even roughly, from other men, apart from their being unmarried. On the other hand, in the case of goodness or rightness, as in the case of birds, there are many characteristics of things, acts, or persons to whom those terms apply which, by and large, set them apart from those which are not right or good. In stating that items having one or more of these characteristics are good or right, we are evaluating. If we happen to use terms for the one or more characteristics which might eventually be taken as *defining* characteristics of goodness or rightness, we are still evaluating. If F is such a characteristic, then not only are Fs good, but a person saying they are good would be evaluating, just as he would be in saying Gs are good, where G is not a defining characteristic. We could also say that F-ness is what we mean by "goodness," in which case we would be *defining* the term "good." In the latter case, one would be asserting that being F is the conventionally recognized truth condition for a thing's being good. This is a different assertion from a sentence asserting simply that Fs are good.

We are able to go through life using many words correctly without knowing or caring how they might be defined. As analytic philosophy has shown, it is notoriously difficult to specify definitions of key terms in the discipline, e.g., "action," "cause," "physical object." Presumably such terms are capable of definition. And, presumably, people utter statements containing them which would be analytic, had a definition been formulated. But not only do we not suppose that these persons have been providing an analysis and not giving information, we do not even know if such a statement would be a correct analysis. In other words, we have a large class of terms, the criteria for the use of which are so complex that we do not know which statements containing them could be considered analytic and which synthetic.

This may be the consequence of any of several factors: (a) the term has not been adequately analyzed; (b) there is no set of necessary and sufficient conditions for the use of the term which adequately reflects its actual employment; or (c) the term is not a descriptive one so that its meaning is not exhausted by its truth conditions. Prior to analysis, we do not know whether a given statement asserts that some item to which a term T is applied has a set of characteristics F which are held by common belief to be true of all and only Ts. If indeed people do hold that "X is T" is true if and only if X is F, then "X is T if and only if X is F" may be analytic, and "X is T" may *mean that* X is F. Nevertheless, such sentences as "That T is F" or "Are all T's F?" and "Bring me that F T" reflect beliefs of speakers just as much as would the same sentences with F replaced by a term G which is *not* analytically related to T.

If there is a characteristic, or set of characteristics, F, such that people not only hold that F is always true of Ts and only Ts, but resist attempts to deny that Ts are Fs on the grounds that they would then be unsure of what was being talked about, analysis may discover this fact. If there is no such characteristic F, then one may be selected more or less arbitrarily. Should this be done, "X is T if and only if X is F" is made true by definition and by explicit convention, and the meaning of T has been stipulated, rather than discovered. In such a case, the meaning of T has been to some extent changed.

If (a) is true of moral terms, as I believe it is, then analytic, as well as synthetic, moral statements may be used to evaluate. These remarks hold true even if we believe that a definition cannot function in the same way that a synthetic statement does—be this function informative, evaluative, or both. But we can have no definitions of any term until we become thoroughly conscious of the way in which these terms are used, in a wide variety of different circumstances, and until we are clear about how we should use them in very peculiar situations.

Consequently, I do not think that Nakhnikian has shown that we cannot have true evaluations which are analytic, if he is trying to work from a general distinction between synthetic sentences and definitions. I am not sure, however, that this is all that he is trying to do. He seems also to want to say, as others have, that moral expressions have an extradescriptive function, which is irreducible and essential to their meaning; namely, the requirement or prohibition of actions. This feature, he would probably argue, is not a part of any descriptive expression, and therefore, no descriptive expression can be equivalent to any moral expression. If this is true, then we could obviously have no definition of a moral expression couched in descriptive terms. I think that the arguments presented in the earlier part of this book have sufficiently shown that there is no nondescriptive, nonassertoric component of evaluations which is a part of their meaning, and therefore, that there is no barrier of this sort to definitions of evaluative terms or analytic evaluations.

Nakhnikian's argument does raise the important question of how we might go about finding definitions for evaluative terms, how to defend their selection against rival alternatives, and how to account for disagreements. If, according to some proposed definition, certain actions are right, and if all persons were to agree that those acts were right, we would have grounds for thinking the definition adequate. However, this would be neither a necessary nor a sufficient ground for showing that the conditions mentioned form a complete set of conventionally recognized truth conditions for "X ought to do A." Unless there is, besides universal agreement, a general determination to accept those conditions as being necessary and sufficient, they cannot serve as an adequate analysis of the meaning of "X ought to do A."

Even in nonmoral contexts people may often not accept the truth even of those statements conventionally recognized by the great majority as analytic. It is perfectly possible that someone may deny that a whale is a mammal, even while admitting that the females of the species nurse their young. That someone *could* deny, for example, that it is wrong to damage the interests of any person when this is not necessary to protect more pressing interests of others, does *not* show that he is not denying an analytic— or potentially analytic—statement.

In many cases we can make a distinction between being wrong about a matter of fact and being wrong about the meaning of a term. We know that the child who asserts both that a figure is a triangle and that it has four sides does not know the meaning of the term "triangle." What of a person who asserts that some action satisfies all the conditions of rightness set out by an almost universally accepted analysis, but denies that it is one the agent in question ought to perform: is he contradicting himself? It is true that we do not accuse people of contradicting themselves when they utter moral judgments which are in conflict with whatever fundamental principles we believe in. But it does not follow that no contradiction is made. We seldom accuse people of contradicting themselves unless we have a clear understanding of what all the terms involved mean. Many terms, which have not been satisfactorily defined, we suppose capable of use in analytic statements. We think that "cause" and "mental" mean something, and that it is possible to utter tautologies and contradictions of a nontrivial sort when using such terms.

How do we recognize such analytically true or false statements when no clear-cut definitions have been set forth? We must consult our sense of the appropriateness of using the terms, which we have acquired, as speakers of the language, in all sorts of circumstances. Would we or would we not apply it under this or that peculiar set of conditions? Sometimes complete answers to the latter question cannot be given, for the term may be open-textured and have no set of necessary and sufficient conditions for its application. By asking such questions, by discussing with others what they think, it becomes possible to map out the meaning of the term, to indicate what are the sufficient conditions, which the necessary, and to what extent the boundaries are fuzzy, and what sort of tasks the terms and the various statements containing them are used to perform. Where such a job has been incompletely performed, it is possible for people to utter contradictions or tautologies without being caught. Those who do make such empty statements are not thought to be doing so; they at least believe themselves to be conveying information.

Now suppose we undertake a mapping project of the sort mentioned above with regard to moral language. There are certain kinds of situations in which our sense of the appropriateness of moral language tells us that we would say that an act was right (or wrong) no matter what—that in any possible world where such an act was performed under these conditions, it would also be right (or wrong). But how are we to respond to a person whose sense of the appropriateness of moral language tells him the contrary—that acts of this sort under these conditions need not be right in every possible world, or, for that matter, even in this one? Could we justly accuse him of not knowing what the term "ought" means? If we are to maintain that there is a complete set of truth

conditions for all moral judgments, then it surely seems that anyone who denies that these conditions hold for a given judgment,
yet asserts the judgment, does not know the meaning of the terms
involved and is contradicting himself.

I do not think, however, that such harsh judgments upon those
who would disagree with even a widely accepted set of truth conditions for moral statements are called for. There are many terms
and statements, as we have seen, whose meanings are in dispute.
For example, I once attended a discussion group whose task was
to consider the problem of skepticism. Debate largely centered
around the question of the meaning of various epistemic terms.
Every one of us knew what these terms meant, in any ordinary
sense of "knowing the meaning." Yet the major source of disagreement concerned whether various statements were analytically true or false, and whether, given odd conditions, these statements would be correctly used. While it has been suggested that
some epistemic statements, e.g., "S knows that p," are performatives rather than declaratives, no one has supposed that all
such statements are nondescriptive, merely because agreement
has not been reached as to just what is their correct analysis. Nor
did those who disagreed about the meaning of the statements in
question, who gave different answers about whether the statement
was true under certain conditions, accuse each other of not knowing the meaning of such terms as "know," "certain," or "believe."[6]

In like manner, I do not think that, even if a faultless analysis
of moral expressions should be presented, any one has the right
to accuse those who disagree with it of contradicting themselves
or of not knowing what those terms mean. The fact that two
people cannot agree on what is the correct analysis of "S is absolutely certain that p," even though both know what the terms involved mean, does not entail that there are no nontrivial analytic
epistemic statements. Similarly, it does not follow that there are
no analytic evaluative statements either. It seems that we do not
really have the right to accuse those who disagree with us about
the proper analysis of a term of not knowing the meaning of the
term or of contradicting themselves in using it, unless and until
the meaning of the term has been settled by lexicographers.

Now, by a lexicographer I do not mean only the compiler of a dictionary. The definitions found in dictionaries, while adequate for ordinary use, are frequently insufficient for persons who need to be very precise about the term in question. Those terms that become of great importance to a particular discipline need to be more carefully explained than they are in any dictionary. Scientists and lawyers, for example, as well as philosophers, need to be far more clear about the meanings of key terms than they can be from reading common dictionaries. They become so by working together, considering how these terms are used in fact, as well as how their meaning might be refined. Often scientists have conferences at which such matters are not only discussed, but decisions are made about how the terms are to be used in the future. Thus a standardized use is adopted, and those who depart from it can rightly be accused of contradicting themselves, and of not knowing what the terms mean.

Philosophers on the contemporary Anglo-American scene do not legislate in this manner, but confine themselves to discussing ordinary use, or, at the most, to making carefully selected stipulations for their own purposes, which they do not impose upon others. And it is right that they should so limit themselves. For if they did legislate the meanings of the terms, the answers that they would provide for various questions might not be answers to the questions raised, since the questions are posed in ordinary, not philosophically refined, language.

On the other hand, while philosophers cannot stipulate the ways in which their terms are to be used with the same freedom that scientists have, they do, in an important sense, function as lexicographers. For as discussion progresses, it is to be hoped—for otherwise why would we engage in such discussion?—that we will draw nearer to one another in our analyses of those terms which are important to us. While we do not hold conferences at which we set the meanings of these terms, gradually we can, through discussion, eliminate eccentric analyses, and those which entail the falsity of statements which are most firmly believed to be true. Someday, agreement may be reached as to how some of these terms ought to be used, and, for a time, at least, philosophers may claim to have the correct analysis of such expressions and be justified in accusing those who employ them eccentrically of not knowing their meaning. Should eccentricity of a particular sort become widespread, however, the expressions in question should certainly be reanalyzed. Their meanings may have changed with time, or the original analyses may have been faulty. But always, unless such analytical activities are to be nothing more than games, we suppose that there is a correct use of such terms which we may discover. If, after much effort, no such use is discovered and the term is, nevertheless, one which it would be desirable to employ, we may resort to legislation, provided that we keep in mind that the legislation is just that. Legislation has, of course, been carried out with fruitful results in logic, as well as in the introduction of terms which have no extraphilosophical use.

When a philosopher presents an analysis of evaluative terms—or of others, for that matter—the ultimate determinant of his opinion must rest upon his intuitions of how the terms in question are used. It is to his sense, as a speaker of philosophical English (or other language), of the appropriateness of the terms in question that he must appeal in the end. Does this analysis permit us to say what we most firmly hold to be true? Does it forbid our saying what we strongly believe to be false? Would a person's using the term in such a way as to imply the falsity of the analysis leave us wondering what he was talking about? If not, then something is wrong with the analysis.

The above discussion clearly implies that there is nothing arbitrary about the kind of linguistic analysis which is so widely employed at the present time and which I think can be used in determining the meaning of moral terms. Knowing the meaning of a term is knowing the linguistic conventions that govern its use, and defining terms is the process of describing these conventions—either those that already exist, or those which are proposed for the future.

If this much is conceded, a new line of argument may be taken against the view that moral terms can be defined. If there is no fundamental difference between evaluations which are true by definition and those which are not, such that the former are statements about a language and the latter prescribe actions and ascribe worth, then on what grounds can one claim the necessary truth of these analytic evaluations? A decision to make "Whatever is conducive to pleasure is good" true by definition—whether this decision is made by fiat or by the unconscious collective formation of a convention of usage by the speakers of a language—would surely be an arbitrary one. If the definition which only describes the fact of this decision's having been made is not arbitrary, the decision itself *is*. Any such decision reflects the values of those who made it, and anyone with a different set of values could construct his own definitions. There would be no reason for supposing that either definition was the true one or that there was any ground for preferring one to the other. To accept either definition would be to accept the one set of values rather than the other, and there would be no justification for the claim that either set was better or truer than the other.

It is true that to accept any given set of evaluations as analytic is to accept certain values and that to accept a different set, not logically equivalent to the first, is to accept different values. It does not follow, however, that there are no grounds for preferring one set of definitions (and values) to another. In the nonmoral as well as the moral case, we are free to change the meanings of terms by accepting different sets of truth conditions. I see no reason to suppose that the meanings of terms are unalterable. Yet what truth conditions are accepted is determined in part by the usefulness of accepting them. In biology, a system of classification is chosen which satisfies criteria of simplicity and ease of expressing known information. The moral concepts we now have also have a greater utility than do certain alternatives, which limits the number of sets of truth conditions that people are likely to accept.

We use evaluative terms to classify objects and actions, persons and their character traits according to the way in which they affect the achievement of our ends. On the whole, we call "good" or "right" things and actions which enable us to achieve our goals, and "bad" or "wrong" those which frustrate them. I do not want to argue here that such terms are so defined by the conventions of the languages containing them. I do think, however, that any analysis of moral expressions which did not entail that we ought to do what would help us achieve our purposes and that we ought to avoid what would frustrate them, would ever be accepted by any group. The reason is that, as purposeful beings, we want things and actions which will further our ends. Moreover, while we may reluctantly accept the restrictions imposed by natural scarcity, no person wishes to see others preventing him from attaining his goals as a result of their having much more of the world's goods than he. Thus we have inborn desires for goal attainment and fairness. Moral systems are established to satisfy these demands. To the extent that following the rules of a system would achieve these purposes, the more likely the rules are to find acceptance—at least among reflective persons. Moral theories are criticized and rejected for failing to incorporate principles which would satisfy one or the other of the two demands. Utilitarians have been accused of neglecting fairness, for example, while deontological systems have been thought defective because of too little attention to human wants.

To see how this is, we might consider the way in which moral beliefs become well-established. There seems to be a general principle which governs whether or not a group accepts a new practice. New practices are accepted when the group likes them or expects them to bring more things they like. Or, if a new practice requires giving up things they like, it promises greater returns of desired things in the future. Old practices are abandoned when people cease to enjoy them or their consequences, and when alternatives seem possible.

Most of us are willing to accept rules of honesty because we like a world in which our goods are protected and in which we can count on others to tell the truth and keep promises. By obeying such rules we give up a few advantages, but if we can be sure that others will generally obey the rules, it is worth the sacrifice, for in the long run we gain more of what we want than we give up. Here is an example of practices accepted for their usefulness in bringing us things we desire.

A contrasting example is the changing sexual mores of the Western world. Because contraceptive measures are generally effective, and, when they do fail, safe abortions provide a convenient back-up, the risk of having unwanted children is minimal. Thus a major reason once set forth against extramarital intercourse is no longer tenable. Consequently, it is often argued that, since sex is fun and hurts nobody, there is no good reason not to enjoy it at will. One may question this argument, but what is important for our purposes is the nature of this justification for abandoning traditional taboos. It is that something we want can be acquired by abandoning former standards, and, at the same time, nothing desirable will be lost—i.e., no harm will be done.

Such an argument could never be brought forward in favor of generalized theft, lying, or deliberate cruelty, and it is almost certain that all societies will keep some clear restrictions on practices of this kind. In general, the reasons offered to justify accepting or rejecting acts, practices, or rules are intimately connected with what people want.

If "ought," "good," etc., came to have radically different meanings we would lose all incentive to do what we ought to do. If what we ought to do had no bearing on our getting anything we might want, or if we ought to pursue what we did not want or, sacrifice what we desired more for what we desired less, then who would wish to do as he ought consistently? If doing as one ought had no bearing on the wishes of others, or if it were to frustrate those wishes, we would have no reason to want people to do by us as we ought to be done by, nor would we wish to treat anyone else for whom we had the slightest concern in the way in which he ought to be treated. If we ought always to put our own desires above those of others, then I grant that we would often be tempted to do our duty, but we would not care to have anyone else do his duty by us. We should take pains to teach children to eschew right action and to punish people who did as they ought. The action-guiding function of "ought" would soon disappear entirely, for it is dependent on the fact that we have a stake in people's doing as they ought—one which society reinforces where nature is lacking. It is this fact which poses restrictions upon the moral concepts and systems that are ever likely to be adopted.

If, indeed, the underlying purpose of having moral codes and making moral judgments is to promote human desires and adjudicate conflicts between the desires of individuals so as to minimize dissatisfaction, then two features often held to be true of moral systems could be explained. First, people can criticize their own or another society's moral tenets, and they seem to have some standard in mind when they do so. Perhaps what enables them to determine how well a given moral code meets this standard is a recognition of the extent to which it fulfills the underlying purpose of desire satisfaction. Secondly, if there is this underlying purpose, it would be possible for a variety of moral codes to be equally valid, for a given purpose can frequently be fulfilled by a number of different means. We may also see how a given rule may be valid in one code but not another. Suppose that Code I consists of rules A and B and Code II consists of rules C and D. While following A and B alone might achieve the purpose of moral systems to a high degree, following A, for example, together with C and D might frustrate that purpose. Rule A might conflict with what is accomplished by following C and D, for example. Thus following A would be right for those living by Code I, but wrong for those living by Code II. A deeper consideration of this matter is, however, beyond the scope of this book.

Can We Know the Meanings of Moral Terms without Knowing Criteria

Some have argued that, even if we were to be quite ignorant of the criteria being used for the goodness of a thing or the rightness of an act, we would still know what the terms "good" and "right" mean.[7] The reason is, they claim, that the descriptive criteria are not a part of the meanings of these terms; rather it is their emotive or prescriptive force which constitutes their sense, the approbation and positive feeling they express.

It is quite true that we do not always know the *specific* criteria for the goodness or rightness of particular classes of things and actions. For example, I know very little of what characteristics make certain power tools good. On the other hand, I do know that if a power tool is a good one, it has properties which make it capable of doing the job—whatever that may be—for which it was designed. Knowledge of this general criterion of goodness does not entail knowledge of specific criteria.

Let us suppose that there is an analysis D of a given form of evaluation, for example, "X ought to do A," such that D provides a full set of criteria for that evaluation, and such that D adequately reflects the current use of "X ought to do A." Suppose that an alternative analysis D' is proposed.

Nondescriptivists would maintain that the change from D to D' would not be a change in meaning, provided "X ought to do A" still had the function of prescribing, or expressing approval of, A. All that would be different would be the criteria people adopted, but these criteria are not part of the meaning. They reflect only different standards.

A descriptivist, however, is committed to the view that a change from D to D'—at least when the change is large—*does* involve a change in meaning. But I think this is tenable. It is not clear that small changes would result in changes of meaning. The meaning of the term "copper" changed only slightly, if at all, when chemists decided to define it as the element with atomic number 32. "Copper" still denoted the same metal with the same physical and chemical properties. If D and D' still supported the same, or very nearly the same, well-established moral beliefs, and if more or less the same actions were considered right under both analyses, then we would not need to suppose a change in meaning.

The case would be otherwise if D and D' were radically different criteria. If chemists were to redefine copper as the element with atomic number 17, and instead of a brightly colored, malleable metal, the term now denoted a poisonous green gas, the meaning of "copper" would certainly have changed. Likewise, if D' were to include statements like "One ought to do whatever one feels like doing, regardless of the effect on others or the long-term effects upon oneself," or "One ought to frustrate as many desires as possible," or "A is wrong if and only if it decreases the size of a rock," as being analytically true, there would be no escaping the conclusion that the meaning of "X ought to do A" had changed.

The test for whether there had been a change of meaning would be to see whether persons adopting the analysis D' could be understood by those who accepted D. To say that the latter would not understand the former is not to say that the latter would find the former unsympathetic or insane, but that they would not be able to comprehend what the former's "ought"-containing sentences conveyed. Let us consider the following dialogue:

A: I ought to go torture my prisoners now.

B: Good God! Are you saying that that is the *right* thing to do?

A: Certainly; why not?

B: I don't agree that people ought to be tortured, but I suppose you have some reason for it. Do you suspect them of harboring secrets dangerous to the government?

A: No, nothing like that. I'm not trying to get information from them.

B: Surely you aren't torturing them for fun!

A: Oh, no, I don't really get any pleasure from that sort of thing. In fact, it rather nauseates me.

B: Do the *prisoners* enjoy it? Are they masochists?

A: Not in the least. They hate every minute of it.

B: Then why torture them at all?

A: To cause pain, of course.

B: Why on earth would you want to do that?

A: One *ought* to cause pain.

B: What on earth *for*? To build character?

A: Not at all. Pain is just a good thing.

B: Do *you* like to be in pain?

A: Of course not. But it is right for others to cause me pain. *Everyone* ought to bring about as much pain to as many people as he can.

B: Surely, because of some good the pain does?

A: Oh, no. Pain is good in itself.

B: But *why*?

A: It's what I prescribe for everybody; I commend it.

B: But how can you prescribe something which neither you nor anyone else wants? How can you commend it? What does prescribing or commending mean in such a case?

A: No, I don't want pain, nor do I want pain to be caused, but causing pain is still what I approve, commend, and prescribe, and it is still right to cause it.

B: It seems as if you only prescribe, commend, and approve things that you and others *don't* want, but people normally prescribe, commend, or approve what they *do* want, or think that others might want, even if *they* don't.

A: Not always.

B: True. But if they prescribe or approve something that they neither want nor think that anyone else might want, they are being misleading. When we do these things we are expressing a belief in the goodness of the thing or action so appraised and in doing this we are saying that the thing or action is wanted or may lead to something that might be wanted by somebody.

A: Well, that's not what *I'm* doing when *I* commend, approve, or prescribe.

B: Then your commending, approving, and prescribing is different from other people's. You must mean something different from what the rest of us do by those words.

A: That may be. But I must get to my torturing; I've neglected my duty long enough. Goodbye. (Exit)

B: Hmm! I wonder what he means when he says *good*bye—wishing me a day of suffering, maybe?

While a person who prescribes, approves, or commends an action need not desire that that action be performed, if he supposes that *nobody* would want that action performed, it is not easy to make sense of his prescribing, approving, or commending. In the absence of a connection with human desires and purposes, what these speech acts amount to stands in need of explanation, and so does the application of such terms as "right" and "good."

That the expressions "good," "right," "approval," "commendation," etc., do not seem understandable apart from their implying conduciveness to furthering human ends and desires, suggests that anyone who uses such terms in such a way as not to have this implication has a different set of concepts and means something different by these terms from what the rest of us mean. This suggests that there is a logical connection between what is right and good, on the one hand, and what is desired, on the other. I will not try to prove this here. For the moment, I am merely appealing to the reader's linguistic intuition in asking whether it does not seem clear to him that A and B in the above dialogue mean entirely different things by the value terms they are using. As for me, I am convinced that I would not understand what a person taking A's position was trying to say. I would not know quite where to begin in trying to find out what he was talking about. Perhaps his use of the words "ought" and "good" differ from mine; perhaps it is his use of the word "pain," or the term "desire" or "commend." I would not know, because there would be no fixed points of reference. Unless A and I were to share some beliefs, fixing the meanings of the terms being used, mutual understanding could never occur.

Without some fixed criteria, then, it is not possible to understand the meanings of moral expressions. Furthermore, these criteria seem grounded in the tendency of positively evaluated items to promote the achievement of human ends. Unless we understand good things or right actions as being positively related to these ends, it is difficult to make sense of evaluative expressions. Even the idea that what is good or right is what we commend, approve, or prescribe is impossible to comprehend unless we suppose that human beings want what is good and right, or want the consequences of good and right actions. The reason for this is that we normally commend, approve, and prescribe things we want or think others might want—or at least things that are likely to bring about desired states of affairs. If we commend, approve, or prescribe things we believe are neither wanted nor apt to lead to anything wanted, we are being deliberately misleading. For this reason, if moral expressions can be defined in terms of human ends and desires, their action-guiding nature is understandable; if not, it is difficult to see how they could have this function.

The end-promoting nature of good things and right action is more fundamental than is the action-guiding nature of the terms. Whether one's actions will be affected as the result of one's acknowledgment of an object's having a given evaluative quality depends also upon one's ends. Where we are indifferent to the ends which an item promotes, the consideration that it is good does not move us, even though we agree that it is good. I have no interest in golf; consequently, that a young man is a good golfer will in no way lead me to approve of him. I might be brought to recommend him for a country club job, but only because I cared to some extent for promoting his well-being or that of his prospective employers. While I may not know what specific criteria make one a good golfer, I do know that generally they are characteristics which promote the ends of those interested in that activity, and that this may, in some, but not all, circumstances lead to approving or prescribing.

WHY SHOULD WE BE MORAL?

People often ask why we should be moral. This question can mean one of two things: (1) why ought one (morally) be moral, i.e., do what one morally ought to do—which, as many have pointed out,[8] is a trivial question upon which I wish to spend no time; or (2) what reasons, other than moral reasons, can be given for acting morally. If we are looking for some consideration which will give everyone an absolutely sufficient motivation to do what he believes he ought on every occasion, the search is vain. Since people do not always do what they think they ought, any supposed reason of this sort would be highly suspect. That some nondescriptivists take it to be a virtue of their systems that the evaluation-performance gap is closed, that holding that one ought to do A has a logical connection with one's doing A, is a strong reason for making us doubt the adequacy of their analyses. Any analysis, where one holds that X ought to do A entails anything about what the speaker *will* do with regard to X and A, flies in the face of moral experience. Only if we make additional suppositions about what the speaker desires, how much he desires it, and what conditions are present, can we make an inference about the way in which his moral beliefs will be reflected in action on a given occasion.

Nevertheless, I must indicate what motives people may have for acting morally when this is contrary to their own interests and does not increase fellow-feeling with others. Unlike Kant, I do not think this desire is simply respect for human rationality as such, but rather I believe it is a motive based on human feeling.

With certain restrictions, morality promotes the wants and interests of persons, and the motive for acting morally is grounded in one's concern for the interests of others. Nearly everyone loves and cares for some people besides himself, and actively wants their interests to be promoted. We approve of actions which do so promote them and favor persons who act morally. We are also, for the most part, endowed with enough sympathy that, other things being equal, at least, it distresses us to see people being hurt and pleases us to see them prosper. So long as our own interests do not conflict with theirs, we are generally content to let them be or even help them in small ways.

In addition to these motives, we have a general desire to be a part of a human community. The person who ignores the desires of others will forfeit this, for he will soon find himself without friends, while the one who is careful of others will be loved and respected. To most people nothing is more important than having good relationships with others, and there is no better way to achieve this than to do what is morally right and good. This desire usually suffices to induce people to behave in morally acceptable ways.

It is not, of course, always sufficient. For many, other things are more important than their relationships with other people. Money, power, professional achievement, and so on, may mean more to one, and, in the case of a conflict between these goals and moral goals, one may be led to do what is wrong. Furthermore, there may be many wrong acts which a person can commit without forfeiting good relationships with those persons who matter to him. If certain practices, like cheating in school work, become widely accepted, then one can keep one's friendships in good repair even though one engages in bad actions. Finally, when certain right actions are not acceptable in one's *milieu*, one will have a definite motive to avoid them. Many Southern whites refrained from participating in the civil rights movement of the 1960s because of the hatred they could expect from their neighbors. In these sorts of circumstances, where one desires other things more than human friendship and where wrong acts are condoned and right acts condemned, most people most of the time fall by the wayside. Only those who have a strong commitment to doing the morally right thing will be able to withstand these temptations. And people who succeed in doing so most or all of the time are comparatively rare. It takes an unusually courageous and morally committed person to do what he thinks right, not only when he will get nothing for himself by doing so, but when he knows he will forfeit the good will of those for whose good will he cares.

Such persons have a stronger motive than those ties of affection and capacity for sympathy which keep most of us acting rightly most of the time. For some, the source of this motive is religious. A religious person may believe, perhaps, that while it is possible to keep human fellowship intact without always doing what is right, his relationship with God will suffer from wrongdoing. He need not believe in divine punishment, but simply that he will draw apart from God if he does wrong. Or, one may believe that God cares for everyone, and hence the value of each person and the extent to which his good should be pursued seems to him enhanced. Nonreligious, as well as religious, persons may have a strong motive to do what is morally right as a result of a particularly well-developed sense of sympathy with others, which they extend even to those they do not know, or who are very different from themselves, or whom they dislike. Still others may have an ideal—a person or group of people whose goodness serves as a model of behavior, and towards whom they feel reverence and a desire to emulate. Any one of these motives, and no doubt others besides, account for the occurrence of outstandingly good actions and people. Thus there are many reasons why people actually do wish to do the right thing; some of these are self-regarding, but others are not. We can hardly expect, however, to find an omnipresent motive to do what is right, nor need we think that we have to justify moral behavior on nonmoral grounds in order to make engaging in it reasonable and palatable.

In this chapter, I have argued that there is less disagreement about the meaning of moral terms among moral philosophers than one might suppose. Also, I have indicated how we can admit that some could ultimately disagree with a correct analysis of such terms without supposing that they blatantly contradict themselves. Also I have tried to show what does account for the fact that the belief that an action is right provides us with a reason for doing it, and—for most of us most of the time—a sufficient motive. If my views are correct, we do not have to suppose that the motives for doing right are built into the meaning of evaluative terms.

Conclusion

In this book I have tried to demonstrate the basic similarity of moral judgments to ordinary descriptive statements. Syntactically and logically, evaluations are much closer to assertions than they are to nonassertoric sentences such as imperatives and performatives of approval. Arguments to the effect that evaluations must have a nondescriptive component to their meaning are, I have maintained, untenable. If all this is true, we have cleared one hurdle that was supposed to stand between us and moral knowledge, for knowledge can be had only of sentences capable of being true or false.

A second hurdle, however, is the problem of deciding how to tell whether a given moral judgment is true or false. I have argued that we do with moral judgments what we do with other descriptive judgments; namely, look for criteria for the application of the relevant terms, which criteria are stated in sentences that are held to be not only true, but reference-fixing. These analytic statements may not always have this status. If they lose it, the meanings of their terms is to some extent changed. This omnipresent possibility makes absolute certainty of definition impossible in any field of inquiry—moral or nonmoral. That there are difficulties in deciding whether or not a moral assertion is true I cannot deny; what I do deny is that these difficulties differ in kind from those we have in determining the truth of other assertions.

A third hurdle is that, while the methods of determining truth conditions of moral judgments do not basically differ from those used in determining the truth conditions of other assertions, those methods may not yield results. Certainly, moral agreement is not as easily come by as is agreement in many other areas. I have not resolved this problem here. To do so is an extensive task, upon which I am still engaged. To show that there is a set of conventionally recognized truth conditions for moral judgments, it will be necessary to show that the kinds of reasons we offer in favor of or against the rightness of acts and practices are basically the same, when pressed to their limits. This requires a broad account of moral beliefs and the ways in which they change as a result of discussion and debate.

What I *have* done here is to propose an answer in general terms: namely, that we argue for the rightness, goodness, etc., of acts and things on the basis of whether or not they satisfy wants. If this is true, the truth conditions for moral assertions lie in this direction. This is not a novel discovery; if it were novel, however, I should be seriously perturbed, for one of the central conclusions of this book has been that moral truth is determined by the most widely and tenaciously accepted moral beliefs.

Appendix
Notes
Selected Bibliography
Index

Appendix

The Formal Structure of Reasoning with Nonassertoric Sentences

The deductive pattern used in this kind of inference is similar to that developed by McArthur and Welker.[1] They introduce as a rule of inference that we may assume as a hypothesis the assertoric form of each nonassertoric sentence, and deduce assertoric conclusions within the scope of that hypothesis. After this subconclusion is reached, the nonassertoric form had by the premise is given to that subconclusion in the subsequent step, via a second transformation rule. The argument "If he is angry, mollify him. He is angry. Therefore, mollify him" may be demonstrated in their system as follows:

*(1) ! (If he is angry, you will mollify him.) (First premise)
**(2) ⊢(If he is angry, you will mollify him.) (Hypothesis, transformation rule)
**(3) ⊢(He is angry.) (Second premise)
**(4) ⊢(You will mollify him.) (From steps 2 and 3, via *modus ponens*)
*(5) !(You will mollify him.) (Transformation rule)

Here, !(You will mollify him.) means "Mollify him!" and ⊢(You will mollify him.) stands for the statement "You will mollify him." The validity of the argument according to their system also depends upon the entailment relations between the conditions under which the premises and the conclusions would be illocutionary acts of the kind in question, and upon certain other formal requirements.

In the pattern of reasoning to be outlined here, these requirements are not necessary, for I am not attempting to show that nonassertoric sentences as such can serve as either premises or conclusions of arguments. I have already indicated that they do not serve as such in the kinds of arguments we actually make, and the pattern of reasoning which I shall now spell out applies to the reasoning patterns we do employ.

$S(\tau\phi)$ asserts that the sentence $\tau\phi$ is satisfied; i.e., if it is an assertion it is true, if a command, it is obeyed, if it is a promise, it is kept, and so forth, in the normal senses of those terms (as opposed to their being only terminated). Since S($\tau\phi$) in every case entails that ⊢ϕ, the following satisfaction rule (S.R.) may be added to those of standard assertoric logic:

(S.R.) To S($\tau\phi$) we may subjoin ⊢ϕ.

The argument used above to illustrate the method of McArthur and Welker can be alternatively expressed as:[2]

Argument 1

**(1) S[!(If he is angry, your mollifying him.)] (Hypothesis)
**(2) ⊢(If he is angry, your mollifying him.) (From step 1, S.R.)
(I.e., If he is angry you will mollify him.)
**(3) He is angry. (Second premise)
**(4) ⊢(Your mollifying him.) (From steps 2 and 3, via *modus ponens*) (I.e., "You will mollify him.")
*(5) If S[!(If he is angry, your mollifying him.)], then you will mollify him. (From steps 1 and 4, conditionalization)

In other words, given the premise that he is angry, we may conclude that if you are to satisfy the imperative "If he is angry, mollify him," you will mollify him.

The following example is more complex. Suppose I say to my children, "I promise that if the weather is good then, and if you behave yourselves all week, I will take you to the circus on Friday," and also, "Please behave yourselves all week." Then let us suppose that the weather is good on Friday.

Argument 2

*(1) The weather is good on Friday. (Premise)
**(2) S[Pr(If the weather is good on Friday and you behave yourselves all week, my taking you to the circus on Friday.)] (Hypothesis)
***(3) S[!(Your behaving yourselves all week.)] (Hypothesis)
***(4) If the weather is good on Friday and you behave yourselves all week, I will take you to the circus on Friday. (From step 2, S.R.)
***(5) You behaved yourselves all week. (From step 3, S.R.)
***(6) I will take you to the circus on Friday. (From 1, 4, and 5, *modus ponens*)
*(7) If {S[Pr(If the weather is good on Friday and you behave

yourselves all week, my taking you to the circus on Friday.)] and S[!(Your behaving yourselves all week.)]}, then I will take you to the circus on Friday. (From 2, 3, and 6, conditionalization)

In other words, provided the children do as I ask and provided that I keep my promise, I will, given the good weather, take them to the circus. The conclusion states what action on my part is necessary for me to fulfill my promise.

To take another example, suppose that a robber says to you, "Give me everything that is in your purse!" and that a copy of Wittgenstein's *Tractatus* is in your purse. We may conclude that to satisfy the robber's demands you must hand over the *Tractatus*:

Argument 3

> *(1) The *Tractatus* is in your purse. (Premise)
> **(2) S[!(x) (If x is in your purse, your giving x to the robber.)] (Hypothesis)
> **(3) (x) (If x is in your purse, you give x to the robber.) (From 2, S.R.)
> **(4) If the *Tractatus* is in your purse, you give the *Tractatus* to the robber. (From 3, universal instantiation)
> **(5) You give the *Tractatus* to the robber. (From 1 and 4, *modus ponens*)
> *(6) If S[!(x) (If x is in your purse, your giving x to the robber.)], then you give the *Tractatus* to the robber. (From 2 and 5, conditionalization)

The conclusions we draw by means of the kind of inference represented by Arguments 1–3 are not always what actions are needed to satisfy a command, promise, etc., but sometimes what conditions must be fulfilled if that sentence is to be satisfied. If I promise to give you the Philosopher's Stone, a necessary condition of my keeping that promise is that the Philosopher's Stone exists.

Argument 4

> **(1) S[Pr(My giving you the Philosopher's Stone.)] (Hypothesis)
> **(2) I will give you the Philosopher's Stone. {I.e., $(\exists x)[(x = $ the Philosopher's Stone) and (I will give you x)]} (From 1, S.R.)
> **(3) $(\exists x)(x = $ the Philosopher's Stone) (From 2, truth functional implication, after appropriate existential instantiations and generalizations)
> *(4) If S[Pr(My giving you the Philosopher's Stone)], then there

is an x such that x is the Philosopher's Stone. (From 1, 3, conditionalization)

Given the basic pattern of inference involving nonassertoric sentences, we may draw other conclusions depending upon what premises are supplied explicitly or by the context. From Argument 4 we know, for example, that my promise to give you the Philosopher's Stone cannot be kept, since there is no such object. The contrapositive of the conclusion (step 4) tells us that the illocutionary act will not be satisfied if the consequent of that conclusion is false.

Notes

CHAPTER 1: THE PROBLEM

1   An exposition of this view, attributed to Protagoras, appears in
    Plato's *Theaetetus* (in *Plato's Cosmology*, ed. F. M. Cornford
    [New York: The Liberal Arts Press, 1937], pp. 161–172). While
    hostile, it evidently reflects accurately the teachings of Protagoras,
    so far as these can be gathered from the extant fragments of his
    work and other indications. (See John M. Robinson, *An Introduc-
    tion to Early Greek Philosophy* [Boston: Houghton-Mifflin Co.,
    1968], pp. 241–250.) A later statement of relativism occurs in Sex-
    tus Empiricus' *Pyrrhonic Sketches* (in *Sextus Empiricus and Greek
    Scepticism*, ed. Mary Mills Patrick [Cambridge: Deighton Bell &
    Co., 1899], pp. 125–132).
        While no philosopher writing today espouses an extreme form of
    individual relativism, this position has been adopted by others—
    some psychologists, in particular. For example, this passage ap-
    pears in a popular self-help book:

>   There are no absolute rights or wrongs. There are things that
>   people do that we wouldn't do; things they do that we
>   consider inappropriate or antisocial; and things we wish they
>   wouldn't do. However, these people are not bad people. . . .
>   If someone doesn't like what we do, we should not become
>   anxious or upset about it. We should recognize that, within
>   their framework, our behavior seems inappropriate. We
>   should not be blamed for that. Nor should we become
>   anxious or depressed about it.

    (C. Eugene Walker, *Learn How to Relax* [Englewood Cliffs, N. J.:
    Prentice-Hall, Inc., 1975], pp. 31–32.)

2   The originator of modern cultural relativism is generally taken to
    be Franz Boas, although cultural, as well as individual, relativism
    was asserted even by Protagoras and Sextus Empiricus. Boas, in
    The Mind of Primitive Man (New York: The Macmillan Co.,
    1911), p. 208, asserts that our own ideas of what is right and
    wrong, and, consequently, our judgments upon other societies, are

183

conditioned by our upbringing. He then suggests—rather cautiously, in fact—that other societies' standards, mores, and values may be just as good as our own. Because of our conditioning we are not competent to judge otherwise. A more recent and stronger version of relativism is held by Melville J. Herskovits, who maintains that the values of every society are valid for all those who live in that society. See especially "Cultural Relativism and Cultural Values," and "Tender and Tough-Minded Anthropology," both reprinted in his collection of essays, *Cultural Relativism: Perspectives in Cultural Pluralism* (New York: Random House, Inc., 1972).

3   This point is made especially well by William K. Frankena in *Ethics* (Englewood Cliffs, N. J.: Prentice-Hall, Inc., 1963), p. 93.

4   Recently Robert Solomon has proposed that emotions are essentially evaluative beliefs and are indeed within rational control (see "The Logic of the Emotions," *Nous* 11 [1977]: 41–49). This is, however, a controversial position, and I think that for the purposes of this chapter we may assume the common view that feelings are only partially under our control and are not merely a kind of belief.

5   That no form of relativism is true by virtue of the meaning of value terms is argued successfully by Richard B. Brandt in *Value and Obligation* (New York: Harcourt, Brace & World, Inc., 1961), pp. 439–440.

6   Frankena, *Ethics*, pp. 92–93.

7   For a statement of this criterion, see A. J. Ayer, *Language, Truth and Logic*, 2d ed. (New York: Dover Publications, Inc., 1950).

8   A. J. Ayer, *Language, Truth and Logic*, chapter 4.

9   See C. L. Stevenson, *Ethics and Language* (New Haven: Yale University Press, 1944), especially chapters 4, 5, 7, 9, and 10.

10   This argument is expounded in G. E. Moore, *Principia Ethica* (Cambridge: At the University Press, 1962), chapter 1. Richard Price's version is in *A Review of the Principal Questions in Morals*, *British Moralists*, ed. Lewis A. Selby-Bigge (New York: Dover Publications, 1965), vol. 2, pp. 105–184, especially sections 587, 605, and 609.

11   See, for example, Frankena's classic paper, "The Naturalistic Fallacy," *Mind* 48 (1939):464–477, Julius Kovesi's *Moral Notions* (London: Routledge and Kegan Paul, Ltd., 1967), chapter 1, Roger Hancock's "The Refutation of Naturalism in Moore and Hare," *Journal of Philosophy* 57 (1960):326–334, and Frank Snare's "The Open Question as a Linguistic Test," *Ratio* 17 (1975):122–129.

12 R. M. Hare's main exposition of his theory is his book *The Language of Morals* (New York: Oxford University Press, Inc., 1964).

13 Roger Scruton, "Attitudes, Beliefs and Reasons," *Morality and Moral Reasoning* (London: Methuen & Co., Ltd., 1972), pp. 25–100.

14 See Patrick Nowell-Smith's *Ethics*, (Baltimore: Penguin Books, Inc., 1954), chapters 7 and 8.

15 The term "illocutionary force" was introduced into philosophical literature by John L. Austin in his William James Lectures, later published as *How to Do Things with Words* (New York: Oxford University Press, Inc., 1965), especially chapter 3.

CHAPTER 2: SENTENCES AND SPEECH ACTS

1 These observations have been made by Hector-Neri Castañeda in "Imperatives, Decisions and Oughts," in *Morality and the Language of Conduct*, eds., Hector-Neri Castañeda and George Nakhnikian (Detroit: Wayne State University Press, 1963), pp. 230–239; Paul Ziff in *Semantic Analysis* (Ithaca, N. Y.: Cornell University Press, 1960), p. 228, and John Searle in "Meaning and Speech Acts," *Philosophical Review* 71 (1962):423–432.

2 These difficulties were first pointed out by Castañeda in "Imperatives, Decisions and Oughts."

3 One of the earliest articles is that by Alf Ross, "Imperatives and Logic," *Philosophy of Science* 11 (1944):30–46. Since then much of the debate has taken place in *Analysis*, beginning with an attack on the notion of imperative inference by B. A. O. Williams (vol. 23), and replies and further discussion by P. T. Geach (vol. 23), André Gombay (vols. 25 and 27), Gary Wedeking (vol. 30), David Clarke (vol. 30), Alfred MacKay (vol. 29 and 31), and Castañeda (vol. 32). R. M. Hare has been the main proponent of the possibility of imperative reasoning, setting forth his views first in *The Language of Morals* (New York: Oxford University Press, Inc., 1964). He has then defended the position that there can be valid imperative inferences against subsequent attacks in "Some Alleged Differences Between Imperatives and Indicatives," *Mind* 76 (1967):309–326. Nicholas Rescher also proposes a system of imperative logic in *The Logic of Commands* (London: Routledge and Kegan Paul, Ltd., 1966), and Castañeda has recently done so in *Thinking and Doing* (Dordrecht, The Netherlands: Reidel, 1975). Searle's work, as summed up in *Speech Acts* (Cambridge: At the

University Press, 1970), introduced the possibility of using illocutionary acts other than imperatives in arguments, and Hare contends in "Meaning and Speech Acts," *Philosophical Review* 79 (1970):3–24, that these can be used in arguments. R. F. Stalley has a reply to Hare ("Intentions, Beliefs and Imperative Logic," *Mind* 81 [1972]:18–28) and Robert P. McArthur and David Welker have set forth a system of nonassertoric logic ("Non-Assertoric Inference," *Notre Dame Journal of Formal Logic* 15 [1974]:225–244).

4 In John L. Austin, *How to Do Things with Words* (New York: Oxford University Press Inc., 1965), Lecture III, 25–38.

5 Ibid., Lecture VIII, 94–107.

6 Among the philosophers who have made a distinction between these two components of meaning are R. M. Hare (see especially *The Language of Morals*, chapter II, and "Meaning and Speech Acts," pp. 19–23); Erik Stenius, "Mood and Language Games," *Synthese* 17 (1967):254–274; John Searle, *Speech Acts*, passim; Stephen Schiffer, *Meaning* (Oxford: Clarendon Press, 1972), especially chapter IV; and Michael Dummett, "What Is a Theory of Meaning?" Part II, in *Truth and Meaning* eds. Gareth Evans and John McDowell (Oxford: Clarendon Press, 1976), pp. 75–76.

Linguists seem to take it for granted that mood is a component of meaning. In the currently debated question of whether meaning is entirely determined in the deep structure of the sentence or whether part of the meaning is a function of the transformational grammar and hence reflected only in the surface structure, we can see this assumption in operation. Jerrold J. Katz and Paul M. Postal, in arguing that the transformations play no part in determining meaning, assert that whether the sentence is declarative, interrogative, or imperative is determined at the level of deep structure (*An Integrated Theory of Linguistic Descriptions* [Cambridge, Mass.: M.I.T. Press, 1972], chapter 4). On the other hand, the fact that mood operators are transformations is taken by Ray S. Jackendoff (*Semantic Interpretation in Generative Grammar* [Cambridge, Mass.: M.I.T. Press, 1977], chapters 7–9) to be evidence that meaning is partly determined by transformations.

While they recognize propositional content and mood as two distinct components of meaning, linguists join most current philosophers in distinguishing between meaning and use. See, for example, Noam Chomsky, *Reflections on Language* (New York: Pantheon Books, 1975), chapter 2; Ruth M. Kempson, *Semantic Theory* (Cambridge: At the University Press, 1977), chapter 4; and

Jerrold M. Sadock, *Toward a Linguistic Theory of Speech Acts* (New York: Academic Press, Inc., 1974), chapter 5.

7   In this account I owe much to W. V. Quine, especially chapter 6 of *Word and Object* (Cambridge, Mass.: M.I.T. Press, 1960).

8   There have been some attempts to limit the number of moods by reducing performatives to declaratives and questions to imperatives. See, for example, Schiffer, *Meaning*, chapter 4, and Kempson, *Semantic Theory*, pp. 64–68. Here questions have been analyzed as nothing more than a request for an answer, and such sentences as "I promise not to tell" and "I pronounce you man and wife" have been construed as ways of saying *that* I am promising not to tell or *that* I am pronouncing you man and wife. David Lewis suggests that all speech acts, even imperatives, can be adequately represented as assertions ("General Semantics," in *Semantics of Natural Language*, ed. Donald Davidson and Gilbert Harman (Dordrecht, The Netherlands: Reidel, 1972), pp. 205–212, and a similar proposal has been made by Michael J. White in "A Suggestion Regarding the Semantical Analysis of Performatives," *Dialectica* 30 (1976):117–134.

While I have much sympathy for a program of this sort which decreases the number and complexity of moods, there are some difficulties which stand in its way. To ask a question is not always to request an answer. If you do not know the answer, I would prefer that you say so, rather than supply an answer to my question; on other occasions, I may ask a question merely to throw out something for your consideration, without wanting or expecting an answer. As for performatives, there seems to be an even clearer difference between them and declaratives than there is between imperatives and interrogatives. If a minister says to a couple, "I now pronounce you man and wife," and it is later discovered that the groom has wives in two other states, then the marriage is void and it is false that the minister has pronounced the couple man and wife, for one of the conditions of their becoming so is unfulfilled. Yet the sentence uttered by the minister is not false; it fails of its purpose, but it does not describe a nonexistent state of affairs.

Perhaps these difficulties can be avoided, and, if so, my own task would be simplified. If performatives are declaratives and evaluations are performatives, then evaluations are also declaratives, and I need only refute the theory that evaluations are imperatives in order to show descriptivism to be tenable. But since the question of the status of performatives is in doubt, my own views will be better supported if I proceed on the assumption that at least some of these sentences are not declaratives and are neither true nor false.

9   See William P. Alston in *Philosophy of Language* (Englewood Cliffs, N. J.: Prentice-Hall, Inc. [1964], chapter 2). White's analysis (see previous note) could be considered a complex elaboration of this kind of theory.

10 That the speaker must intend this understanding of his intention on the part of his audience was brought out by H. Paul Grice in "Meaning," *Philosophical Review* 66 (1957):377–388. Since then Peter F. Strawson ("Intention and Convention in Speech Acts," in Strawson's *Logico-Linguistic Papers* [London: Methuen & Co. Ltd., 1971], pp. 157 and 166), and Schiffer (*Meaning*, chapters 1 and 2) have elaborated upon this theme. I am not sure, however, that the speaker must have this intention for his utterance to have the usual illocutionary force. It is unclear whether "I will be there" uttered in a context where a promise is expected but where the speaker does not intend to promise does in fact constitute a promise. I think it does not, though the speaker may be held morally responsible for doing what he *said* he would do since the expectations he unwittingly raised are just what would have been raised by a promise.

11 Austin, *How to Do Things with Words*, Lecture II.

12 See Grice's paper "Logic and Conversation," in *The Logic of Grammar*, ed. Gilbert Harman and Donald Davidson (Encino, Calif.: Dickinson Press, 1975), pp. 64–75.

13 Donald Davidson, "Truth and Meaning," *Synthese* 17 (1967):304–323.

14 See especially Jerrold J. Katz, "Logic and Language: An Examination of Recent Criticisms of Intensionalism," in *Language, Mind and Knowledge*, ed. Keith Gunderson. *Minnesota Studies in the Philosophy of Science* (Minneapolis: University of Minnesota Press, 1975), vol. 7, pp. 63–76; J. A. Foster, "Meaning and Truth Theory," *Truth and Meaning*, eds. Gareth Evans & John McDowell (Oxford: Clarendon Press, 1976), pp. 11–14; and Brian Loar, "Two Theories of Meaning," also in *Truth and Meaning*, eds. Gareth Evans and John McDowell, pp. 139–143.

15 That a certain amount of agreement in belief among the speakers of a language is necessary to fix the reference of terms in that language is maintained by Davidson (see "Belief and the Basis of Meaning," *Synthese* 27 [1974]:309–323, and "Thought and Talk," in *Mind and Language*, ed. Samuel Guttenplan [Oxford: Clarendon

Press, 1975], pp. 7–23). Dummett critically discusses this view, but ends with qualified agreement, in "What Is a Theory of Meaning" Part I, also in *Mind and Language*, ed. Guttenplan, pp. 67–137.

16 The similarity to some of the views expressed by Hilary Putnam in "The Analytic and the Synthetic," in *Scientific Explanation, Space and Time*, eds. Herbert Feigl and Grover Maxwell. *Minnesota Studies in the Philosophy of Science* (Minneapolis: The University of Minnesota Press, 1962), vol. III, pp. 358–398, may well strike the reader. I am heavily indebted to that paper.

17 The possibility of robot animals is suggested by Putnam in "The Meaning of Meaning," in *Language, Mind and Knowledge*, ed. Keith Gunderson, *Minnesota Studies in the Philosophy of Science*, vol. 7, pp. 131–93.

18 Primarily in Quine, "Two Dogmas of Empiricism," in *From a Logical Point of View*. (Cambridge, Mass.: Harvard University Press, 1953), pp. 20–46.

19 As Quine has argued in "Truth by Convention," in *The Ways of Paradox* (Random House, Inc., 1966), chapter 9, we cannot consider all truth conventional on the following grounds. Suppose we take all truths of logic as conventional. Then, presumably, all the consequences of these truths will also be conventionally true. But we cannot know what the consequences are without adopting certain rules of inference. Yet rules of inference are not themselves premises or statements, and hence are not conventional truths. Thus we might hold both "p" and "If p, then q" to be true, by convention, but we cannot pass from these premises to q without the use of *modus ponens*. *Modus ponens*, however, is not itself a premise or something true by convention. It could be argued, however, that a decision to use *modus ponens* is a sort of convention; although not a decision to hold certain beliefs come what may, it could be a decision to count as true certain statements when certain other statements are true. And, although, it is not itself a tautology, *modus ponens*, and rules of inference in general, do express a recognition of a tautology, as May Brodbeck has pointed out (in "Explanation, Prediction and 'Imperfect' Knowledge," in *Scientific Explanation, Space and Time*, eds. Feigl and Maxwell, *Minnesota Studies in the Philosophy of Science*, vol. 3, pp. 231–272).

20 See David Lewis, *Convention* (Cambridge, Mass.: Harvard University Press, 1969), especially chapter V.

21 Lewis, "Language and Languages," in *Language, Mind and*

Knowledge, ed. Gunderson, *Minnesota Studies in the Philosophy of Science*, vol. 7, pp. 34–35.

22 Putnam has written several articles ("The Meaning of 'Meaning,'" in *Language, Mind and Knowledge*, ed. Gunderson; "Language and Reality," in *Mind, Language and Reality*, *Philosophical Papers* (New York: Cambridge University Press, 1975), vol. 2, pp. 272–290; and "Explanation and Reference," in *Conceptual Change*, eds. Glenn A. Pearce and Patrick L. Maynard (Dordrecht, The Netherlands: Reidel, 1973), pp. 199–221), in each of which he develops a different view of meaning; i.e., that the meaning of a term does not consist in the necessary and sufficient conditions of its application, but is rather a *stereotype*. The stereotype for a given term consists of those features by which we generally identify the referents of the term. For example, the stereotype of a tiger is a four-legged orange beast with black stripes, fierce and cat-like in behavior. Yet some tigers are white, so that, while being orange and black striped is a part of what we mean by "tiger" this criterion does not serve as a necessary and sufficient condition of tigerhood and does not determine the extension of, or fix the reference of, the term "tiger." To use another example, the swan stereotype is white and whiteness constitutes part of the meaning of "swan," but it is not one of the truth conditions of statements asserting that some creature is a swan, since the existence of black swans is recognized.

I do not think that the identification of meaning with stereotypes is irreconcilable with my views expressed here. It is a broader notion of meaning than is any theory which affirms that meaning is identical with truth conditions—conventionally recognized or otherwise. However, in most, though not in all, cases truth conditions form a part of the stereotype. In those situations where we are unclear what criteria to use for the application of a term, it is to the stereotype we look to decide which are most central to our concept of what that term means. And while conventionally recognized necessary and sufficient conditions do not always form a part of the stereotype for a term, they generally underlie the characteristics which do. Thus water's consisting of two hydrogen atoms and one oxygen atom is not part of what people think of when they think of water, but its molecular structure explains the properties of water which do constitute the stereotype and may, as a result, come, in time, to be a part of that stereotype.

23 See, for example, Strawson, "Intention and Convention in Speech

Acts," and also "Meaning and Truth," in his *Logico-Linguistic Papers.*

24 Some think that the necessity for bringing intentions and beliefs into a theory of meaning can be avoided by the expedient of introducing possible worlds. A sentence of the form "S is true if and only if p" would, according to such an analysis, be equivalent to "S means that p" if and only if it were true not just in the actual world, but in every possible world; that is, no matter what the factual circumstances might be, and under every possible combination of conditions. No combination of states of affairs would result in "S is true if and only if p" 's being false. Such a theory would rule out "'Snow is white' is true if and only if grass is green" as a meaning postulate because it is possible that there is a world in which snow is white even though grass is not green. (See Lewis, "General Semantics," and Foster, "Meaning and Truth Theory," pp. 23–32.)

The value of using a possible worlds analysis for a theory of meaning has been questioned on good grounds by Jerrold J. Katz ("Logic and Language: An Examination of Recent Criticisms of Intensionalism," pp. 117–120). We may only decide, he says, what is or is not logically possible (true in some possible world) on the grounds of whether or not statements describing the states of affairs in question are consistent. But this question of consistency can only be decided if we know already the meanings of the terms involved. Consequently, the notion of possible worlds is logically dependent upon a concept of meaning, so that meaning cannot be defined in terms of possible worlds.

25 Hare, "Meaning and Speech Acts," pp. 19–23. The symbols I am using closely resemble the notation employed by Searle in *Speech Acts.*

Chapter 3: Nonassertoric Inferences

1 All three kinds of logics are spelled out by Alf Ross in "Imperatives and Logic," *Philosophy of Science* 11 (1944):30–46, although he rejects one of being-in-force as unworkable (p. 35). R. M. Hare in "Some Alleged Differences Between Imperatives and Indicatives," *Mind* 76 (1967):309–326, also describes logics of satisfaction and acceptance. Nicholas Rescher's system is a logic of satisfaction (see *The Logic of Commands* [London: Routledge and Kegan Paul,

Ltd., 1966], and Robert P. McArthur and David Welker (in "Non-assertoric Logic," *Notre Dame Journal of Formal Logic*, 15 [1974]:225–244), develop a logic of speaker commitment. A logic of being-in-force is suggested, but not worked out by André Gombay ("Imperative Inference and Disjunction," *Analysis* 25 [1965]:58–62, and the system of Hector-Neri Castañeda (*Thinking and Doing* [Dordrecht, The Netherlands: Reidel, 1975], chapters 4 and 5) is one of justification.

2   That this holds true of commands was recognized by Ross ("Imperatives and Logic," pp. 37–38) and by Rescher (*The Logic of Commands*, chapter 5).

3   I am indebted to James Forrester of the University of Wyoming for suggesting this possibility.

4   Similar observations are made by McArthur and Welker in an unpublished appendix to "Non-assertoric Logic."

5   *The Logic of Commands*, chapter 1.

6   "Imperatives and Logic," p. 37.

7   "Non-assertoric Logic," pp. 234–237.

8   I am basing this interpretation upon a general consideration of Hare's moral theory, especially as spelled out in *Freedom and Reason* (New York: Oxford University Press, Inc., 1965), chapter 3.

9   R. F. Stalley, in "Intentions, Beliefs and Imperative Logic," *Mind* 81 (1972):18–28, makes this point.

10   *Thinking and Doing*, pp. 73–76 and chapter 4.

11   Ibid., chapters 4 and 5.

12   This thesis is also maintained by Bruce Aune, *Reason and Action* (Dordrecht, The Netherlands: Reidel, 1977), pp. 173–176.

13   Many points raised in this chapter were discussed when I read an earlier version of it at the University of Nebraska in Lincoln in October 1976. I received many helpful criticisms and suggestions from the members of the Philosophy Department there, particularly Charles Sayward, Philip Hugly, and Robert Audi.

CHAPTER 4: THE ILLOCUTIONARY STATUS OF EVALUATIONS

1   The main argument in this chapter is essentially that presented in my "An Argument for Descriptivism," *Journal of Philosophy* 71 (1974):759–769, although I have made a number of changes in the presentation. I wish to thank the editor of the *Journal of Philosophy* for permission to reuse some of the material from this article.

2   James Martin of the University of Wyoming first pointed this out to me.

3   The necessity for considering this possibility was made clear to me by James Forrester of the University of Wyoming. Since then it has been brought to my attention by Alfred MacKay's paper "The Principle of Mood Constancy," *Analysis* 31 (1971):91–96, and by Hector-Neri Castañeda in *Thinking and Doing* (Dordrect, The Netherlands: Reidel, 1975), pp. 67–68. In his earlier work (see "Imperatives, Decisions and Oughts," in *Morality and the Language of Conduct*, eds. Hector-Neri Castañeda and George Nakhnikian [Detroit: Wayne State University Press, 1963]), Castañeda denied that imperatives could serve as the antecedents of conditionals, but he now thinks that this is so because the emphasis of conditionals containing imperatives is always on the imperative, and that such conditionals may always be expressed in the form "Not-p or q."

4   R. M. Hare discussed this distinction both in "Some Alleged Differences Between Imperatives and Indicatives," *Mind* 76 (1967):309–326 and in "Meaning and Speech Acts," *Philosophical Review* 79 (1970):6–16.

5   See John Searle's consideration of this point, *Speech Acts* (Cambridge: At the University Press, 1970).

6   See especially George C. Kerner, *The Revolution in Ethical Theory* (New York: Oxford University Press, Inc., 1966), pp. 202–216, and J. O. Urmson's *The Emotive Theory of Ethics* (New York: Oxford University Press, Inc., 1968), especially chapter 11.

7   Hare, "Meaning and Speech Acts," *Philosophical Review* 79 (1970); section IV.

8   I am grateful to James Martin for this example.

9   See Paul Taylor, *Normative Discourse* (Englewood Cliffs, N. J.: Prentice-Hall, Inc., 1961), chapters 5–7.

10 By Roger Pilon of the Hoover Institution, Stanford University, as well as by a reviewer of this manuscript.

11 As in Charles L. Stevenson's analysis, see *Ethics and Language* (New Haven: Yale University Press, 1944), especially p. 22.

Chapter 5: Emotivism

1   This view is expressed by J. O. Urmson in The *Emotive Theory of Ethics* (New York: Oxford University Press, Inc., 1968), chapter 11; by Roger Scruton in "Attitudes, Beliefs and Reasons," in *Mo-*

rality and Moral Reasoning, ed. John Casey (London: Methuen & Co., Ltd., 1971), pp. 25–100; and by George C. Kerner in *The Revolution in Ethical Theory* (New York: Oxford University Press, Inc., 1966), pp. 202–216.

2 Cf. H. Paul Grice, "Logic and Conversation," in *The Logic of Grammar*, eds. Gilbert Harmon and Donald Davidson (Encino, Calif.: Dickinson Press, 1975), as well as his earlier paper "The Causal Theory of Perception." *Proceedings of the Aristotelian Society*, Supplementary Volume 35 (1961):121–152.

3 In Mary Forrester, "A Note on Commendation and Approval," *Ethics* 85 (1975):148–150.

4 As discussed in the articles cited in footnote 2 of this chapter.

5 The attitude of approval or commendation and the expressions thereof differ from performative approvals ("I approve the report") and commendations ("I hereby commend you for your bravery"). The latter are official acts whose vehicles are sentences having a distinctly nonassertoric mood, while the former may be expressed by a variety of different sentences having different moods.

CHAPTER 6: PRESCRIPTIVISM

1 R. M. Hare, *Freedom and Reason* (New York: Oxford University Press, Inc., 1965), chapter 5.

2 The arguments given here also apply to some other theories of *akrasia*, or weakness of will. According to Aristotle's famous analysis of the phenomenon, (*Nichomachean Ethics*, ed. and trans. W. D. Ross [London: Oxford University Press, 1954], Book VII), weak action occurs when the agent, who knows the *principle* according to which he ought to act, becomes temporarily unaware of the circumstances, like one who is drunk or out of his senses, so that he does not know how to apply the principle. But the typical case of moral weakness occurs when the agent is fully aware of what he ought to do, yet fails to do it. Still the notion of *akrasia* as a cognitive failure has persisted. In a recent paper ("Perversity," *Philosophical Quarterly* 26 [1976]:229–242), L. S. Carrier argues that a weak-willed person is confronted with conflicting reasons for and against the act, but fails to deliberate with sufficient care, and, consequently, acts contrary to what a perfectly rational man would choose. Another point of view is taken by Donald Davidson ("How is Weakness of the Will Possible?" in *Moral Concepts*, ed. Joel Feinberg [London: Oxford University Press, 1969], pp. 12–13),

who suggests that, while the weak person knows the better alternative, he chooses the worse, and this choice, being irrational, cannot be given an explanation in terms of desires or motives. Thus Davidson seems to regard *akrasia* as a sort of psychological compulsion, which the agent neither understands nor is able to control; in this way, his account closely resembles Hare's. Whether or not Davidson considers the agent able to do the better thing, his analysis fails, for weak-willed action generally, if not always, is motivated by desires and dispositions of which the agent is very much aware, such as fear or greed. These motives are such that he considers them less worthy of being acted upon than are courageous or selfless impulses, but they are, nevertheless, stronger in him at the time of action.

3 Among these writers are: Niel Cooper, "Two Concepts of Morality," *Philosophy* 41 (1966):19–33, and "Morality and Importance," *Mind* 77 (1968):118–121, both reprinted in G. Wallace and A. D. M. Walker, *The Definition of Morality* (London: Methuen & Co., Ltd., 1969); W. D. Falk, "Morality, Self and Others," in *Morality and the Language of Conduct*, eds. Hector-Neri Castañeda and George Nakhnikian (Detroit: Wayne State University Press, 1963), pp. 25–67; C. K. Grant, "Akrasia and the criteria of assent to practical principles," *Mind* 65 (1956):400–407; Peter F. Strawson, "Social Morality and the Individual Ideal," *Philosophy* 36 (1961): 1–17, reprinted in Wallace and Walker, *Defintion of Morality*, pp. 98–118. William K. Frankena gives a long and useful discussion of the distinction in question in "On Defining Moral Judgments, Principles and Codes," in *Perspectives in Morality*, ed. K. E. Goodpaster (Notre Dame, Ind.: Notre Dame University Press, 1976), pp. 184–192, and again in *Thinking About Morality* (Ann Arbor: The University of Michigan Press, 1980), pp. 18–30.

4 See the debate between Alan Gewirth and L. W. Sumner, for example, as well as Frankena's discussions in the papers cited in the previous footnote. Gewirth's initial paper on the subject is in "Metaethics and Normative Ethics," *Mind* 69 (1960):187–205. Sumner's reply is in "Normative Ethics and Metaethics," *Ethics* 77 (1967):95–106, and Gewirth's rejoinder appears in "Metaethics and Moral Neutrality," *Ethics* 78 (1968):214–225.

5 See William K. Frankena, "On Defining Moral Judgments, Principles and Codes," and also "'Ought' and 'Is' Once More," in *Perspectives in Morality*, ed. K. E. Goodpaster, pp. 141–142. Frankena expounded this point in more detail while visiting the

University of Wyoming in May 1977. This view has also been held by Niel Cooper. See his "Oughts and Wants" and "Further Thoughts on Oughts and Wants," both in *Weakness of Will*, ed. Geoffrey Mortimore. (London: Macmillan and Co., Ltd., 1971), pp. 190–199 and 216–225, respectively. He rejects here the idea that ought judgments are necessarily overriding, as well as Hare's belief that prescriptivism entails this view.

6 Professor Daniel Lyons, of Colorado State University, has suggested a position of this sort; namely, that "S believes that X ought to do A" entails "S desires (to some extent) that X do A." There is a difficulty here about what creates the entailment. Is S's desire a consequence of the fact of S's being in a state of belief or a consequence of "X ought to do A" proper? To make it the former would be to alter the notion of what it is to believe a statement, for belief does not entail anything about the believer's desires. And "X ought to do A" does not, by itself, entail anything about the desires of anyone. If believing that X ought to do A were equivalent to or entailed accepting the imperative "X (and everyone else) do A!" then S's desire might well be a consequence of this different sort of belief. But the imperativist analysis is, as I have argued throughout, unacceptable for other reasons.

Chapter 7: Fundamental Criteria

1 I am indebted to Ronald Moore of the University of Washington and Hardy Jones of the University of Nebraska for many excellent suggestions and criticisms. They are responsible for much of whatever value this chapter may have.

2 See Ludwig Wittgenstein, *Philosophical Investigations*, trans. G. E. M. Anscombe (New York: The Macmillan Company, 1953), especially paragraphs 69–75.

3 For example, the force of Gettier cases lies in the fact that the justified true belief analysis of knowledge allows us to say that S knows that p in situations where we are firmly convinced that S does not know that p. See Edmund L. Gettier, "Is Justified True Belief Knowledge?" *Analysis* 23 (1963):121–123.

4 In John Rawls, *A Theory of Justice* (Cambridge, Mass.: Harvard University Press 1971), paragraph 44.

5 For a good discussion of linguistic methods for determining ambiguity, see Jerrold M. Sadock, *Toward a Linguistic Theory of Speech Acts* (New York: Academic Press, Inc., 1974), chapter 5.

6 John Searle makes similar points in *Speech Acts* (Cambridge: At the University Press, 1970), chapter 2. So also does J. M. Brennan in *The Open-Texture of Moral Concepts* (New York: Barnes and Noble, Inc., 1977), especially pp. 89–149.

CHAPTER 8: SOME OBJECTIONS TO DESCRIPTIVISM

1 In G. E. Moore, *Principia Ethica* (Cambridge: At the University Press, 1962), chapter 1.
2 These arguments are found in *The Ethics*, Book III, Propositions 3–5, and the Definitions of the Emotions, 1; and Book IV, Propositions 18–37, and Definitions. See the edition edited and translated by Robert H. M. Elwes, *The Chief Works of Benedict de Spinoza*, (New York: Dover Publications, Inc., 1951), vol. 2.
3 In Søren Kierkegaard, *Fear and Trembling*, ed. and trans. Walter Lowrie (Garden City, N. Y.: Doubleday & Company, Inc., 1954).
4 See, for example, Friedrich Nietzsche, *Beyond Good and Evil*, ed. and trans. Marianna Cowan (Chicago: Henry Regnery Company, 1955), fifth and ninth articles.
5 In George Nakhnikian, "On the Naturalistic Fallacy," in *Morality and the Language of Conduct*, eds. Hector-Neri Castañeda and George Nakhnikian (Detroit: Wayne State University Press, 1963), pp. 145–159.
6 Cf. John Searle's discussion in *Speech Acts* (Cambridge: At the University Press, 1970), chapter 1.
7 See, for example, Roger Scruton, "Attitudes, Beliefs and Reasons," in *Morality and Moral Reasoning*, ed. John Casey (London: Methuen & Co., Ltd., 1971), pp. 67–68, but the approach is at least as old as David Hume's *An Enquiry concerning the Principles of Morals, in Hume's Enquiries*, ed. Lewis A. Selby-Bigge (Oxford: Clarendon Press, 1902), especially paragraphs 136, 242, and 327.
8 Cf. Kurt Baier, *The Moral Point of View* (Ithaca, N. Y.: Cornell University Press, 1958), chapter 12, and William K. Frankena, *Ethics* (Englewood Cliffs, N. J.: Prentice-Hall, Inc., 1963), pp. 96–98.

APPENDIX: THE FORMAL STRUCTURE OF REASONING WITH
NONASSERTORIC SENTENCES

1 Robert P. McArthur and David Welker, "Non-assertoric Inference," *Notre Dame Journal of Formal Logic* 15 (1974):225–244.

2 The deduction method used in the following arguments, and the notation (apart from special expressions defined earlier in this book) follow that of W. V. Quine, *Methods of Logic*, 3d ed. (New York: Holt Rinehart & Winston, Inc., 1972), especially chapter 37. The asterisks indicate a premise that is being accepted only conditionally (i.e., an hypothesis). Once the conclusion reached from assuming the hypothesis has been stated, the asterisk may be removed in the subsequent step. Every promise is accepted conditionally, since the argument is designed to show what may be concluded *if* the premise is true, so all premises receive an asterisk.

Selected Bibliography

Alston, William P. *Philosophy of Language*. Englewood Cliffs, N. J.: Prentice-Hall, Inc., 1964.

Aune, Bruce. *Reason and Action*. Dordrecht, The Netherlands: Reidel, 1977.

Austin, John L. *How to Do Things with Words*. New York: Oxford University Press, Inc., 1965.

Ayer, A. J. *Language, Truth and Logic*. 2d ed. New York: Dover Publications, Inc., 1950.

Baier, Kurt. *The Moral Point of View*. Ithaca, N. Y.: Cornell University Press, 1958.

Brandt, Richard B. *Value and Obligation*. New York: Harcourt, Brace & World, Inc., 1961.

Brennan, J. M. *The Open-Texture of Moral Concepts*. New York: Barnes and Noble, Inc., 1977.

Carrier, L. S. "Perversity." *Philosophical Quarterly* 26 (1976):229–242.

Castañeda, Hector-Neri. "Imperatives, Decisions and Oughts." In *Morality and the Language of Conduct*, edited by Hector-Neri Castañeda and George Nakhnikian, pp. 219–300. Detroit: Wayne State University Press, 1963.

Castañeda, Hector-Neri. "There are Command sh-Inferences." *Analysis* 32 (1971):13–19.

Castañeda, Hector-Neri. *Thinking and Doing*. Dordrecht, The Netherlands: Reidel (1975).

Chomsky, Noam. *Reflections on Language*. New York: Pantheon Books, 1975.

Clarke, David. "Mood Constancy in Mixed Inferences." *Analysis* 30 (1970):100–103.

Cooper, Niel. "Further Thoughts on Oughts and Wants." In *Weakness of Will*, edited by Geoffrey Mortimore, pp. 215–225. London: Macmillan and Co., Ltd., 1971.

Cooper, Niel. "Morality and Importance." *Mind* 77 (1968):118–121.

Cooper, Niel. "Oughts and Wants." In *Weakness of Will*, edited by Geoffrey Mortimore, pp. 190–199.

Cooper, Niel. "Two Concepts of Morality." *Philosophy* 41 (1966):19–33.

Davidson, Donald. "Belief and the Basis of Meaning." *Synthese* 27 (1974):309–323.

Davidson, Donald. "How is Weakness of the Will Possible?" In *Moral Concepts*, edited by Joel Feinberg, pp. 93–113. London: Oxford University Press, 1969.

Davidson, Donald. "Thought and Talk." In *Mind and Language*, edited by Samuel Guttenplan, pp. 7–23. Oxford: Clarendon Press, 1975.

Davidson, Donald. "Truth and Meaning." *Synthese* 17 (1967):304–323.

Dummett, Michael. "What is a Theory of Meaning?" Part I. In *Mind and Language*, edited by Samuel Guttenplan, pp. 97–138; Part II. In *Truth and Meaning*, edited by Gareth Evans and John McDowell, pp. 67–137. Oxford: Clarendon Press, 1976.

Foot, Philippa. *Virtues and Vices and other Essays in Moral Philosophy*. Berkeley: University of California Press, Inc., 1978.

Forrester, Mary. "A Note on Commendation and Approval." *Ethics* 85 (1975):148–150.

Forrester, Mary. "An Argument for Descriptivism." *The Journal of Philosophy 71* (1974):759–769.

Foster, J. A. "Meaning and Truth Theory." In *Truth and Meaning*, edited by Gareth Evans and John McDowell, pp. 1–23. Oxford: Clarendon Press, 1976.

Frankena, William K. *Ethics*. Englewood Cliffs, N. J.: Prentice-Hall, Inc., 1963.

Frankena, William K. "The Naturalistic Fallacy." *Mind* 48 (1939):464–477.

Frankena, William K. "On Defining Moral Judgments, Principles and Codes." In *Perspectives in Morality*, edited by K. E. Goodpaster, pp. 184–192. Notre Dame, Ind.: Notre Dame University Press, 1976. (Originally in *Etycka* [1973].)

Frankena, William K. "'Ought' and 'Is' Once More." In *Perspectives in Morality*, edited by K. E. Goodpaster, pp. 133–147. Notre Dame, Ind.: Notre Dame University Press, 1976.

Geach, P. T. "Imperative Inference." *Analysis* 23 (Suppl.) (1963):37–42.

Gewirth, Alan. "Metaethics and Moral Neutrality." *Ethics* 78 (1967–1968):214–225.

Gewirth, Alan. "Meta-ethics and Normative Ethics." *Mind* 69 (1960):187–205.

Gombay, André. "Imperative Inference and Disjunction." *Analysis* 25 (1965):58–62.

Selected Bibliography

Gombay, André. "What *Is* Imperative Inference?" *Analysis* 27 (1967):145–152.

Grice, H. Paul. "Logic and Conversation." In *The Logic of Grammar*, edited by Gilbert Harman and Donald Davidson, pp. 64–75. Encino, Calif.: Dickinson Press, 1975.

Grice, H. Paul. "Meaning." *Philosophical Review* 66 (1957):377–388.

Hancock, Roger. "The Refutation of Naturalism in Moore and Hare." *The Journal of Philosophy* 57 (1960):326–334.

Hare, R. M. *Freedom and Reason.* New York: Oxford University Press, Inc. 1965.

Hare, R. M. *The Language of Morals.* New York: Oxford University Press, Inc. 1964.

Hare, R. M. "Meaning and Speech Acts." *Philosophical Review* 79 (1970):3–24.

Hare, R. M. "Some Alleged Differences Between Imperatives and Indicatives." *Mind* 76 (1967):309–326.

Harman, Gilbert. *The Nature of Morality: an Introduction to Ethics.* New York: Oxford University Press, Inc., 1977.

Hume, David. *Enquiry concerning the Principles of Morals.* Reprint. *Hume's Enquiries*, edited by Lewis A. Selby-Bigge. Oxford: Clarendon Press, 1902.

Jackendoff, Ray S. *Semantic Interpretation in Generative Grammar.* Cambridge: M.I.T. Press, 1977.

Katz, Jerrold J. "Logic and Language: An Examination of Recent Criticisms of Intensionalism." In *Language, Mind and Knowledge*, edited by Keith Gunderson, pp. 36–130. *Minnesota Studies in the Philosophy of Science*, vol. VII. Minneapolis: University of Minnesota Press, 1975.

Katz, Jerrold J., and Postal, Paul M. *An Integrated Theory of Linguistic Descriptions.* Cambridge, Mass.: M.I.T. Press, 1972.

Kempson, Ruth M. *Semantic Theory.* Cambridge: At the University Press, 1977.

Kenny, Anthony. "Practical Inference." *Analysis* 26 (1966):65–75.

Kerner, George C. *The Revolution in Ethical Theory.* New York: Oxford University Press, Inc., 1966.

Kierkegaard, Søren. *Fear and Trembling.* Edited and translated by Walter Lowrie. Garden City, N. Y.: Doubleday & Company, Inc., 1954.

Lewis, David. *Convention*, Cambridge, Mass.: Harvard University Press, 1969.

Lewis, David. "General Semantics." In *Semantics of Natural Language*, edited by Donald Davidson and Gilbert Harman, pp. 169–218. Dordrecht, The Netherlands: Reidel, 1972.

Lewis, David. "Languages and Language." In *Language, Mind and Knowledge*, edited by Keith Gunderson, pp. 3–35. *Minnesota Studies in the Philosophy of Science*, vol. 7. Minneapolis: University of Minnesota Press, 1975.

Loar, Brian. "Two Theories of Meaning." In *Truth and Meaning*, edited by Gareth Evans and John McDowell, pp. 138–161. Oxford: Clarendon Press, 1976.

MacKay, Alfred. "Inferential Validity and Imperative Inference." *Analysis* 29 (1969):145–156.

MacKay, Alfred. "The Principle of Mood Constancy." *Analysis* 31 (1971):91–96.

McArthur, Robert P. and Welker, David. "Non-Assertoric Inference." *Notre Dame Journal of Formal Logic* 15 (1974):225–244.

Moore, G. E. *Principia Ethica*. Cambridge: At the University Press, 1962.

Nakhnikian, George. "On the Naturalistic Fallacy." In *Morality and the Language of Conduct*, edited by Hector-Neri Castañeda and George Nakhnikian, pp. 145–158. Detroit: Wayne State University Press, 1963.

Nietzsche, Friedrich. *Beyond Good and Evil*. Edited and translated by Marianne Cowan. Chicago: Henry Regnery Company, 1955.

Peetz, Vera. "Imperative Inference." *Analysis* 39 (1979):109–112.

Price, Richard. *A Review of the Principal Questions in Morals*. British Moralists, edited by Lewis A. Selby-Bigge, vol 2. New York: Dover Publications, Inc., 1965, pp. 105–184.

Putnam, Hilary. "Explanation and Reference." In *Conceptual Change*, edited by Glenn A. Pearce and Patrick L. Maynard. Dordrecht, The Netherlands: Reidel, 1973.

Putnam, Hilary. "It Ain't Necessarily So." *The Journal of Philosophy* 59 (1962):658–671.

Putnam, Hilary. "Language and Reality." In *Mind, Language and Reality*. (*Philosophical Papers*, vol. 2). New York: Cambridge University Press, 1975, pp. 272–290.

Putnam, Hilary. "The Analytic and the Synthetic." In *Scientific Explanation, Space and Time*, edited by Herbert Feigl and Grover Maxwell, *Minnesota Studies in the Philosophy of Science*, vol. 3, pp. 358–398.

Putnam, Hilary. "The Meaning of 'Meaning'." In *Language, Mind and Knowledge*, edited by Keith Gunderson, *Minnesota Studies in the*

Philosophy of Science, vol. VII, pp. 131–193. Minneapolis: University of Minnesota Press, 1975.

Quine, Willard van Orman. "Truth by Convention." In *The Ways of Paradox*, pp. 70–99. New York: Random House, Inc., 1966.

Quine, Willard van Orman. "Two Dogmas of Empiricism." In *From a Logical Point of View*, pp. 20–46. Cambridge, Mass.: Harvard University Press, 1953.

Quine, Willard van Orman. *Word and Object*. (Cambridge, Mass.: M.I.T. Press, 1960).

Rescher, Nicholas. *The Logic of Commands*. London: Routledge and Kegan Paul, Ltd., 1966.

Ross, Alf. "Imperatives and Logic." *Philosophy of Science* 11 (1944):30–46.

Sadock, Jerrold M. *Toward a Linguistic Theory of Speech Acts*. New York: Academic Press, Inc., 1974.

Schiffer, Stephen R. *Meaning*. Oxford: Clarendon Press, 1972.

Scruton, Roger. "Attitudes, Beliefs and Reasons." In *Morality and Moral Reasoning*, edited by John Casey, pp. 25–100. London: Methuen & Co., Ltd., 1971.

Searle, John. "Meaning and Speech Acts." *Philosophical Review* 71 (1962):423–432.

Searle, John. *Speech Acts*. Cambridge: At the University Press, 1970.

Snare, Frank. "The Open Question as a Linguistic Test." *Ratio* 17 (1975):122–129.

Spinoza, Benedict de. *The Ethics. The Chief Works of Benedict de Spinoza*, edited and translated by Robert H. M. Elwes, vol. 2. New York: Dover Publications, Inc., 1951.

Stalley, R. F. "Intentions, Beliefs and Imperative Logic." *Mind* 81 (1972):18–28.

Stenius, Erik. "Mood and Language Games." *Synthese* 17 (1967):254–274.

Stevenson, C. L. *Ethics and Language*. New Haven: Yale University Press, 1944.

Strawson, P. F. "Intention and Convention in Speech Acts." In *Logico-Linguistic Papers*, edited by Peter F. Strawson, pp. 149–69. London: Methuen & Co., Ltd., 1971. (Originally in *Philosophical Review* [1964]:439–460.)

Strawson, P. F. "Meaning and Truth." In *Logico-Linguistic Papers*, edited by Peter F. Strawson, pp. 170–189. London: Methuen & Co., Ltd., 1971.

Sumner, L. W. "Normative Ethics and Metaethics." *Ethics* 77 (1967):95–106.

Taylor, Paul. *Normative Discourse*, Englewood Cliffs, N. J.: Prentice-Hall, Inc., 1961.

Urmson, J. O. *The Emotive Theory of Ethics*. New York: Oxford University Press, Inc., 1968.

Warnock, G. J. *The Object of Morality*. London: Methuen & Co., Ltd., 1971.

Watson, Gary. "Skepticism About Weakness of Will." *Philosophical Review* 86 (1977):316–339.

Wedeking, Gary. "Are There Command Arguments?" *Analysis* 30 (1970):61–66.

White, Michael J. "A Suggestion Regarding the Semantical Analysis of Performatives." *Dialectica* 30 (1976):117–134.

Williams, B. A. O. "Imperative Inference." *Analysis* 23 (Suppl.) (1963):30–36.

Wittgenstein, Ludwig. *Philosophical Investigations*. Translated by G. E. M. Anscombe. New York: The Macmillan Company, 1953.

Ziff, Paul. *Semantic Analysis*. Ithaca, N. Y.: Cornell University Press, 1960.

Index

Abortion: and who counts as a person, 150

Abraham: Kierkegaard on, 147

Acceptance: of sentences associating terms with states of affairs, 36–37; of sentences, by speaker, 68; of moral principles, as assent to imperatives, 108; of definitions of evaluative terms, 161–63; of moral practices, 163–65. *See also* Commitment

Action: as sole criterion of belief, 113–14; relation between evaluative terms and, 169–70

Action guides: moral judgments as, 15–16, 169

Actions: effects of, compared with integral parts of, 32–33

Agreement: on moral judgments, limitations on, 16, 20–21, 22; on truth of reference-fixing sentences, 46–50; on criteria for application of terms, 50–51; on meanings of terms, 159–61

Akrasia, 194–95*n2*. *See also* Moral weakness, Weakness of will

Alston, William P.: on meaning as illocutionary act potential, 39–40

Alternation: conditional evaluative premises expressed as, 83–87

Ambiguity of terms, 136–37

Analogues for truth values: discussed, 57–73 *passim*; conditions for, as not specified, 76; in evaluations, according to emotivist theories, 97–99. *See also* Being-in-force; Justification; Orthotic sentences; Satisfaction; Speaker, commitment of; Termination; Truth values

Analysis of meaning; methods of, 132–33; disagreement on correct method of, 144–45; contrasted with knowledge of meaning, 157–59; differing as not entailing nondescriptive nature of terms, 159; nonarbitrariness of, 161; role of intuition in, 161; sense of appropriateness and, 161. *See also* Analyticity; Analytic statements; Definitions; Self-contradiction

Analytic evaluations: possibility of, 142,151–65 *passim*; as arbitrary, 161–62; claims for necessary truth of, 161–65; acceptance of as acceptance of values, 162. *See also* Analytic statements; Definitions of evaluative terms

Analyticity: discovery of, versus assignment of, 51

Analytic moral statements: as not true evaluations, 151

Analytic statements: how determined, 50–51; as true by definition, 152; as distinguished from definitions, 152–53; as distinguished from synthetic statements, 152–53; as informative, 152–56, 157–59; as evaluations, 153–55; recognition of, 158; relation of, to reference-fixing criteria, 174. *See also* Definitions; Necessary and sufficient conditions for application of terms

Animal rights: compared to those of Nietzsche's natural slaves, 149–50

Antecedent of conditional. *See* Subordinate clause of conditional

Appropriateness, sense of: role in association of terms with referents, 35–36; role in analyses of meaning, 161

Approval: as part of meaning of

Index

moral codes, 119–21. *See also* Values

Being-in-force: relation to felicity conditions, 72; relation to obligations, 72; analogue of truth, 72–73. *See also* Justification; Orthotic sentences; Validity of nonassertoric arguments

Belief: Stevenson on, disagreement in, 16–17; agreement in, concerning criteria for identifying referents, 51–53; challenges to and meaning change, 52–53; as value corresponding to commitment of speaker, 71; and attitudes, 102–6; in goodness, 104; that one accepts a moral principle, 110–13; in worth of moral principle, 111–13

Beliefs. *See also* Evaluative beliefs; Moral beliefs; Well-established moral beliefs

—religious: as motive for acting morally, 172

—reluctance to relinquish, 46–47, 138–40

—shared: as needed for communication, 46–47, 51–53, 168–69

Bets, mood of, 38

Beyond Good and Evil (Nietzsche), 149

Blame: and inability to act, 115–16

Boas, Franz: cultural relativism of, 183*n2*

Brandt, Richard B.: criticism of ethical relativism, 184*n5*

Brennan, J. M.: speakers' awareness of criteria for application of terms, 197*n6*

Brodbeck, May: on rule of inference, 189*n19*

Cancellation: of conversational implicature, 42; of contextual implication, 104

Carrier, L. S.: on weakness of will, 194*n2*

Castañeda, Hector-Neri: on logic of endorsement, 71; on logic of imperatives, 71–72; on differences between imperatives and evaluations, 185*n1*; on imperatives and subordinate clauses of conditionals, 185*n2*; on imperative inference, 185*n3*; on justification as analogue of truth, 192*n1*; on conditionals expressed as alternations, 193*n3*

Categorical premises: and validity of arguments containing evaluations, 82–83; compared with conditional premises, 88–89

Causal relations: difference of, from sameness of meaning, 46

Certainty: possibility of, in definition, 174

Changing one's mind: as abandonment of intention, 110–11

Choice: in evaluations, 22–23

Chomsky, Noam: on distinction between meaning and use, 186*n6*

Clarke, David: on imperative inference, 185*n3*

Classes of states of affairs: denoted by propositional content, 34–35, 37

Classification systems: utility of as determinants of definitions, 162–63

Coercion: in rejection of moral practices, 138–39

Commands: and moral judgments, 19–21

Commendation: evaluations as, 26, 86–87, 96; relation of, to desire, 168

Commitment: to accepting beliefs, 45–54 *passim*; to moral principles, 110–13. *See also* Hare, R. M.; Prescriptivism; Speaker, commitment of; Weakness of will

Communication: and reference-fixing sentences, 46–50, 52–54; and con-

Index

133; means of determining, 127–31, 135–41; as necessary and sufficient conditions for application of terms, 128–29; confirmation of theories about, 129, 131–35; use in justifying well-established moral beliefs, 129–30; awareness of, in use of arguments, 132, 140; uncertainty about, 135; changes in, 135–37; absence of, 136–37, 141; noncircularity of method of determining, 140–41; and desire satisfaction, 168–70

Criticism: and well-established moral beliefs, 129–31, 137–40; as test of reliability of data, 133–34

Customs: as partial determinants of illocutionary force, 42–43

Davidson, Donald: and characterization of meaning in terms of truth conditions, 44–45; on agreement in belief to fix reference, 188n15; on weakness of will, 194–95n2

Declarative sentences: satisfaction of, 60–61; in arguments, differences from nondeclaratives, 76. See also Assertions; Descriptions

Defining terms: as asserting conventionally recognized truth conditions, 155; as describing linguistic conventions, 161

Definitions

—of evaluative terms: impossibility of, according to Moore, 16–17; reasons for lack of agreement on, 142–43; conditions for adequacy of, 157; methods of determining, 157–58; acceptance of, as acceptance of values, 161–62

— of philosophical terms: uncertainty concerning, 155. See also Analysis; Meaning

—of terms: as not clearly articulated, 132–33; as stipulations about language, 151–52; as incapable of being evaluations, 151–52; distinguished from analytic statements, 151–53; as metalinguistic statements, 152–53; as chosen on grounds of utility, 162–63; possibility of certainty of, 174. See also Analytic statements; Goodness; Metalinguistic statements; Right and wrong; Truth by definition

Denials of attitudes: as not expressing attitudes, 100–102

Deontological theories: as neglecting human wants, 163

Descriptions: as sharing universalizability with moral judgments, 20; evaluations as different from, 23–24; of types of states of affairs, propositional content as, 34–35, 37; moral judgments as, 83, 89–92, 174; subordinate, conditioning clauses as, 83; moral standards as, 90–92. See also Assertions; Declarative sentences

Descriptive conjuncts: of evaluations, 15–17, 193n11; evaluations as having, 83, 91–92, 93–95

Descriptive predicates: as not comprising meaning of moral terms, 17–19, 143. See also Criteria; Evaluations

Descriptivism: compared with naturalism, 17; as true, 93–95; reputation of, since Moore, 145; and change in criteria and meaning, 165–70

Desires: expressions of, compared with evaluations, 4–5; and justification, 4–5; and rational control, 5, 184n4; differences in and willingness to act on beliefs, 113–14; Spinoza's account of, 146; prescribing, approving, commending and, 168

Desire satisfaction: as criterion of goodness, x–xi; as standard for moral codes, 164–65. See also Ends, promotion of; Interests of persons

Index

Determinism: and ability to act otherwise, 115

Disagreement: in attitude and belief, 15–17; on moral questions, 130; on analysis of moral terms, 142–51 *passim*; on method of analysis, 144–45. *See also* Moral arguments

Disconfirmation: of hypotheses concerning fundamental criteria, 133–34

Dissonance: between feelings and values, 6–8; absence of, in association between terms and referents, 36

Doubt, expressions of: difference between evaluations and performatives in, 26–27

Dummett, Michael: on components of sentence meaning, 186*n6*; on agreement in belief and fixing of reference, 189*n15*

Ejaculations: and evaluations, 14–15

E-making characteristics, 97–99

Emotions: as contrasted with attitudes, 21–22, 96–97; as evaluative beliefs, 184*n4*

Emotivism: Ayer's version of, 14–15; distinguished from relativism, 14–15; Stevenson's version of, 15–17; Scruton's version of, 21–22, 25; as type of general exposition of, 95–99; objections to, 99–107. *See also* Performatives

Empirical statements: contrasted with evaluations, 12–13

Endorsement of sentences. *See* Speaker, commitment of

Ends, promotion of: as basis for accepting moral systems, 162–63, 169–70

Equality: Nietzsche on, 149–50

Ethical disagreements. *See* Disagreement, on moral questions

Evaluations: as assessments, ix; rationality and universalizability of, 4–9, 15–17, 22, 96–97, 108; changes

in, and changes in taste, 6–8; as meaningless, 12–13; as incapable of being verified, 12–13; contrasted with empirical statements, 12–13; as nondescriptive, nonassertoric, nonfactual sentences, 13–14, 23–24; as similar to ejaculations, 14–15; as imperatives, 14–15, 26, 85–89, 108–23 *passim*; contrasted with imperatives, 15, 122–23; as containing nonassertoric conjunct, 15–17, 92–93; compared with attitudes, 21–22, 96–97; as expressions of pro and con attitudes, 23; as performative expressions of approval or commendation, 26, 86–87; in form of questions and doubt, 26–27; in subordinate clauses of conditional premises, 29, 81–83, 89–92; compared with assertoric and nonassertoric sentences, 57, 81, 85–87; use in arguments, 57, 82–83, 89–92; as assertions, 82–83, 89–92, 93–95, 123; negations of, 85–87, 99; as justified by standards, principles, and fundamental criteria, 89–92, 125–27; emotivist analysis of, 97–99; as contrasted with expression of attitude, 106–7; as contrasted with performatives, 122–23; determining truth conditions of, 123, 124–41 *passim*; analytic, possibility of, 142, 154–58; analytic, claims for necessary truth of, 161–65; gap between performance and, 170. *See also* Moral judgments

Evaluative arguments: requirements for validity of, 94–95

Evaluative beliefs: conflict between, xi, 15–17, 131–32, 137–40

Evaluative terms: and other philosophical terms, 132–33; understanding of, 142; disagreements on analysis of, 142–51 *passim*; action guiding nature of, 169–70

Evidential relations: contrasted with

Index

sameness of meaning, 46

Extension of terms: decisions concerning, 48–49

External negation: defined, 84–85; of evaluations and attitudes, 85–87, 99–100; effect on arguments, 86–87

Factual content of evaluations: as forming no part of meaning of, 23–24

Fairness: demand for in moral theories, 163–64

Faith, moral demands and: Kierkegaard on, 147–48

Falk, W. D.: on distinction between social norms and personal values, 195*n3*

Feelings: dissonance between values and, 6–8; contrasted with attitudes, 21–22, 96–97; as essential to attitudes, 102–6. *See also* Emotions

Felicity conditions: for illocutionary acts, 40–41, 67–68; being-in-force and, 72; for expressing attitudes, 98. *See also* Austin, J. L.; Illocutionary force; Speech acts

Fiat, determination of meaning by, 50–51

Forrester, James: on primacy of assertion, 192*n3*; conditionals expressed as alternations, 193*n3*

Foster, J. A.: criticism of Davidson, 188*n14*; on possible worlds, 191*n24*

Frankena, William K.: on different senses of "morality," 119–21; weak prescriptivism of, 121–23; on contrast between value judgments and expressions of taste, 184*n3*; criticism of Moore, 184*n11*; on moral reasons for being moral, 197*n8*

Freedom of action: senses of, 115–17

Fundamental criteria. *See* Criteria, fundamental, for application of terms

Geach, P. T.: on imperative inference, 185*n3*

Gettier, Edmund: on knowledge as justified true belief, 196*n3*

Gewirth, Alan: on distinction between a morality and the morally right, 195*n4*

God: will of, as criterion of goodness, x; commands of, and moral rules, according to Kierkegaard, 147–48

Gombay, André: on imperative inference, 185*n3*; on being-in-force, 193*n3*

Good-making characteristics: cited as justifying evaluations, 7–9; as insufficient to constitute definition of "good," 135–54. *See also* Criteria; Definitions; Goodness

Goodness: judgments of, 4–9, 17; meaning of, 11; and criteria for, 13, 153–54; criteria of, according to Stevenson, 16; Moore's argument against defining, 17–19; as capacity to satisfy wants, 174–75

Grading, evaluations as, 97

Grant, C. K.: distinction between social norms and personal values, 195*n3*

Grice, H. P.: on conversational implicature, 42; on contextual implication, 104, 194*n2*; on role of speaker's intention in speech acts, 188*n10*

Guilt: in moral weakness, 111, 118; in perversity, 118

Hancock, Roger: criticism of Moore, 184*n11*

Hare, R. M.: imperativism of, 19–21, 108; semantic theory of, 31; on components of sentence meaning, 55, 87–89, 186*n6*; commitment logic of, 68–71; on subordinate clauses of conditionals, 87–89; on moral weakness and perversity, 109–19, 194*n2*; on imperative inference, 186*n3*: on satisfaction and acceptance as analogues of truth, 191*n1*; on internal and external negation,

Index

Intention: meaning and, 53–54; to act, 108–11, 117; in speech acts, 188n10
Interests of persons: conclusions concerning, in nonassertoric arguments, 79; as promoted by moral systems, 162–65, 171
Internal negations: of nonassertoric sentences and evaluations, 84–87, 99–101
Interrogative mood, 37
Intuition: role of in determining analysis of meaning, 161
Invalidity: of arguments with performatives as premises, 73–76, 87–89

Jackendoff, Ray S.: on mood as component of sentence meaning, 186n6
Jones, Hardy, 196n1
Justification: of evaluations, compared with causes of likes and dislikes, 4–6; failure of relativism to provide, 9–11; of moral judgments, as willingness to prescribe universally, 20–21; as analogue of truth for nonassertoric sentences, 71–73; of moral beliefs, 125–30; of morality, on nonmoral gounds, 147, 170–73; of changes in moral practices, 163–64. *See also* Being-in-force; Criteria, fundamental, for application of terms; Moral arguments; Orthotic sentences

Katz, Jerrold: on mood as component of meaning, 186n6; criticism of Davidson, 188n14; on possible worlds, 191n24
Kempson, Ruth M.: on distinction between meaning and use, 186n6
Kerner, George C.: on evaluations as performatives, 193n6, 194n1
Kierkegaard, Søren: on religious faith and moral demands, 147–48
Knowledge, moral. *See* Moral knowledge

Knowledge of meaning: as requiring acceptance of truth of reference-fixing sentences, 46–47; of evaluative terms, 142; as contrasted with knowledge of facts, 157; as contrasted with ability to analyze, 157–59; of moral and nonmoral terms, 159; as knowledge of linguistic conventions, 161. *See also* Analysis; Reference; Truth conditions
Kovesi, Julius: criticism of Moore, 184n11

Language, learning of, 35–37
Legislation: role of, in determining meanings of terms, 51, 159–60
Lewis, David: on linguistic conventions, 52; on reduction of all speech acts to assertions, 187n8; on meaning and possible worlds, 191n24
Likes and dislikes: contrasted with values, 4–9; as not needing justification, 9. *See also* Desires; Tastes, changes in
Linguistic competence, 36
Linguistic conventions: origins of, 51–53; in expressions of attitudes, 97–99; knowledge of, as knowledge of meaning, 161. *See also* Conversational implicature; Felicity conditions; Illocutionary force; Meaning of utterance; Truth by convention; Truth conditions
Loar, Brian: criticisms of Davidson, 188n14
Logic: of satisfaction, 58–68, 70–71; of imperatives, 62–63, 66–72; of commitment, 68–71; of being-in-force, 72–73; of evaluations as similar to that of assertions, 81–95 *passim*, 174. *See also* Assertoric logic; Nonassertoric logic
Lyons, Daniel: on evaluations as entailing desires, 196n6

Index

McArthur, Robert P., and David Welker: rules of inference for nonassertoric arguments, 66–68; system of nonassertoric inference, 179–82, 186n3; speaker commitment as analogue of truth, 191–92n1; primacy of assertion and truth, 192n4

MacKay, Alfred: on imperative inference, 185n3; on conditionals expressed as alternations, 193n3

Martin, James, 193n2, 193n8

Mavrodes, George I., 63–64

Meaning: of unuttered sentences, 43; sameness of, compared with causal, evidential relations, 46; changes in, 49–50, 135–37; intention and, 53–54; role of intuition in analysis of, 161; in terms of possible worlds, 191n24

—of evaluative expressions: according to relativists, 11; as not exhausted by descriptive criteria, 19, 157–58; as expressions of commitment, 20, 108–19 *passim*, 121–23; as expressions of attitudes, 21–22, 23, 96–107 *passim*; as descriptions, 81–95 *passim*; changes in, 166–68. *See also* Descriptivism; Emotivism; Nondescriptivism; Prescriptivism

—of sentences: as independent of circumstances of utterance, 31; relation to use, 31–33, 186–87n6; relation to illocutionary force, 31–43, 94; and perlocutionary force, 33; propositional content and, 34–37, 43, 124–25; mood and, 34, 37–38, 43, 124–25, 186n6; as illocutionary act potential, 39–40; analysis of, in terms of truth conditions, 44–56; conventionally recognized truth conditions and, 46–50, 124; characterized, 54–56; as function of grammatical and logical behavior, 57; attitudes, use, and, 106–7. *See also* Mood of sentences; Propositional content; Truth conditions

—of terms: as determined by reference-fixing sentences, 46–47, 154, 174; role of legislation in determining, 51, 159–61; philosophical means of reaching agreement on, 160–61; stereotypes and, 190n22. *See also* Analysis; Criteria for application of terms; Definitions

—of utterance, 54

Meaningfulness, 35–36, 49

Meaninglessness, 12–13

Meaning postulates, 44, 50, 81, 95. *See also* Analytic sentences; Definitions; Reference-fixing sentences

Meaning rules: for termination, 63–65

Metaethical relativism, 11–12

Metalinguistic statements: as premises and conclusions in arguments involving nonassertoric sentences, 76–80; definitions as, 152–53

Mood

—of evaluations: as indicative, 124–25. *See also* Meaning of evaluative expressions

—of sentences: relation to illocutionary force, 33–34, 38–41; as component of meaning, 34, 37–38, 43, 186n6; as manner of representing states of affairs, 37–38, 66; compared with mood of verb, 38; changes in, and changes in meaning, 43; compared with Hare's trophic, 55; symbols for, 55; use of symbols to represent sentences and illocutionary acts, 60–63, 179–82; negations and, 82–87, 99–102; as determined by mood of conditioned clause, 91; attempts to reduce types of, 187n8

Mood morphemes: conditions of meaningfulness of, 38; convention in meaning of, 55

Mood operators, 55

Index

Moore, G. E.: and open question argument, 17–18; on disagreements among moral philosophers, 142; Nakhnikian's views compared to, 153

Moore, Ronald, 196*n1*

Moral arguments: nature of, 125–26; as used in justifying actions, 90–92, 125–26, 129–31; major premises of, as determinants of fundamental criteria, 132–33. *See also* Moral principles

Moral beliefs: and revision of moral theories, xi, 134–35; reasons for holding, 137–41; relationship to moral truth, 174–75. *See also* Well-established moral beliefs

Moral codes: as contrasted with behavioral norms, 119–21; as concerned with behavior affecting sentient beings, 120; purposes of, 164–65; different, as being equally valid, 165. *See also* Moral principles; Moral standards

Moral disagreement: as due to complexity of moral issues, 130. *See also* Disagreement

Moral issues: as concerned with behavior affecting persons, 120. *See also* Moral codes

Morality: as behavioral norm, moral code, or moral rightness, 119–21; as concerned with behavior, 120; as in interest of agent, 146–47; reasons for acting in accordance with, 170–73

Moral judgments: universality and rationality of, 15, 17; as prescriptions, 19–21, 108; as not inferable from factual statements, 20; as expressions of commitment, 20, 108; distinguished from practical judgments, 120; means of determining truth conditions of, 124–44 *passim*; consensus on, and criteria for application of moral terms, 134; as de-

scriptive statements, 174. *See also* Evaluations

Moral knowledge: requirements for possibility of, xi–xii; and truth or falsity of moral judgments, 174

Moral language: similarity of, to factual language, xii, 133–34, 174. *See also* Evaluations; Moral judgments

Moral practices: rejection of, 138–40; acceptance of, and end promotion, 163–64; basis for changes in, 163–64. *See also* Moral beliefs; Well-established moral beliefs

Moral principles: conflicts between, ix–x; use of, in moral arguments, 89–92, 125–27, 130; acceptance of, as intending action on, 109–10; acceptance of, as belief in worthiness of, 113–14

Moral relativism, 3

Moral responsibility: ability to act and, 116

Moral rules: Kierkegaard and justification for breaking, 147–48; ability to follow, and personhood, 149–51. *See also* Moral codes: Moral principles

Moral skepticism, 11

Moral standards, 89–92, 120–21. *See also* Moral principles

Moral terms: hypotheses about meaning of, 134–35; complexity of, 143–44; agreement on meaning of, among philosophers, 151; definitions of, as arbitrary, 162; use of, to classify objects and actions, 162–63. *See also* Criteria, fundamental, for application of terms; Evaluations; Meaning of evaluative expressions

Moral theories: need for compatibility of, with common beliefs, xi, 131–41 *passim*, 175; basis for criticism of, 162–65

Moral weakness: common notion of, 109; incompatibility with strong prescriptivism, 109; distinguished

Index

from perversity, 109, 118–19; Hare's account of, 109–17; contrasted with weakness of will, 110, 118; guilt in, 111; as failure to act on principles, 111–15; as inability to act on principles, 114–17; as weak desire to do right, 116–17; role of self-deception in, 118; as compatible with weak prescriptivism, 121–22

Morphemes: as mood indicators, 38, 55; contrasted with context of utterance, 40

Motives for acting morally, 147, 170–73

Nakhnikian, George: on analytic evaluations, 151–65; compared with Moore, 153

Naturalism: defined, 17; contrasted with descriptivism, 17; Price and Moore on, 17

Naturalistic fallacy, 18

Necessary and sufficient conditions for application of terms: relation of, to meaning, 44–45, 124–25, 157; fundamental criteria and, 128–29. See also Truth conditions, conventionally recognized

Necessary truth; of analytic evaluations, 161–65

Negations: of evaluations as opposed to negations of performatives and expressions of attitude, 83–87, 99–102, 122

Neustic of sentences, 55, 88–89

Nietzsche, Friedrich, 145; on slave morality, 149–50; on obligations of natural masters, 149; on who counts as a person, 150

Nonassertoric arguments: artificiality of, 73; conclusions of, 73–76, 180–82; and application of truth analogues, 76; contrasted with evaluative arguments, 94–95

Nonassertoric logic: parallelism of, with assertoric logic, 59–63; system of, by McArthur and Welker, 66–68, 179; as dependent on assertoric logic, 72–76. See also Logic, of satisfaction, of commitment, of being-in-force

Nonassertoric sentences: defined, 23–24; as incapable of taking form of question or doubt, 26–27; as incapable of appearing in subordinate clause of conditional premise, 27–29, 82–89; inferences involving, 30–33, 73–79, 179–82; validity of arguments involving, 57–58, 87–89; values of, 57–73; as not used as premises or conclusions, 73–76; negations of, 85–87. See also Imperatives; Performatives

Noncognitivism, 11. See also Nondescriptivism

Nondeclarative sentences. See Nonassertoric sentences

Nondescriptive components: in evaluations, 13–23, 92–95, 157–58

Nondescriptivism: defined, 3, 13; showing truth of, 95; as explanation of moral disagreement, 143; popularity of, since Moore, 145; as solution to problem of moral motivation, 147, 170; and relation between change in criteria and change in meaning of evaluative terms, 165–67. See also Emotivism; Imperativism; Prescriptivism

Norms: as standards of behavior, 89–90; used to justify more specific evaluations, 89–92; social, 119; behavioral, as contrasted with moral codes, 119–21

Nowell-Smith, P. H.: nondescriptivism of, 22–23, 25

Obligations: as incurred by performance of illocutionary acts, 72; being-

Index

Index

Nonassertoric sentences; Reference-fixing sentences

Sextus Empiricus: ethical relativism of, 183$nn1$–2

Sign of subscription, 55, 87–89

Slave morality: Nietzsche on, 149–50

Snare, Frank: criticism of Moore, 184$n11$

Solomon, Robert: on emotions as evaluative beliefs, 184$n4$

Speaker
—commitment of: moral judgments as expressions of, 20; as analogue of truth, 68–71; as entailing investment in realizing states of affairs, 68; interpretation of validity of arguments in terms of, 68; as corresponding to belief, 71. *See also* Acceptance
—expectations of: meaning and, 52–56; illocutionary force and, 55–56

Speech acts: illocutinary force of, 31–32; potential, as determinants of meaning, 39–40, 67; as performed in nonstandard conditions, 41–42; operators for, 55; analysis of, 55–56; necessity for performance of, for satisfaction values to apply, 60–61; felicity conditions for, 67–68; of evaluation, emotivist analysis, 97–99; role of speaker's intention in success of, 188$n10$. *See also* Illocutionary acts

Spinoza, B. de: egoism of, contrasted with ordinary concept of moral rightness, 145–46; on virtue, 146; on justification of morality as rational, 146–47

Stability: as reason for accepting cultural relativism, 10

Stalley, R. F.: on consistency of desires, 192$n9$

Standardization of terminology: role of, in science and philosophy, 144–45

Standards, absolute moral: existence of, xi. *See also* Moral standards

Standing for: relation of, 35–36

States of affairs: types of, as described in propositional content, 34–36; manner of representing, as function of mood, 37–38; incompatibility between, and commitment logic, 69–71; holding of, as necessary condition for satisfaction of illocutionary acts, 77, 179–80; represented as holding by subordinate clauses, 83

Stenius, Erik: on components of sentence meaning, 186$n6$

Stereotypes: and meanings of terms, 190$n22$

Stevenson, C. L.: imperativism of, 15–17, 23; on evaluations as conjunction of assertion and imperative, 193$n11$

Strawson, P. F.: on role of speaker's intention in succcess of speech acts, 188$n10$; on speaker's intention as part of meaning, 190–91$n23$; on distinction between social norms and personal values, 195$n3$

Subjectivism: contrasted with Frankena's weak prescriptivism, 122

Subordinate clause of conditional: assertoric nature of, 26–29, 82–83

Sumner, L. W.: on distinction between a morality and moral rightness, 195$n4$

Sympathy: as motive for acting morally, 171–72

Synonymy, conditions of, 46. *See also* Analyticity; Meaning; Meaning of terms.

Syntax: similarity of evaluations and assertions in, 26, 57, 174

Synthetic statements: distinguished from analytic, 50–51, 152–53

Tarski, Alfred: definition of truth, 65

Tastes, changes in: compared with

220

Index

of satisfaction, 58–68; consideration of mood in defining, 66; according to McArthur and Welker, 66–68; in terms of commitment, 68–71; in terms of justification, 71–73; as dependent on validity of assertoric arguments, 77–80, 81. *See also* Nonassertoric arguments; Nonassertoric logic

Value judgments. *See* Evaluations; Moral judgments

Values: conflicts between, x; dissonance between feelings and, 6–8; as analogous to truth, 58–73, 97–98; as contrasted with moral codes, 119–21; acceptance of, as implied by acceptance of definitions of evaluative expressions, 161–62. *See also* Moral beliefs: Truth values

Value terms. *See* Meaning of evaluative expressions; Moral terms

Verifiability theory of meaning, 12

Verification of evaluations, 12–13

Vienna Circle, 12

Virtue: according to Aristotle and Spinoza, 146

Wants. *See* Desires; Desire satisfaction

Warnings: satisfaction of, as being heeded, 59

Weakness of will: as indecisiveness, 110; contrasted with moral weakness, 110, 118

Wedeking, Gary: on imperative inference, 185*n3*

Welker, David. *See* McArthur, Robert P., and David Welker

Well-established moral beliefs: as justified by use of fundamental criteria, 129–30; as having withstood criticism, 130–31; compared with widespread beliefs, 130–31; evidence for, 131–32; likelihood of truth of, 131–34; as indicating consensus on fundamental criteria, 134; as supported by good reasons, 137–41

White, Michael J.: on reduction of all speech acts to assertions, 187*n8*

Williams, B.A.O.: on imperative inference, 185*n3*

Ziff, Paul: on differences between imperatives and evaluations, 185*n1*

JACKET DESIGNED BY ED FRANK
COMPOSED BY GRAPHIC COMPOSITION, INC., ATHENS, GEORGIA
MANUFACTURED BY CUSHING MALLOY, INC., ANN ARBOR, MICHIGAN
TEXT AND DISPLAY LINES ARE SET IN TIMES ROMAN

Library of Congress Cataloging in Publication Data
Forrester, Mary Gore, 1940–
Moral language.
Bibliography: pp. 199–204
Includes index.
1. Language and ethics. I. Title.
BJ44.F67   170′.42   81–50825
ISBN 0–299–08630–5   AACR2